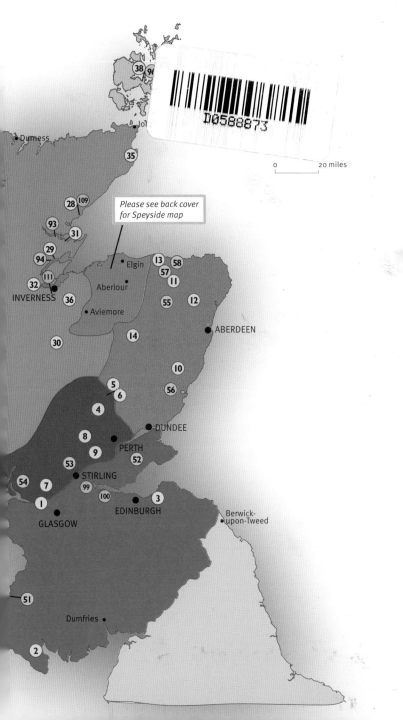

Dunness

38 96

Jo...

35

28 109

93

31

29

94

32 111

INVERNESS   36

30

• Elgin

13 58

57

11

Aberlour

55

12

• Aviemore

14

ABERDEEN

10

5

6

56

4

8

• DUNDEE

9

PERTH

53

52

54   7

STIRLING

99

1

100

EDINBURGH

3

GLASGOW

Berwick-
• upon-Tweed

51

Dumfries •

2

*Please see back cover
for Speyside map*

0   20 miles

D0588873

Discovering *Scotland's* Distilleries

Gavin D Smith & Graeme Wallace

Publishing

GW Publishing

Acknowledgements

Grateful thanks are due to the many people who contributed in various ways to this project. They include
Michael Alexander (Diageo plc), Sonia Bastian (Chivas Bros Ltd), Michael Beamish (Tullibardine Distillery
Ltd), Kirsteen Beeston (Morrison Bowmore Distillers Ltd), Robin Bell (Isle of Arran Distillers Ltd),
Sarah Bottomley (Glengoyne Distillery/Ian Macleod Distillers Ltd), Stephen Bremner (Tomatin Distillery Co
Ltd), Neil Cameron (Glenturret Distillery/The Edrington Group), John Campbell (Laphroaig Distillery/Beam
Global UK Ltd), Jane Cattanach (Morrison Bowmore Distillers Ltd), Ian Chapman (Gordon & MacPhail),
Marco di Ciacca (Burn Stewart Distillers Ltd), John and Frances Clotworthy (Loch Ewe Distillery),
Chris Conway, Graham Coull (La Martiniquaise), Jason Craig (Highland Park Distillery/The Edrington
Group), Francis Cuthbert (Daftmill Distillery), Robert Fleming (Glencadam and Tomintoul Distilleries/
Angus Dundee plc), Jane Grimley (John Dewar & Sons Ltd), Anna Hall (The Glenmorangie Co), Mari
Laidlaw (Morrison Bowmore Distillers Ltd), Libby Lafferty (William Grant & Sons Ltd), Frank McHardy
(Springbank and Glengyle Distilleries/J&A Mitchell & Co Ltd), Ian Macmillan (Burn Stewart Distillers Ltd),
Dennis Malcolm (Campari Group), Tracy Markey (The Edrington Group), Des McCagherty (Signatory
Vintage Scotch Whisky Co Ltd), Linda Mellis (Diageo plc), Caroline Mitchell (Chivas Bros Ltd), Richard
Paterson (Whyte & Mackay Ltd),Robert Ransom (J&G Grant), Mark Reynier (Bruichladdich Distillery
Co Ltd), John Robertson (Tullibardine Distillery Ltd), Vicky Stephens (Laphroaig Distillery/Beam Global
UK Ltd), Morag Swanson (Dalmore Distillery/Whyte & Mackay Ltd), Mark Tayburn (Abhainn Dearg
Distillery), Alistair Walker (The BenRiach-GlenDronach Distilleries Company Ltd), Malcolm Waring
(Pulteney Distillery/Inver House Distillers Ltd), Claire Watson (Gordon & MacPhail), Anthony Wills
(Kilchoman Distillery Co Ltd), Stuart Nickerson, Glenglassaugh Distillery Co Ltd.

Design – Melvin Creative
Printing – Color Print Offset, China

Published by
GW Publishing, PO Box 6091, Thatcham, Berks RG19 8XZ.

Tel + 44 (0)1635 268080
www.gwpublishing.com

ISBN 978-0-9561211-5-8

CONTENTS

Photographs: Front Cover - Dalwhinnie Distillery

CRAIGELLACHIE VILLAGE

4

HOW TO USE THIS GUIDE

The majority of this book comprises a listing of every working malt whisky distillery in Scotland. The first section (pages 70-171) lists the working distilleries that encourage visitors and have permanent facilities to cater for such. Presented in alphabetical order but within each geographical region (see below), there is a helpful colour-coordinated index on page 71 that links to the coloured tabs at the top of each page to help find a distillery close to where you plan to travel.

The second section (pages 172-221) lists working distilleries that do not generally provide a visitor experience, although some offer tours with varying degrees of flexibility. This section is also listed by region, then alphabetically within that, with the section index being on page 173. Finally, the third section (pages 222-237) highlights a selection of distilleries that are no longer in operation, but which offer something worthwhile to see from the outside. Of these, Dallas Dhu is now a distillery museum and also offers excellent tours of the internal operation.

Every page has a space in which to record your experience, and you can even collect managers' or guides' signatures as a true memento of your visit.

Inside the front and back covers are maps of Scotland and of Speyside, showing the location of each distillery.

A full alphabetical list of all distilleries in the book is on page 240.

Finally, pages 16-63 provide useful information regarding facilities such as whisky bars, whisky shops and some suggested itineraries, based around popular cities and towns which serve as ideal centres for distillery exploration.

Geographical Whisky Regions (colour coding in page top corners)

Lowland ⸻

Highland (South) ⸻

Highland (East) ⸻

Speyside ⸻

Highland (North and West) ⸻

Islay and Campbeltown ⸻

Island ⸻

GLENTAUCHERS DISTILLERY

FOREWORD

France has its wine; Spain its sherry and Germany its lager, each adding to its country's international reputation. However, none are more synonymous, and globally recognised, than Scotland and Scotch whisky. The world's leading premium spirit has done more than any other drink to spread a positive image of its country of origin around the globe. Sold in almost every nation in the world, and one of Scotland's most valuable exports, it has done much to bring a small country to the attention of a massive audience. It is no doubt for this reason that tourists to Scotland envisage visiting a Scotch whisky distillery as one of their 'must-do' activities. In fact, over a million of them visit a distillery every year – about eight per cent of all Scotland's tourists.

From the 'whisky island' of Islay to the heart of the industry in Speyside, enthusiasts and novices alike are welcomed to have a look behind the scenes. With more than half of Scotland's distilleries open to the public, and dispersed through the Lowlands, Highlands and Islands, they provide an opportune theme through which to experience Scotland.

For those planning a tour of Scotland and its distilleries **Discovering Scotland's Distilleries** provides an excellent place to start. Built on Gavin's encyclopaedic knowledge of the whisky industry, his long-standing personal contacts and, as ever, thorough research, Gavin has produced the first true whisky tourist's companion. **Discovering Scotland's Distilleries** is full of practical advice and thoughtful suggestions. It has interwoven fascinating distillery profiles with recommended routes and suggested places of interest. It is an excellent reference guide for those wanting to add a whisky element to their tour of Scotland or those wishing to 'bag' the lot. Written by one of the leading whisky writers, someone with so much passion for the industry, I hope it inspires you to come and see for yourself.

Slàinte!

Chris Conway

ScotlandWhisky [www.scotlandwhisky.com]

ScotlandWhisky, is a partnership between the public and private sectors, with the aim of exploring where the tourism and Scotch whisky industries can work together to realise mutual commercial benefits. It is supported by the Scotch Whisky Association, The Scotch Whisky Experience, Scottish Enterprise, Highlands and Islands Enterprise, and VisitScotland.

SCOTCH WHISKY

Scotch whisky has become a major Scottish icon, inextricably associated with the country by people from all around the globe. Whisky is Scotland's greatest export and also its greatest 'ambassador.'

Scotch whisky currently sells in more than 200 countries, and in 2008 exports broke through the £3 billion barrier for the first time. During that year the equivalent of 1,080 million bottles of whisky were sent overseas. Scotch whisky is one of the UK's top five export-earners, and accounts for an estimated one in 50 jobs in Scotland.

Whisky-making is a business, and as such it has to be responsive to commercial pressures, producing more spirit during the good times, and cutting back in the bad. Accordingly, new distilleries are built and existing ones fall silent, are mothballed or even close forever. At the time of writing, a number of 'micro-distilleries' are at the planning or fund-raising stage in locations from south-west Scotland to the Outer Hebrides. Scotch whisky never stands still.

There are currently 97 Scotch malt whisky distilleries either active or nominally active. This compares with 329 in 1825, 161 in 1899 and 123 in 1979. In addition to the 97 working malt whisky distilleries there are six operational grain distilleries. Whereas the total malt whisky output from close to 100 distilleries in 2009 is estimated at 202.5 million litres, the handful of grain distilleries produced some 260 million litres, highlighting the very large scale on which grain distilleries operate.

BALBLAIR DISTILLERY

LOCATION

It is worth considering just why Scotland's distilleries are situated where they are: often in places that seem logistically inconvenient in relation to blending and bottling facilities and to the centralised warehousing complexes so often used by larger companies today.

The answer is that distilleries were usually constructed close to the source of raw materials required for whisky-making; a particularly important factor in the days before modern road transport was developed. Malt whisky is distilled using malted barley, so a location close to arable farm land capable of nurturing cereal crops was desirable. North-east Scotland has a long heritage of growing high quality barley, hence the concentration of distilleries in the Speyside region. Abundant supplies of pure water are also essential for distillation, so a reliable water source - river, loch, well, mains supply - was a prerequisite that determined the location of distilleries. Peat was another important raw material, being burnt for fuel and 'flavouring' in the days when each distillery malted its own barley on site. Again, a local supply of peat was highly desirable when choosing a site on which to build your distillery.

Transportation was a further factor to take into account, and many distilleries were constructed on coastal sites so that boats could be used to deliver barley, coal and empty casks and in return take away with them casks of spirit destined for the blenders and/or bottlers. Part of the attraction of Campbeltown, on the Kintyre peninsula of Argyllshire, was the fact that while the road journey to Glasgow was torturous and extremely lengthy, it was only a distance of some 50 miles by sea.

From around the middle of the 19th century, a new transport-related element entered the distillery location equation - namely the railway. As the rail network spread across Britain, reaching into many remote parts of the Scottish Highlands, distillers were presented with a comparatively quick and efficient means of getting barley, coal and empty casks into their distilleries, and getting casks filled with spirit out and into the marketplace. Many Victorian distilleries were constructed close to railway lines, often with their own sidings which linked to the public system.

DEANSTON DISTILLERY

WHISKY HISTORY

The true origins of whisky are lost in the mists of time.

Although the art of distillation is documented by the Greeks, Egyptians and Arabs, a strong case can be made for the Chinese as the first distillers, probably using barley and rye. From China the mysterious art is believed to have travelled to Arabia, and by the 10th century, the Spanish-Arabian physicist Albucasis had written extensively on the distillation of vinegar, water and wine.

The Arabians are credited with the innovation of cooling the tube leading from the still head with water, and the Greeks were also in on the distilling act at quite an early stage. Aristotle (384-322BC) wrote about the chemistry of distillation, while the Egyptians were practising the craft during the time of Diocletian (AD285-305). However, it is thought that knowledge of the distillation of alcohol did not reach Europe until the 11th or 12th century, being passed on by the Moors, or by soldiers returning to Britain from the Crusades.

EARLY SCOTCH

The first surviving written record of Scotch whisky occurs in 1494, in the Scottish Exchequer Rolls, where it is written 'Eight bolls of malt to Friar John Cor wherewith to make aquavitae." However, it seems likely that distilling was taking place in Scotland for some considerable time prior to that, as eight bolls is the equivalent of around half a ton, so the friar was distilling on quite a considerable scale.

There are claims that the Irish were making whisk(e)y before the Scots, and that the art of whisk(e)y distillation spread from Ireland to Scotland by way of the Hebrides and Kintyre. The fact is that we will probably never know for certain.

Whoever made it first, the Scots took to distilling whisky with great enthusiasm, and in 1579 the Scottish parliament banned the use of grain for distilling purposes for a year due to a serious crop failure, suggesting that the practice was certainly widespread by that time. In 1644 duty (2s 8d Scots per Scots pint) was imposed on whisky for the first time, and by the mid-18th century a growing number of comparatively large distilleries were in operation, particularly in the Lowlands.

However, illicit distilling was rife in the Highlands, and a number of measures were introduced in order to curb the illegal trade and encourage legal whisky-making. These culminated in the 1823 Excise Act, which liberalised existing excise laws, significantly reducing levels of duty, and laid the foundations of the modern Scotch whisky industry we know today.

THE ADVENT OF BLENDING

For Scotch whisky, the most significant feature of the second half of the 19th century was the development of the art of blending together malt and grain whiskies to create a cheaper, lighter- flavoured and more consistent drink.

The increasing global demand for blended Scotch whisky led to the creation of new distilleries in Scotland, with no fewer than 33 being constructed during the last decade of the 19th century alone. However, bust inevitably follows boom, and before too long over-supply became a disastrous feature of the industry. The bubble finally burst with the high profile failure of the Leith firm of Pattison's Ltd in 1899, and redundancies and distillery closures followed.

THE 20TH CENTURY AND BEYOND

Remarkably, it was to be half a century before the next new Scottish distillery was created, but the years following the Second World War saw the gradual development of a new Scotch whisky bonanza to mirror that of the late 19th century.

Once again, though, bust was to follow boom, with an international decline in whisky sales during the 1970s. In order to reduce the level of what was termed the 'whisky loch,' many companies closed distilleries, with the giant Distillers Company Ltd shutting no fewer than 21 in 1983 and 1985. In total, 29 distilleries fell silent during the first half of the 1980s.

One significant feature of the Scotch whisky industry during the past half century has been an increasing level of consolidation, with ownership of distilleries becoming concentrated into ever fewer hands, and today a large percentage of the industry is controlled by the two leading players, Diageo and Pernod Ricard, who own many distilleries and world-leading brands. Overall, Scottish distilleries are owned by companies from a diverse range of countries, including France, Italy, Japan, Thailand, Trinidad & Tobago and the USA.

Despite the trend towards consolidation and internationalisation, in recent years there has also been a trend for distilleries surplus to the requirements of the major distillers to be acquired by smaller, independent companies, in some cases blenders and bottlers. These include Benromach, Edradour and Glengoyne. Additionally, new, small-scale distilleries such as Abhainn Dearg, Arran, Daftmill and Kilchoman have been built from scratch.

Relatively small-scale, flexible distillers have been able to cash in on the steadily growing interest in single malt whiskies, and the development of 'finished' whiskies and exclusive single cask bottlings, though the larger distillers have also been quick to see opportunities offered by the specialist malt market.

In the early years of the 21st century, it is clear that economic factors continue to dictate the fate of the Scotch whisky industry, but whatever financial crises occur, love of whisky distilled in Scotland is geographically so widespread that the future of the world's greatest spirit is certainly assured.

SCOTCH WHISKY REGIONS

For many years, Scotch malt whiskies and the distilleries in which they are produced have been categorised on a geographical basis. The usual classifications are Lowland, Highland, Speyside, Campbeltown, Islay and Islands, though sub-divisions are frequently made within the larger of those regions, most notably in the case of Highland and Speyside. It should be emphasised that the categories exist for geographical convenience rather than because whiskies within each grouping necessarily share stylistic similarities.

LOWLAND

Lowland single malts are distilled south of a theoretical line which runs between Greenock on the Firth of Clyde in the west and Dundee on the Firth of Tay in the east, separating the Lowlands from the Highlands. Despite it once being the powerhouse of Scotch whisky distillation, history has not been kind to the Lowland area, and a few years ago only Auchentoshan, near Glasgow and Glenkinchie, south of Edinburgh, were in production. Now, however, the region has gained greater impetus, with distilling having been revived at Bladnoch in Galloway, while a small-scale, farm-based distillery has been developed at Daft Mill in Fife, and Ailsa Bay distillery has opened at Girvan, on the Ayrshire coast.

HIGHLAND

Historic excise legislation dictates that Highland malt whiskies are distilled north of a line stretching between Greenock and Dundee. The vast Highland region is often sub-divided into a number of smaller areas, within which there may be some stylistic similarities. References to Northern, Western, Eastern and Southern Highland areas of production are common. Geographically, the Highland region of malt whiskies embraces Scotland's most northerly mainland distillery of Pulteney, in the Caithness port of Wick, and its most westerly in the shape of Oban. Leading Highland single malts include Old Pulteney and Clynelish from the far north of the region, Glenmorangie and Dalmore from the east, Oban and Ben Nevis from the west, and Glengoyne, Aberfeldy and Edradour from the south.

SPEYSIDE

More than half of Scotland's working malt whisky distilleries are located within the Speyside region of north-east Scotland. The Speyside whisky industry grew significantly during the late 19th century, with the increasing popularity of blended whisky. The smooth, relatively subtle character of many Speyside malts was ideally suited for blending purposes, and no fewer than 21 distilleries were built on Speyside during the 1890s alone.

Speyside remains home to many of the greatest names in Scotch whisky, such as Glenfiddich, Glenfarclas, Glen Grant, The Glenlivet and The Macallan.

CAMPBELTOWN

Once the 'whisky capital' of Scotland, with no fewer than 21 working distilleries during the 1880s, Campbeltown lies near the southern tip of the remote Kintyre peninsula in Argyllshire. Today, Campbeltown's whisky-making industry is a shadow of its former self, with just Springbank, Glen Scotia and Glengyle in operation, though Springbank remains a classic malt with a worldwide reputation for excellence. Distilling recommenced at Glengyle in 2004, after almost eight decades of silence, and the Scotch Whisky Association subsequently reinstated Campbeltown as a separate whisky region, having previously included its whiskies in the Highland category for a number of years.

ISLAY

If Campbeltown was formerly Scotland's 'whisky capital', then Islay is the country's 'whisky island.' It is home to eight working distilleries, the most recently established being Kilchoman, a 'boutique,' farm-based operation which commenced production in 2005. Once principally used for blending purposes, Islay single malts have become extremely fashionable during the past couple of decades, with Ardbeg, Bowmore, Lagavulin and Laphroaig all gaining something approaching cult status with drinkers. One of the great recent success stories of Islay has been the renaissance of Bruichladdich distillery since its re-opening in 2001 after several years of silence.

ISLANDS

The Islands category of malt whiskies is geographically very diverse. It embraces Scapa and the world-renowned Highland Park from the Orkney Islands to the north of mainland Scotland, along with western distilleries such as Arran, Jura, Talisker and Tobermory. The most recent addition to the classification is Abhainn Dearg, located on the west coast of the Isle of Lewis.

BENRIACH DISTILLERY

WHISKY TOURISM

Modern 'whisky tourists' almost have an embarrassment of riches at their disposal in Scotland. Distilleries that welcome visitors are to be found the length and breadth of the country, from Bladnoch in the south-west to Highland Park on the Orkney Islands in the north, from Kilchoman in the west to Glengarioch in the east. During 2008 nearly one million people toured Scotch whisky distilleries, with Tullibardine in Perthshire claiming the number one spot with 130,000 visitors passing through its doors

Many of Scotland's distilleries are to be found in beautiful locations, and visiting them provides a great way of exploring Scotland – its landscape, history and culture. Around half of Scotland's working malt whisky distilleries are open to the public and the welcome is invariably warm. The visitor experience varies from a low-key informal tour of the site to the high-tech and interactive.

Once upon a time it was enough for a distillery to offer brief, guided tours of the plant, followed by a dram and the chance to buy a souvenir item or bottle of the product, but in an increasingly sophisticated and competitive leisure market, a number of distilleries, such as Aberfeldy and Glenturret, now offer more elaborate visitor facilities. Some provide a 'menu' of tours, increasing in exclusivity and price, giving the true enthusiast an opportunity to engage in tutored tastings of older and rarer whiskies and perhaps fill and label their own bottle from the cask.

SPEYSIDE DISTILLERY

Distillery visitor centres tend to use history and company heritage a great deal to encourage an emotional connection with the particular whisky being promoted, for ultimately a sense of ongoing brand loyalty is the principal aim of the distilling company whose premises are being visited. Selling a box of shortbread and a cup of tea and a sticky bun at the end of the tour is just the icing on the cake, as it were.

Distilleries are very sensuous places, often announcing their presence even before they are first glimpsed with an alluring aroma created by the mashing process. Inside, the senses are assailed by the roar of the mill grinding malt into grist, the hiss of the curvaceous, copper stills, the heat they generate, the gasp of breathe from exposure to carbon dioxide in the washbacks and the cool, damp atmosphere of a traditional, stone-built, earth-and-cinder-floored warehouse, with its heady scents of slowly maturing whisky.

Externally, distilleries vary enormously, from 'classic' stone-built Victorian structures with pagoda-topped maltings and rows of mould-covered warehouses to the modern, compact and functional. Only a handful of distilleries continue to make malt on site, with the rest buying in malt prepared to their specifications from large-scale, commercial maltsters. Therefore, distilleries built, or rebuilt, since the 1960s do not possess malting facilities. Similarly, casks are no longer filled at a significant number of distilleries. Instead, the newly made (new make) spirit is tankered away for centralised filling into casks, which then mature in large warehouse complexes remote from the distilleries where the spirit was created. Accordingly, a number of distilleries constructed during the last few decades do not have on-site warehousing.

GLENROTHES DISTILLERY

AROUND EDINBURGH

Edinburgh is Scotland's capital city, home to the Scottish Parliament and the second-largest settlement in the country after Glasgow. Widely regarded as one of the most attractive cities in Europe, due to its spectacular setting and high incidence of historic buildings, areas of Edinburgh were listed as a UNESCO World Heritage Site in 1995.

Edinburgh consists of the Old Town and the New Town, with the latter, to the north of Princes Street Gardens, being developed during the Georgian period. Edinburgh subsequently became known as the 'Athens of the North' due to its characteristic neo-classical architecture. Natural features to explore include the extinct volcano of Arthur's Seat and Salisbury Crags, while the coastline of the Firth of Forth is also close by.

The city attracts around one million overseas visitors each year, making it the second most visited city in Britain after London, and principal events include the Edinburgh International Festival, the 'Fringe' Festival and the Edinburgh Military Tattoo.

The Edinburgh International Festival, incorporating The Edinburgh Military Tattoo, staged over three weeks in late summer, is a world-class cultural event, established in 1947. It spawned the 'Fringe' Festival, which is now the biggest arts festival in the world.

The Edinburgh International Festival. The Hub, Castlehill, Edinburgh, EH1 2NE, tel. 0131 473 2099, email: marketing@eif.co.uk, website: www.eif.co.uk.

The Edinburgh Festival Fringe. 180 High Street, Edinburgh, EH1 1QS, tel. 0131 226 0026, email: admin@edfringe.com, web: www.edfringe.com.

The Tattoo Office. 32 Market Street, Edinburgh, EH1 1QB, tel. 0131 225 1188, email: edintattoo@edintattoo.co.uk, web: www.edintattoo.co.uk.

Once famed as a centre for brewing, Edinburgh also has a lengthy, whisky-related heritage, having been home to 10 distilleries since the late 18th century, and today the North British grain distillery carries on the city's whisky-making heritage. Opened in 1887, the 'NB' as it is affectionately known, is one of six operational Scottish grain distilleries. It is owned in partnership by Diageo and The Edrington Group

The last Edinburgh distillery to close was Caledonian, established in 1855, and at one time the largest grain distillery in Britain. The distillery chimney and distinctive still house remain, having been converted into accommodation units.

Edinburgh's historic port of Leith has been home to many of Scotland's whisky brokers, bottlers and blending companies over the years and also boasted two distilleries, namely Leith, which operated from the 1790s until the 1850s, and Lochend, which was in production from around 1825 until the outbreak of the First World War in 1914.

LOWLAND

GETTING TO EDINBURGH

The A1 and A68 roads provide major links from the south-east, while the M8 and M9 motorways connect the city to Glasgow and Stirling respectively. The M90 provides access north, to Perth and beyond.

Edinburgh has good rail links with the rest of the UK via its two main stations, with Glasgow being just 30 minutes away via Haymarket Station, see www.nationalrail.co.uk for details of all timetables and fares.

Waverley Station. Waverley Bridge, Edinburgh, EH1 1YH, **tel. 0845 748 4950**.

Haymarket Railway Station. Haymarket Ter, Edinburgh, EH12 5EZ, **tel. 0845 748 4950**.

Edinburgh Bus Station. St Andrews Sq, Edinburgh, EH1, **tel. 0131 555 6363**.

This is the terminus for long-distance coaches, while express bus services to Edinburgh International Airport depart from Waverley Bridge, adjacent to Waverley Station.

Edinburgh International Airport. Edinburgh, EH12 9DN, **tel. 0870 040 0007**, www.edinburghairport.com. The airport is eight miles west of the city centre, off the A8.

WHISKY SHOPPING

■ **Robert Graham Ltd.** 194a Rose Street, Edinburgh, EH2 4AZ and 254 Canongate, EH8 8AA, tel. 0131 226 1874, www.whisky-cigars.com.

■ **Royal Mile Whiskies**. 379 High Street, The Royal Mile, Edinburgh, EH1 1PW, tel. 0131 225 338, www.royalmilewhiskies.com.

■ **The Whisky Shop.** Princes Mall, Edinburgh, EH1 1BQ and 28 Victoria Street, EH1 2JW, tel. 0131 558 7563, www.thewhiskyshop.com.

■ **William Cadenhead Ltd.** 172 Canongate, Edinburgh, EH8 8DF, tel. 0131 556 5864, www.wmcadenhead.com.

RECOMMENDED BARS

■ **The Abbotsford Bar.** 3 Rose Street, Edinburgh, EH2 2PR, tel. 0131 225 5276, www.theabbotsford.com.

■ **Bow Bar**. 80 West Bow, Edinburgh, EH1 2HH, tel. 0131 226 7667.

■ **Café Royal**. 19 West Register Street, Edinburgh, EH2 2AA, tel. 0131 556 1884.

■ **Canny Man's**. 237 Morningside Road, Edinburgh, EH10 4QU, tel. 0131 447 1484.

■ **Forth Floor Bar**. Harvey Nichols, 30-34 St Andrews Sq, Edinburgh, EH 2 2AD, tel. 0131 524 8350.

■ **Halfway House**. 24 Fleshmarket Close, Edinburgh, EH1 1BX, tel. 0131 225 7101, www.halfwayhouse-edinburgh.com.

■ **Leslie's Bar**. 45 Ratcliffe Terrace, Edinburgh, EH9 1SU, tel. 0131 667 7205, www.lesliesbar.com.

■ **The Whisky Lounge**. The Vintners Rooms, The Vaults, 87 Giles Street, Leith EH6 6BZ, tel. 0131 554 6767, www.thevintnersrooms.com

■ **Whiski Bar**. 119 High Street, Edinburgh, EH1 1SG, tel. 0131 556 3095, www.whiskibar.co.uk.

ITINERARIES AND AMENITIES

PLACES TO VISIT

The dramatically-located **Edinburgh Castle** dominates the city and is a must-see for every visitor. There was a fortress on the site as long ago as AD600.
Castlehill, Edinburgh, EH1 2NG, **tel. 0131 225 9846,**
email: hs.ticketing@scotland.gsi.gov.uk, web: www.scotland.gsi.gov.uk.

The **Palace of Holyrood House**, the Queen's official Scottish residence, once home to Mary Queen of Scots, stands at the eastern end of the Royal Mile, and in the shadow of Arthur's Seat.
Canongate, Edinburgh, EH8 8DX, **tel. 0131 556 5100,**
e-mail: bookinginfo@royalcollection.org.uk, web: www.royalcollection.org.uk.

The **National Gallery Complex** houses the National Gallery of Scotland and showcases and conserves one of the world's finest collections of western art, dating from the Middle Ages to the present day.
The Mound, Edinburgh, EH2 2EZ, **tel. 0131 624 6200,**
email: enquiries@nationalgalleries.org, web: www.nationalgalleries.org.

The Scottish Parliament building is a highly individualistic expression of modern architecture, situated close to the Palace of Holyrood. The modern parliament was established in 1999, and it is the successor to a Scottish parliament that had previously not been convened since the Act of Union in 1707.
The Scottish Parliament, Edinburgh, EH99 1SP, **tel. 0131 348 5200,**
email: sp.info@scottish.parliament.uk, web: www.scottish.parliament.uk.

FURTHER GENERAL INFORMATION

Edinburgh & Scotland Information Centre, 3 Princes Street, Edinburgh, EH2 2QP, **tel. 0845 2255121,** www.edinburgh.org.

EDINBURGH CASTLE

RECOMMENDED HOTELS

- **Caledonian Hilton.** Princes Street, Edinburgh, EH2 2AB,
  tel. 0131 222 8888, www.hilton.co.uk/caledonian (STB ★★★★★) £125+

- **Dovecot House.** (B&B) 6 Dovecot Road, Edinburgh, EH2 7LE,
  tel. 0131 367 7467, www.dovecothouse.co.uk (STB ★★★★) Under £50

- **Dunstane City Hotel.** 4 West Coates, Edinburgh, EH12 5JQ,
  tel. 0131 337 6169, www.dunstane-hotel-edinburgh.co.uk (STB ★★★★) £75-£125

- **King James by Thistle.** 107 Leith Street, Edinburgh, EH1 3SW,
  tel. 0871 376 9016, www.thethistle.com (STB ★★★★) £75-£125

- **Mercure Point Hotel.** 34 Bread Street, Edinburgh, EH3 9AF,
  tel. 0131 221 5555, www.accorhotels.com (STB ★★★) £75-£125

- **Old Waverley Hotel.** 43 Princes Street, Edinburgh, EH2 2BY,
  tel. 0131 556 4648, www.oldwaverely.co.uk (AA ★★★) £75-£125

- **Premier Inn (Edinburgh Central).** 82 Lauriston Place, Edinburgh, EH3 9DG,
  tel. 08709 906610, www.premierinn.com (STB approved) Under £75

- **Scotsman Hotel.** 20 North Bridge, Edinburgh, EH1 1YT,
  tel. 0131 556 5565, www.theetoncollection.com (STB ★★★★★) £125+

- **23 Mayfield.** (guest house) 23 Mayfield Gardens, Edinburgh, EH9 2BX,
  tel. 0131 667 5806, www.23mayfield.co.uk (STB ★★★★) Under £50

RECOMMENDED RESTAURANTS

- **Amber Restaurant** at the Scotch Whisky Experience. (Scottish) 354 Castlehill, Edinburgh, EH1 2NE,
  tel. 0131 477 8477, www.amber-restaurant.co.uk Under £35

- **Dubh Prais.** (Contemporary Scottish) 123b High Street, Royal Mile, Edinburgh, EH1 1SG,
  tel. 0131 557 5732, www.dubhpraisrestaurant.com Under £35

- **Grain Store.** (Scottish/French) 30 Victorian Street, Edinburgh, EH1 2HE,
  tel. 0131 225 7635, www.grainstore-restaurant.co.uk £35+

- **The Indian Cavalry Club.** (Indian) 22 Coates Crescent, Edinburgh, EH3 7AF,
  tel. 0131 220 0138, www.indiancavalryclub.co.uk Under £35

- **Indigo Yard.** (Eclectic) 7 Charlotte Lane, Edinburgh, EH2 4QZ,
  tel. 0131 220 5603, www.indigoyardedinburgh.co.uk Under £25

- **Mussel Inn.** (Seafood) 61-65 Rose Street, Edinburgh, EH2 2NH,
  tel. 0131 225 5979, www.musssel-inn.com Under £35

- **Santini Ristorante.** (Italian) 8 Conference Square, Edinburgh, EH3 8AN,
  tel. 0131 229 9131, www.santiniedinburgh.co.uk Under £35

- **Oloroso.** (Contemporary) 33 Castle Street, Edinburgh, EH2 3DN,
  tel. 0131 226 7614, www.oloroso.co.uk £35+

- **The Witchery.** (Scottish) 352 Castlehill, Royal Mile, Edinburgh, EH1 2NF,
  tel. 0131 225 5613, www.thewitchery.com £35+

ITINERARIES AND AMENITIES

EASTERN LOWLAND TRAIL ▪▪▪▪▪▪▪ 🚗

This tour takes in **The Scotch Whisky Experience** *in Edinburgh and one of Scotland's best-known Lowland single malt distilleries, namely* **Glenkinchie**.

Allow half a day to visit The Scotch Whisky Experience plus half a day to visit Glenkinchie.

The Scotch Whisky Experience is an STB five-star Visitor Attraction, situated on Castlehill, close to Edinburgh Castle, and at the head of the historic Royal Mile. Housed in a former school building, the Experience provides whisky novices with the perfect introduction to Scotland's national spirit, equipping them to get the most out of future distillery visits. There is also much to inform and entertain the more knowledgeable visitor.

The Scotch Whisky Experience underwent a £3 million makeover early in 2009, and features an innovative 'barrel ride' through the various whisky-making processes, an interactive exploration of the art of blending, and the chance to marvel at the world's largest assembly of Scotch whiskies. The Diageo Claive Videz Collection of Scotch Whiskies comprises some 3,500 bottles, amassed over a period of 35 years by Brazilian collector Claive Videz.

An extensive selection of whisky, books and related gifts are on sale in the Experience's own shop, and also now via its online retail outlet www.scotchwhiskyshop.co.uk, while the Amber Restaurant allows visitors to sample fine, fresh Scottish produce and more than 300 different Scotch whiskies in the adjacent bar.

The Scotch Whisky Experience is open seven days a week, 364 days of the year, from 10am to 6pm (last tour at 5pm) and in June, July and August, from 8.30am to 6.30pm, with the last tour being at 5.30pm.

The 'standard' adult tour admission price is £11.00, which includes a complementary dram and Glencairn whisky glass, while other options include a Collection Tour (£20) which showcases the Diageo Claive Videz Collection in detail.

Written guides are available in French, German, Italian, Spanish, Dutch, Portugese, Russian, Japanese and Chinese.

354 Castlehill, The Royal Mile, Edinburgh, EH1 2NE, **tel. 0131 220 0441**, www.scotch-whisky-experience.co.uk.

Glenkinchie Distillery (see p.76) is the closest working malt whisky distillery to Edinburgh, tucked away in the village of Pencaitland, 17 miles (30 minutes' drive) south-east of the city, via the A68 and the A6093. It is worth noting that peak-time traffic is best avoided, as it can significantly lengthen the journey.

CENTRAL SCOTLAND TRAIL ▪▪▪▪▪▪▪▪ 🚗

*This trail features one of Central Scotland's less well known distillery visitor attractions, namely **Deanston**, which is open to the public by prior appointment.*

Allow at least half a day to visit Deanston.

Deanston Distillery (see p176) is situated a mile west of the historic town of Doune, 44 miles (one hour's drive) from Edinburgh, via the M8, M9, A84 and B8032.

Deanston is a relative newcomer to the ranks of distilleries open to the public, and is unique in being housed in a former mill. One idiosyncratic warehouse occupies what was formerly a vaulted weaving shed. While visiting the distillery it is worth taking a stroll around the pretty, neighbouring village of Deanston, which stands on the south bank of the River Teith. It was developed during the 1780s for workers in the Adelphi cotton mill, now home to Deanston distillery.

Doune was once noted as a centre for Scottish pistol manufacture and Doune Castle, in the care of Historic Scotland, dates from the late 14th century. It gained cult status among Monty Python fans after featuring in the film *Monty Python and the Holy Grail.*

Back in Edinburgh, the **Scotch Malt Whisky Society** (SMWS) was founded during 1983 by accountant Pip Hills, and it offers members a vigorous programme of cask strength, single cask bottlings from almost all of Scotland's distilleries. These are not mentioned by name on the labels or in the tasting notes, but are given only a numerical identity. However, broad hints are dropped as to the origins of each whisky in the exuberant and extravagant tasting notes written by the Society's sampling panel.

Society members can enjoy the hospitality of two venues in Edinburgh, one based in Leith's 18th century Vaults building and the other in a Georgian townhouse in the New Town's Queen Street. The Dining Room and bar of the Queen Street property are also open to non-members, **tel. 0131 220 2044**. Additionally, the Society has Members' Rooms in Greville Street, London and branches in a growing number of countries around the world. It hosts an eclectic line up of whisky-related events in a wide geographical range of locations, as well as in its two Edinburgh premises. Tel. 0131 555 2929, email: sales@smws.com, web: www.smws.com.

Edinburgh is also home to the **Scotch Whisky Association** (SWA), based at 20 Atholl Crescent, Edinburgh, EH3 8HF, **tel. 0131 222 9200** and the guardian of Scotch whisky and its integrity around the world. The SWA produces informative guides to whisky-related topics and has a useful website www.scotch-whisky.org.uk.

AROUND GLASGOW

Glasgow is the largest city in Scotland, with a population of more than one million people living within the Greater Glasgow Urban Area. It was first settled in Prehistoric times as a crossing point of the River Clyde.

21st century Glasgow stands at the centre of the former heartland of Scotland's industrial might, having grown, during the 18th and 19th centuries into what was often referred to as 'The second city of the British Empire,' after London. Much of its wealth was based on the importation of tobacco during the 18th century and later on heavy industry, with engineering and shipbuilding at its core.

Glasgow boasts a proud whisky heritage, too, having been home to seven distilleries over the years, though today only Chivas Brothers' Strathclyde grain distillery remains operational. It is situated in Moffat Street (G5 0QB) but is not open to the public and is located in an area that is well off the tourist track.

The city and its environs have also long been a centre for blending and bottling, with malt whisky being shipped via the River Clyde from distant distilleries in the days when the Scottish road network was comparatively primitive, especially in remote, Highland areas.

Today, Glasgow remains home to the distillers and blenders Whyte & Mackay Ltd www.whyteandmackay.com, to Morrison Bowmore Distillers Ltd www.morrisonbowmore.co.uk, John Dewar & Sons Ltd www.dewars.com and The Edrington Group www.edringtongroup.com. The area around Glasgow is the base of a number of major packaging operations for the world's largest Scotch whisky distillers – Diageo plc and Chivas Brothers Ltd - who occupy sites at Shieldhall and Kilmalid respectively.

Since the decline of traditional heavy industry during the second half of the 20th century, Glasgow has, to an extent, reinvented itself as a major cultural and tourist destination, as well as broadening its overall employment base. The 'Lonely Planet Guide' lists Glasgow as one of the top ten tourist cities in the world, and in 1990 it was designated European City of Culture.

Glasgow plays host to the **National Theatre of Scotland, tel. 0141 221 0970,** www.nationaltheatrescotland.com, **Scottish Opera, tel. 0141 248 4567,** www.scottishopera.org.uk, **Scottish Ballet, tel. 0141 331 2931,** www.scottishballet.co.uk, **Royal Scottish National Orchestra, tel. 0141 226 3868,** www.rsno.org.uk, and offers a vibrant night life with clubs, restaurants and bars to suit all tastes and pockets, while whisky lovers are spoilt with a fine selection of well-stocked bars.

GETTING TO GLASGOW

Glasgow is well served by rail, with direct trains from most major British cities to the **Central Station**, Gordon Street, Glasgow G1, **tel. 0141 335 4352**. Edinburgh is just 30 minutes away by rail, and frequent services run from **Queen Street Station**, North Hanover Street, Glasgow, G1 2AF, **tel. 0141 204 2844**. See www.nationalrail.co.uk for details of all timetables and fares.

Buchanan Street Bus Station. Buchanan Street, Glasgow G2 3NP, **tel. 0141 332 9191** is the terminus for long-distance coaches and also the point of arrival/departure for frequent bus services to Glasgow International Airport.

Glasgow International Airport. Paisley, PA2 3ST, **tel. 0141 887 1111**, www.glasgowairport.com is seven miles from the city centre, and close to the M8 motorway, which, along with the M74 to the south, provides one of the principal road links to Glasgow.

Edinburgh International Airport. Edinburgh, EH12 9DN, **tel. 0844 461 8989**, www.edinburghairport.com is 40 miles away, via the M8, but it is worth noting that this Edinburgh-Glasgow motorway route can become extremely congested at peak times.

WHISKY SHOPPING

- **Robert Graham Ltd.** 10-14 West Nile Street, G1 2PP, **tel. 0141 248 7283**, www.whisky-cigars.co.uk
- **The Whisky Shop.** Buchanan Galleries, G1 2GF, **tel. 0141 331 0022**.
- **The Whisky Shop.** Unit 12, Princes Square, G1 3JN, **tel. 0141 226 8446** www.whiskyshop.com

---

RECOMMENDED BARS

- **Ben Nevis.** 1147 Argyle Street G3 8TB, tel. 0141 576 5204.
- **Corinthian.** 191 Ingram Street G1 1DA, tel. 0845 166 6030.
- **Horseshoe Bar.** 17-21 Drury Street G2 5A, tel. 0141 229 5711.
- **Oran Mor.** 731-735 Great Western Road G12 8QX, tel. 0141 357 6200, www.oran-mor.co.uk.
- **The Pot Still.** 154 Hope Street G2 2TH, tel. 0141 333 0980, www.thepotstill.co.uk.
- **Strata.** 45 Queen Street G1 3EH, tel. 0141 204 2110, www.strataglasgow.com.
- **The Lismore.** 206 Dumbarton Road G11 6UN, tel. 0141 576 0103.
- **Uisge Beatha.** 234-246 Woodlands Road G3 6ND, tel. 0141 564 1596.

For a bar with a difference, try **The Clockwork Beer Co**, 1153-1155 Cathcart Road, Glasgow, G42 9BH, tel. 0141 649 0184, www.clockworkbeer.com or **West Brewery Bar and Restaurant**, Binnie Place, Glasgow Green, Glasgow G40 1AW, www.westbeer.com. Both boast on-site micro-breweries, with Clockwork also having a very good whisky range, while West offers authentic, Munich-style beers and cuisine with a German twist.

ITINERARIES AND AMENITIES

PLACES TO VISIT

The Burrell Collection, assembled by Glasgow shipping magnate Sir William Burrell, is located in Pollok Country Park, and showcases a fascinating range of paintings, sculptures, furniture and exotic artefacts from all over the world. Pollokshaws Road, Glasgow, G43 1AT, **tel. 0141 287 2550**, www.glasgowmuseums.com.

Kelvingrove Art Gallery & Museum was established in 1901, and between 2003 and 2006 it underwent a £28 million refurbishment programme. It is the largest civic museum and art gallery in the UK, and houses collections of international importance.
Argyle Street, Glasgow, G3 8AG, **tel. 0141 276 9599**, www.glasgowmuseums.com.

The People's Palace and Winter Gardens opened on Glasgow Green in 1898, and The People's Palace presents a lively and absorbing view of the social life of the city.
Glasgow Green, Glasgow, G40 1AT, **tel. 0141 276 0788**, www.glasgowmuseums.com.

Glasgow is also closely associated with the celebrated artist and designer **Charles Rennie Mackintosh** (1868-1928). Mackintosh was a native of Glasgow, and some of his finest work can be seen in his home city. The Charles Rennie Mackintosh Society can be contacted on **tel. 0141 946 6600**, www.crmsociety.com.

FURTHER GENERAL INFORMATION

Glasgow City Marketing Bureau, 11 George Square, Glasgow G2 1DY, tel. 0141 566 0800, www.seeglasgow.com.

GEORGE SQUARE

LOWLAND

RECOMMENDED HOTELS

- **Carlton George Hotel**. 44 West George Street, Glasgow, G2 1DH, tel. 0141 353 6373, www.carltonhotels.co.uk (STB ★★★★) £75-£125

- **City Inn**. Finnieston Quay, Glasgow, G3 8HN, tel. 0141 240 1002, www.cityinn.com (STB ★★★) £125++

- **Glasgow Marriott.** 500 Argyle Street, Glasgow, G3 8RR, tel. 0141 226 5577, www.marriott.co.uk (STB ★★★★) £75-£125

- **Hilton Glasgow.** 1 William Street, Glasgow, G3 8HT, tel. 0141 204 5555, www.hilton.co.uk (STB ★★★★★) £125+

- **Holiday Inn City Centre.** 161 West Nile Street, Glasgow, G1 2RL, tel. 0141 352 8305, www.higlasgow.com (STB ★★★★) £75-£125

- **Hotel du Vin @ One Devonshire Gardens**. Glasgow, G12 0UX, tel. 0141 576 2260, www.the-devonshire.co.uk (STB ★★★★★) £125++

- **Manor Park Hotel.** (guest house). 28 Balshagray Drive, Glasgow, G11 7DD, tel. 0141 339 2143 (STB★★★) Under £50

- **Newton Guest House.** 248-252 Bath Street, Glasgow, G2 4JW, tel. 0141 332 1666, (STB ★★★) £50-£75

- **Radisson SAS.** 301 Argyle Street, Glasgow G2 8DL, tel. 0141 204 3333, www.glasgow.radissonsas.com (STB ★★★★★) £125+

RECOMMENDED RESTAURANTS

- **1 Bistro@Downstairs.** (Mediterranean and Middle Eastern) 192 Pitt Street, Glasgow G2 4DY, tel. 0141 332 5300. Under £25

- **City Merchant.** (Seafood) 97/99 Candleriggs, Glasgow, G1 1NP, tel. 0141 553 1577. Under £25

- **La Vallee Blanche.** (French) 360 Byres Road, Glasgow G12 8EB, tel. 0141 334 3333. Under £35

- **Malmaison.** (Classic/Scottish) 278 West George Street, Glasgow, G2 4LL, tel. 0141 572 1000, www.malmaison.com £35+

- **Osteria Piero.** (Italian) 11 West Regent Street, Glasgow, G2 2RU, tel. 0141 248 3471. Under £25

- **Rogano.** (Italian/Seafood) 11 Exchange Place, Glasgow, G1 3AN, tel. 0141 248 4055 (£35+)

- **Salty Dog.** (Eclectic) Second Floor Terrace, Princes Square, Glasgow, G1 3JN, tel. 0141 221 7800. Under £35

- **Shish Mahal.** (Indian) 1348 Maryhill Road, Glasgow, G20 9DG, tel. 0141 334 7899, www.shishmahal.co.uk Under £35

- **The Living Room.** (International) 150 St Vincent Street, Glasgow, G2 5NE, tel. 0141 229 0607. Under £35

- **The Ubiquitous Chip.** (Classic/Scottish) 12 Ashton Lane, Glasgow, G12 8SJ, tel. 0141 334 5007. www.ubiquitouschip.co.uk £35+

ITINERARIES AND AMENITIES

SOUTHERN HIGHLAND TRAIL ▬▬▬▬▬▬ 🚗

*This tour takes in **Auchentoshan** and **Glengoyne** Distilleries, both of which produce a comparatively light style of whisky with Auchentoshan being famed for the use of triple rather than double distillation, while Glengoyne is promoted as the 'unpeated' malt whisky.*

Allow a full day to visit both distilleries. Alternatively, either one can be visited on a half-day drive from Glasgow.

Auchentoshan Distillery (see p.72) is the closest working malt whisky distillery to Glasgow, located just 8.5 miles (20 minutes' drive if avoiding peak times) north of the city centre, via the A82. The historic, neighbouring town of Dumbarton used to boast a major grain distillery and has long been known for its many whisky maturation complexes.

The drive from Auchentoshan to **Glengoyne Distillery** (see p.84) is some 14 miles long, and takes approximately 30 minutes (via the A814/A810/B8050/A809/B821/A81).

Just a few miles to the north-west of Glengoyne lies one of Scotland's great tourist attractions, Loch Lomond, which is extremely popular with visitors and locals alike. Loch Lomond is some 24 miles in length and, in terms of surface area, is the largest lake/loch in Britain. It is part of the Loch Lomond and The Trossachs National Park. A great place to rest at the end of your day and watch the sun set over the loch.

Loch Lomond Shores at Balloch **tel. 01389 751035**, www.lochlomondshores.com presents a blend of retail and leisure opportunities, and serves as a good point to begin exploration of the loch. It is situated eight miles from Glengoyne distillery, via the A81 and A811.

Also close to Loch Lomond is the Loch Lomond Distillery (see p.177), situated in the town of Alexandria. Functional and modern in appearance, it is the only distillery in Scotland to produce both grain and malt whisky. The distillery is located on the Lomond Industrial Estate (G83 0TL), off the B857 in Alexandria, although it is not open to the public.

LOCH LOMOND

SOUTHERN WEST COAST TRAIL ▪▪▪▪▪▪▪▪ 🚗

*This tour takes in just one distillery, named after the **Isle of Arran**, but it offers a stunning and rewarding trip to a tranquil island, even if whisky is not necessarily the main priority.*

Allow a full day, though an overnight stop may be advisable in order to get the best of this excursion.

Often described as 'Scotland in miniature,' The Isle of Arran www.arran.info.com offers a great opportunity to experience island life in all its variety. The 30 miles car journey from Glasgow to the ferry port of Ardrossan in Ayrshire takes around one hour (via the M8 and A737) and there are regular car ferry crossings to Brodick, the small island 'capital' with Caledonian MacBrayne www.calmac.co.uk. There is also a train service from Glasgow Central Station to Ardrossan, see www.nationalrail.co.uk for details.

Once on Arran, the **Isle of Arran Distillery** (see p.144) is just 14 miles and 20 minutes north (via the A841) at Lochranza. **Catacol Bay Hotel** www.catacol.co.uk, **tel. 01770 830231** and **Ormsdale Hotel** www.ormisdale-hotel.co.uk, **tel. 01770 302293** are noted for good food, local ales and accommodation. The opposite (western) side of the island has a remote feel, and the open, twisting road provides beautiful views of the coastline and out to sea.

Rather than return by ferry from Brodick to the mainland, a scenic alternative involves taking a short trip on a small car ferry from Lochranza to Claonaig, on the Mull of Kintyre. From here, an excursion to **Springbank Distillery** (see p.170) in the historic whisky-making centre of Campbeltown is possible (28 miles, via the B842), and for anyone wishing to extend their trip to Islay (see p.58), Caledonian MacBrayne ferries www.calmac.co.uk run from Kennacraig, PA29 6YF, **tel. 01880 730253**, just 10 miles from Claonaig on the A83.

The return journey to Glasgow from Claonaig (on the A83 and A82) is 100 miles long and lasts some two and a half hours. It provides spectacular, West Highland 'mountain and loch' scenery, and the chance to stop off at one of Scotland's finest whisky retailers – **Loch Fyne Whiskies** www.lfw.co.uk, tel. **01499 302219** in the beautiful loch-side village of Inveraray.

Also worthy of a stop en route to Glasgow is the Loch Fyne Oyster Bar and Restaurant www.lochfyne.com, **tel. 01499 600236** situated beside the A83 at Cairndow. Local fish and meat dishes are on offer, while the Birlinn Bar gives travellers the chance to try Fyne Ales www.fyneales.com, brewed in a nearby farm setting, plus a variety of other drinks. There is also a well-stocked shop, providing food and gift items.

As an alternative to driving, there is a regular Citylink www.citylink.co.uk coach service between Glasgow and Campbeltown, via the Kennacraig ferry terminal.

AROUND PERTH

Perth stands on the banks of the River Tay, and enjoys a strategic location in central Scotland, making it an idea centre from which to explore distilleries. It also serves as an ideal stepping stone into the Highlands.

The origins of the settlement often known as 'The Fair City' lie in the Roman fort of Bertha, constructed in AD83. The location has long had a strategic importance as the lowest crossing point of the Tay and the highest navigable part of the river.

With the development of the railway network throughout Scotland from the mid-19th century onwards, Perth was ideally placed between the Highlands, where most malt whisky was distilled, and the principal British markets for blended whisky in the south of Scotland and in England. Accordingly, it became a centre for blending and bottling, with three companies in particular putting Perth firmly on the 'whisky map.'

The youthful Arthur Bell joined the Perth wine and spirits firm of TH Sandeman as company traveller in 1837, going on to become partner and ultimately setting up in business on his own in 1851. Bell was one of the pioneers of mixing grain and malt whiskies to create blends, and by the time of his death in 1900, the company of Arthur Bell & Sons had an international client base.

John Dewar was a contemporary of Arthur Bell, and followed the same pattern of working for a wine and spirits merchant before branching out on his own, in 1846. The firm of John Dewar & Sons grew dramatically under the control of John's sons, John and Tommy, during the late 18th and early 19th centuries, with salesman Tommy being one of the best-known and most charismatic figures in the Scotch whisky industry. The family also built Aberfeldy distillery (see p.78) to provide malt whisky for blending purposes.

The third major whisky company to be established in Perth was Matthew Gloag & Son, formed by yet another wine and spirits merchant, one who purchased whiskies from distilleries around Scotland for retail sale.

Gloag's son, William, took over the business in 1860 and began to blend whiskies. It was his son, Matthew, who created the Grouse Brand, later renamed The Famous Grouse, in 1897. The firm remained in family ownership until 1970, when it was sold to Highland Distilleries Co Ltd, now part of The Edrington Group.

Today, The Edrington Group www.edringtongroup.com is the only distiller to retain its connections with Perth, through a modern office complex close to the River Tay at Walnut Grove. However, Bell's Cherrybank Gardens (PH2 0PF), tel. 01738 472800 is home to the National Heather Centre, and the former Bell's offices now house the Pride of Perth Exhibition, which documents Perth's whisky heritage and offers visitors a dram of the Bell's blend.

In addition to its blending and bottling activities, Perth also boasted its own licensed distillery, located in what is now the suburb of Bridgend, on the eastern bank of the Tay. It was operating in 1851 as Clockserrie, later becoming known as Isla distillery. Like so many other Scottish distilleries, Isla failed to survive the turbulent economic times of the inter-war years, closing in 1926. Today the site, at the junctions of Isla Road and Strathmore Street, is occupied by a small, triangular area of parkland.

GETTING TO PERTH

Perth is located some 40 miles north of Edinburgh (via the M90), 60 miles north-east of Glasgow (via the M9 and M8), 110 miles south of Inverness (via the A9) and 85 miles south-west of Aberdeen (via Dundee and the A90).

Perth Railway Station. Leonard Street, Perth, PH2 8RT, **tel. 0845 601 5929** offers regular links to all of Scotland's cities and into England. See www.nationalrail.co.uk for details of all timetables and fares.

Perth Bus Station. Leonard Street, Perth, PH2 provides bus and coach links throughout Scotland. See www.citylink.co.uk, **tel. 08705 505050** for timetables and fares.

The nearest airport offering regular, commercial flights is **Edinburgh International Airport**, **tel. 0844 461 8989**, www.edinburghairport.com.

WHISKY SHOPPING

■ **Robertson's of Pitlochry.** 46 Atholl Road, Pitlochry, Perthshire, PH16 5BX, tel. 01796 472011. Pitlochry is 26 miles north of Perth, via the A9.

RECOMMENDED BARS

- ■ **The Capital Asset.** 26 Tay Street, Perth, PH1 5LO, tel. 01738 580457.
- ■ **The Foundry.** 3 Murray Street, Perth, PH2 8G, tel. 01738 636863.
- ■ **Greyfriars Bar.** 15 South Street, Perth, PH2 8PG, tel. 01738 633036, www.greyfriarsbarperth.co.uk.
- ■ **The Old Ship Inn.** 31 High Street, Perth, PH1 5TJ, tel. 01738 624929.
- ■ **Roca Blu.** 1 Speygate, Perth, PH2 8PJ, tel. 01738 620539, www.rocablu.co.uk.
- ■ **The Sandeman.** 14-16 Kinnoull Street, Perth, PH1 5EZ, tel. 01738 443944.

CASTLE MENZIES

ITINERARIES AND AMENITIES

PLACES OF INTEREST

The Black Watch Regimental Museum is located in Balhousie Castle, close to Perth's historic North Inch, an extensive area of recreational parkland which borders the Tay. Now a battalion within the Royal Regiment of Scotland, The Black Watch was formerly the oldest Highland Regiment, being raised in 1739, and the museum provides a fascinating and poignant focus for its story. Balhousie Castle, Hay Street, Perth, PH1 5HR, **tel. 01738 643245**, email: rhq@theblackwatch.co.uk, web: www.theblackwatch.com.

Perth Theatre is an Edwardian gem in the city centre, which hosts a year round programme of drama. 185 High Street, Perth, PH1 5VW, **tel. 0845 6126323**, www.horsecross.co.uk. Since 2005 Perth has also boasted a state-of-the-art concert hall. Mill Street, Perth, PH1 5HZ, **tel. 01738 621031**, www.horsecross.co.uk. It offers classical and popular music, comedy, drama and children's entertainment.

Perth Racecourse is located in picturesque Scone Palace Park, where the sport has been staged since 1908. Today, National Hunt meetings are held between April and September. Perth is the most northerly racecourse in Britain and attracts horses to contest its events from as far away as Southern Ireland and the West Country.
Scone Palace Park, Perth, PH2 6BB, **tel. 01738 551597**, www.perth-races.co.uk.

Scone Palace is a five-star visitor attraction and home to the Earl of Mansfield. It was formerly the coronation venue for Scottish monarchs, and the Palace houses a notable collection of paintings, furniture and porcelain. It is set in more than 100 acres of gardens, which boast Perthshire's only maze. Perth, PH2 6BD, **tel. 01738 552300**, www.scone-palace.co.uk.

FURTHER GENERAL INFORMATION

Tourist Information Centre, Lower City Mills, West Mill Street, Perth PH1 5PQ, tel. **01738 450600**, www.perthcity.co.uk and www.perthshire.co.uk.

ABERFELDY BIRKS

RECOMMENDED HOTELS

■ **Achnacarry Guest House**. 3 Pitcullen Crescent, Perth, PH2 7HT,
tel. 01738 621421, www.achnacarry.co.uk (STB ★★★★ Guest House) Under £50

■ **Express By Holiday Inn**. 200 Dunkeld Road, Perth, PH1 3AQ,
tel. 01738 636666, www.ichotelsgroup.com (STB ★★★ Metro Hotel) Under £75

■ **Best Western Huntingtower Hotel**. Crieff Road, Perth, PH1 3JT,
tel. 01738 583771, www.huntingtowerhotel.co.uk (STB ★★★) £75-£125

■ **Best Western Queen's Hotel**. Leonard Street, Perth, PH2 8HB,
tel. 01738 442222, www.symphonyhotels.com (STB ★★★) £75-£125

■ **Murrayshall House Hotel and Golf Courses**. Scone, Perth, PH2 7PH,
tel. 01738 551171, www.murrayshall.com (★★★★) £75-£125

■ **Parklands Hotel**. 2 St Leonard's Bank, Perth, PH2 8EB,
tel. 01738 622451, www.theparklandshotel.com (★★★★) £75-£125

■ **Quality Hotel**. Leonard Street, Perth, PH2 8HE,
tel. 01738 624141, www.qualityinn.com (STB ★★★) Under £75

■ **Royal George Hotel**. Tay Street, Perth, PH1 5LD,
tel. 01738 624455, www.theroyalgeorge.co.uk £75+

■ **Salutation Hotel**. South Street, Perth, PH2 8PH,
tel. 01738-630066, www.strathmorehotels.com (STB ★★) Under £75

■ **Sunbank House Hotel**. 50 Dundee Road, Perth, PH2 7BA,
tel. 01738 624882, www.sunbankhouse.com (STB ★★★★ Metro Hotel) Under £50

RECOMMENDED RESTAURANTS

■ **Arts Restaurant**. (Bistro) West Mill Street, Perth, PH1 5QP,
tel. 01738 628281, www.ramadajarvis.co.uk Under £25

■ **Cafe Tabou**. (French) 4 St John's Place, Perth, PH1 5SZ,
tel. 01738 446698, www.cafetabou.co.uk Under £35

■ **The Italian Corner**. (Italian) 33 Princes Street, Perth, PH2 8LJ,
tel. 01738 629645. Under £35

■ **Keracher's Restaurant**. (Seafood) 168 South Street, Perth, PH2 8NY,
tel. 01738 449777, www.kerachers-restaurant.co.uk Under £35

■ **1747 Restaurant**. (Contemporary) Lovat Hotel, Glasgow Road, Perth, PH2 0LT,
tel. 01738 636555, www.symphonoyhotels.co.uk £35+

■ **63 Tay Street**. (Contemporary Scottish) 63 Tay Street, Perth, PH2 8NN,
tel. 01738 441451, www.63taystreet.com £35+

ITINERARIES AND AMENITIES

PERTHSHIRE TRAIL ▪▪▪▪▪▪▪▪ 🚗

*This tour includes three Perthshire distilleries which are very popular with visitors. The single malt from **Aberfeldy** and **Blair Athol** is principally used for blending, although both malts are well respected in their own right. In recent years, the tiny, picturesque distillery of **Edradour** has been responsible for an increasingly wide range of single malt expressions and although one of the smallest, it is also one of the most visited distilleries in Scotland.*

Allow a full day if visiting two or more distilleries, or half a day for any one of them.

Aberfeldy Distillery (see p.78) is located some 30 miles (50 minutes' drive) north-west of Perth, via the A9 north and the A827 (at Ballinluig). Alternatively, there is a more scenic route via the A822 and A826, off the A9 at Dunkeld. Aberfeldy is a charming holiday town on the banks of the River Tay and with Aberfeldy Watermill, The Birks of Aberfeldy (a beautiful, wooded area immortalised by Robert Burns) and Castle Menzies, it is well worth visiting in its own right.

Rural Perthshire has been home to many small distilleries over the years, but three of the most enduring were located in the area between the hamlet of Aberfeldy and Ballinluig, to the east. These were Auchnagie at Tulliemet (1827-1912), Ballechin, near Ballinluig (1810-1927) and Grandtully (1825-1910).

As well as travelling by road, it is also possible to take a Stagecoach bus from Perth to Aberfeldy. **Tel. 0138 629339** or see www.stagecoachbus.com for details.

The picturesque, small town of Pitlochry boast two working distilleries, both offering excellent tours. A journey of 26 miles (40 minutes' drive) from Perth, 14 miles from Aberfeldy, brings you to **Blair Athol Distillery** (see p.80), on the south-eastern outskirts of the town. Take the A9 from Perth, or the A827 from Aberfeldy to the A9 junction at Ballinluig, and head north (via the A924) into Pitlochry. This is a very popular holiday destination with many opportunities for shopping and refreshments. Pitlochry can also be reached by rail, as the main Perth-Inverness line passes through the town. See www.nationalrail.co.uk for details.

Located in a hamlet near Pitlochry, **Edradour Distillery** (see p.82) is just 2.5 miles (10 minutes' drive) via the A924, and is well signposted. En route you pass through the hamlet of Moulin, where the Moulin Inn was established in 1695. Today, it operates a micro-brewery which can be visited, and its excellent ales are available on draught in the Inn and in bottles for off-sales purchase. **Tel. 01796 472196**, www.moulininn.co.uk.

EAST PERTHSHIRE TRAIL ▬▬▬▬▬▬▬ 🚗

The Eastern Perthshire Trail features Scotland's two most visited distilleries, namely **Glenturret** *and* **Tullibardine**.

Allow half a day per distillery.

Glenturret Distillery is promoted as the spiritual home of The Famous Grouse blended whisky brand, and boasts one of the most technologically advanced visitor experiences of any Scottish distillery. Tullibardine Distillery, on the other hand, offers a traditional visitor experience and is conveniently located just of the main Stirling to Perth road

Glenturret Distillery (see p.86) is situated 18 miles (30 minutes' drive) from Perth, via the A85 Crianlarich road. The distillery is located just off the A85, after passing through the small Perthshire town of Crieff, where a stroll through the streets offers an enticing array of gift and antique shops. Glenturret Distillery has a fine café/restaurant and also boasts the Fasan Ur restaurant, offering unforgettable whisky and food fusions, although the latter is only available for private functions.

Tullibardine Distillery (see p.88) in the Perthshire village of Blackford is a short drive south along the A822, then via the A9. An 18 miles' journey along the A9 returns you to Perth.

A number of retail outlets are located in the Tullibardine complex, including one showcasing the products of Scottish family food group Baxter's. It contains a food hall, kitchenware and tasteful gift items, along with an excellent line up of whiskies, wines and bottled beers from Scottish breweries, not to mention a restaurant where menu items are made using Baxter's own products.

The world-famous Gleneagles Hotel and golf course is also situated close to the village of Blackford and stocks a healthy range of malts produced by hotel owner Diageo, alongside many other premium expressions.

FALLS OF DOCHART, KILLIN

ITINERARIES AND AMENITIES

AROUND ABERDEEN

Aberdeen is Scotland's third-largest city, after Glasgow and Edinburgh, and is nicknamed the 'Granite City,' due to the widespread use of locally-quarried grey granite for construction from the mid-18th to the mid-20th centuries. The exuberant gothic Marischal College is the world's second-largest granite structure, after El Escorial, near Madrid.

The area around Aberdeen has been settled for at least 8,000 years, and until Glasgow began to develop as a major industrial centre, Aberdeen was Scotland's 'second city.' The key to its prosperity was its port, and by the 13th century Aberdeen was the country's most significant exporter of wool to the continent.

Aberdeen was granted Royal Burgh status in 1319 and traded extensively with Germany, the Baltic and Scandinavia. Fishing, shipbuilding and whaling were major activities for the city, at various times, reflecting its important maritime status.

The 1970s saw the economy of the north-east of Scotland transformed by the discovery and exploitation of large deposits of crude oil in the North Sea, and today Aberdeen is effectively the 'oil capital' of Europe. The port continues to be extremely active, and Aberdeen Heliport is one of the busiest commercial heliports in the world. The harbour is also home to the mainland terminal for vehicle ferries to the Shetland Isles, along with a service to Orkney. See www.northlinkferries.co.uk.

Aberdeen has a long and distinguished Scotch whisky heritage, having been the historical home of a number of well-known blending companies as well as several distilleries. Blenders based in the city included James Catto & Co Ltd, Gordon Graham & Co Ltd, who established the Black Bottle blend, now in the hands of Burn Stewart Distillers, and most famously of all, Chivas Brothers. The Pernod Ricard-owned Scotch whisky subsidiary traces its origins back to an Aberdeen grocery store in 1801.

Of the various distilleries to have been established in the city, three, in particular, were notable for their longevity. Bon Accord came into existence in 1856, and was based in substantially renovated and upgraded premises on Hardgate, formerly occupied by the Union Glen distillery, which was sequestrated in 1853, and an adjacent 18th century brewery, which ceased trading the following year.

Bon Accord was one of the largest Highland malt whisky distilleries in Scotland, surviving until the early years of the 20th century, while Devanha distillery had earlier origins than Bon Accord, being established by the Devanha Brewery in 1837, on an extension of its existing site. Although the distillery closed in 1910, some buildings remain largely intact, and are clearly visible from trains on the neighbouring Dundee to Aberdeen railway line.

The third of Aberdeen's trio of distilleries which survived into the 20th century was its oldest, smallest, and most enduring. Strathdee was established in 1821 and traded until the Second World War.

GETTING TO ABERDEEN

The main road north to Aberdeen is the A90 from Perth and Dundee, which continues north of the city to the busy fishing port of Fraserburgh. The A96 leads north-west to Inverness, while the A93 passes through Royal Deeside to Braemar, and ultimately south to Perth.

Aberdeen Train Station. Guild St, Aberdeen, AB9 2DQ, **tel. 0845 601 5929,** www.nationalrail.co.uk. Aberdeen is connected by rail to Dundee, Edinburgh, Perth and Glasgow, and there is a sleeper service to London.

Aberdeen Bus Station. Guild St, Aberdeen, AB11 6GR, **tel. 01224 212266.** Regular buses link Aberdeen with other communities in the north-east, and express coach services run to the main cities of Scotland and the rest of the United Kingdom. **Citylink tel. 08705 505050,** www.citylink.co.uk

Aberdeen Airport. Aberdeen, AB21 7DU, **tel. 01224 722331,** www.aberdeenairport.com. The airport is seven miles north-west of the city, off the A96 Aberdeen-Inverness road, near Dyce. There are scheduled flights to a wide range of UK and continental destinations, including the London airports of Gatwick, Heathrow and Luton.

WHISKY SHOPPING

■ **SR&E Barron (Dyce Ltd).** 119 Victoria Street, Dyce, Aberdeen, AB21 7BJ, tel. 01224 722208, www.maltman.co.uk.

■ **Single Malts Direct.** 36 Gordon Street, Huntly, AB54 8EQ, tel. 0845 606 6145, www.singlemaltsdirect.com. Huntly is 22 miles from Aberdeen, via the A96 and A920. Single Malts Direct is the retail outlet of independent whisky bottler Duncan Taylor & Co Ltd. (www.duncantaylor.com).

■ **Parkers Whisky.** 27 Low Street, Banff, AB45 1AU, tel. 01261 812353, www.parkerswhisky.co.uk. Banff is 45 miles from Aberdeen, via the A947.

RECOMMENDED BARS

■ **The Albyn.** 11 Albyn Place, Aberdeen, AB10 1YE, tel. 01224 211666.

■ **Archibald Simpson.** 5 Castle Street, Aberdeen, AB11 5BQ, tel. 01224 621365.

■ **Enigma Bar.** Unit 17, The Academy Centre, Aberdeen, AB10 1LB, tel. 01224 637373.

■ **Moorings Bar.** 2 Trinity Quay, Aberdeen, AB11 5AA, tel. 01224 587 602.

■ **Prince of Wales.** 7 St Nicholas Lane, Aberdeen, AB10 1HF, tel. 01224 640597.

■ **Union Grill.** 213 Union Street, Aberdeen, AB11 6BA, tel. 01224 573530, www.thegrillaberdeen.co.uk.

ITINERARIES AND AMENITIES

PLACES OF INTEREST

Aberdeen city centre boasts three complementary entertainment venues, namely **His Majesty's Theatre**, **The Music Hall** and **The Lemon Tree**. His Majesty's Theatre opened in 1906 and underwent a £7.8 million redevelopment during 2004/5. It offers a diverse range of dramatic entertainment all year round. The Music Hall was created in 1858/59, while the more contemporary Lemon Tree functions as an intimate centre for drama, dance, music and comedy.

His Majesty's Theatre. Rosemount Viaduct, Aberdeen, AB25 1GL, **tel. 01224 641122.**
Music Hall. Union Street, Aberdeen, AB10 1QS, **tel. 01224 632080.**
The Lemon Tree. 5 West North Street, Aberdeen, AB24 5AT, **tel. 01224 337688.**
For online information on all three venues visit www.boxofficeaberdeen.com.

Aberdeen Art Gallery is an STB five-star Visitor Attraction and one of the city's most popular tourist venues. A particularly fine example of late 19th century architecture, it houses one of the best art collections in Britain with paintings, sculpture and graphics from the 15th century to the present day.
Schoolhill, Aberdeen, AB10 1FQ, **tel. 01224 523700,** www.aagm.co.uk.

Dating from 1545, **Provost Skene's House** takes its name from one of Aberdeen's most famous residents, Lord Provost George Skene. The property is now an STB four-star Visitor Attraction and houses a series of period rooms, furnished to show how people lived in the 17th, 18th and early 19th centuries. Visitors can admire an unusual collection of religious paintings in the Painted Gallery and enjoy changing displays of dress in the Costume Gallery.
Guestrow (between Broad Street and Flourmill Lane), Aberdeen, AB10 1AS, **tel. 01224 641086,** www.aagm.co.uk.

Aberdeen Maritime Museum tells the story of the city's long relationship with the sea, housing a unique collection covering shipbuilding, sailing ships, fishing and port history. It is also the only place in the UK with displays on the North Sea oil and gas industry. This STB five-star Museum Attraction is located in historic property on Shiprow, with fine views of the busy harbour.
Shiprow, Aberdeen, AB11 5BY, **tel. 01224 337700,** www.aagm.co.uk.

FURTHER GENERAL INFORMATION

Visitor Information centre, 23 Union Street, Aberdeen, AB11 5BP, **tel. 01224 288828,** www.aberdeen-grampian.com.

HIGHLAND (EASTERN)

RECOMMENDED HOTELS

- **Copthorne Hotel.** 122 Huntly Street, Aberdeen, AB10 1SU,
  tel. 01224 630404, www.millenniumhotels.co.uk (STB ★★★★) £125+

- **The Douglas Hotel.** 43-45 Market St, Aberdeen, AB11 5EL,
  tel. 01224 582255, www.aberdeendouglas.com (STB ★★★) £75-£125

- **Express By Holiday Inn.** Chapel Street, Aberdeen, AB10 1SQ,
  tel. 01224 623500, www.ichotelsgroup.com (STB ★★★ Metro Hotel) Under £75

- **The Jays Guest House.** 422 King Street, Aberdeen, AB24 3RB,
  tel. 01224 638295. (STB ★★★★ Guest House) Under £75

- **Marcliffe at Pitfodels.** North Deeside Road, Aberdeen, AB15 9YA,
  tel. 01224 861000, www.marcliffe.com (STB ★★★★★) £125+

- **Premier Inn Aberdeen. (City Centre)** Inverlair House, West North Street,
  Aberdeen, AB24 5AS,
  tel. 070 990 6300, www.premierinn.com (STB Budget Hotel) Under £75

- **Royal Hotel.** 1/3 Bath Street, Aberdeen, AB11 6BJ,
  tel. 01224 585152. (STB ★★) £75-£125

- **St Elmo's Guest House.** 64 Hilton Drive, Aberdeen, AB24 4NP,
  tel. 01224 483065, www.ensuitedreams.com (STB ★★★★ Guest House)
  Under £75

- **St Magnus Court Soprano Hotels.** 20/22 Guild Street, Aberdeen, AB11 6NF,
  tel. 01224 589411. (★★★) £75-£125

- **Station Hotel.** 78 Guild Street, Aberdeen, AB11 6GN,
  tel. 01224 573350, www.stationhotelaberdeen.com (STB★★★) £125+

RECOMMENDED RESTAURANTS

- **Dizzys Bar & Restaurant** (Eclectic). 70 Carden Place, Aberdeen, AB10 1UL,
  tel. 01224 625577, www.dizzys.co.uk Under £35

- **Howies Aberdeen** (Contemporary/Scottish). 50 Chapel Street, Aberdeen, AB10 1SN,
  tel. 01224 639500, www.howies.co.uk Under £25

- **The Olive Tree Restaurant** (Mediterranean). 32 Queen's Road, Aberdeen, AB15 4YF,
  tel. 01224 208877, www.olivetreegroup.co.uk Under £35

- **Poldino's Restaurant** (Italian). 7 Little Belmont Street, Aberdeen, AB10 1JG,
  tel. 01224 647777, www.poldinos.co.uk Under £35

- **Silver Darling** (Seafood). Pocra Qua North Pier, Aberdeen, AB11 5DQ,
  tel. 01224 56229, www.silverdarlingrestaurant.com £35+

- **Stage Door Restaurant** (Classic). 26 North Silver Street, Aberdeen, AB10 1RL,
  tel. 01224 642111, www.pbdevco.com Under £35

EASTERN HIGHLANDS TRAIL ▬▬▬▬▬▬ 🚗

This trail takes in one of the last remaining Eastern Highland distilleries, namely **Fettercairn**, *with the likes of Glenury Royal at Stonehaven, Glenesk at Montrose and North Port at Brechin all having ceased production. Brechin still boasts Glencadam Distillery (see p.179), which is open to the public by prior appointment, and is hidden away in the back streets of the small town.*

Allow at least half a day to visit Fettercairn from Aberdeen.

Fettercairn Distillery (see p.90) is situated on the outskirts of the pretty village of the same name, 34 miles (55 minutes' drive) south-west of Aberdeen, via the A90 and B966, in the fertile 'Howe of Mearns.' The village of Fettercairn has strong historic connections with the Gladstone family, who formerly owned the Fasque Estate. William Ewart Gladstone was four times Prime Minister of the United Kingdom during the second half of the 19th century.

Just beyond Fettercairn, along the B966, is Edzell Castle and Garden, which boasts a finely manicured renaissance rose garden. If heading back to Aberdeen, stop off in the port of Stonehaven, with its quaint, old harbour area. Also well worth a visit is the stunning Dunottar Castle, precariously located close to the cliff-tops, just south of the town.

PENNAN

ABERDEENSHIRE TRAIL ▪▬▪▬▪▬▪▬▪▬▪ 🚗

*An excursion encompassing two very old distilleries in rural Aberdeenshire,
namely* **Glengarioch** *and* **GlenDronach**.

**Allow half a day to visit Glengarioch and a full day if also taking in
GlenDronach.**

Glengarioch Distillery (see p.94) is located in the small town of Oldmeldrum,
18 miles (35 minutes' drive) north-west of Aberdeen by way of the A947.
 The north-east of Scotland is famed for its castles, with Tolquhon Castle being
the closest to Oldmeldrum. Also nearby, and well worth a visit, are Haddo House
and the immaculate, walled Pitmedden Garden.
 GlenDronach Distillery (see p.92) is surrounded by fertile, arable land, close to
the hamlet of Forgue, within sight of the B9024, nine miles east of Huntly, off the
A97 Huntly to Banff road. If travelling directly to GlenDronach Distillery from
Aberdeen, take the A96 and A97. The distance is 43 miles (one hour's drive).
While Glengarioch is classified as an Eastern Highland single malt, like
Fettercairn, GlenDronach is usually categorised as a Speyside.
 If time permits, a drive north along the coastline, taking in Portsoy, Banff,
Gardenstown, Pennan and Fraserburgh provides an excellent introduction to the
north east's fishing heritage. It is worth noting that travel on these roads is
relatively slow, and a full day can easily be spent just touring the fishing towns
and villages of the area.
 In addition to the distilleries noted above, the city of Aberdeen also provides a
good base for exploring into the heartland of the Speyside region of distilleries, as
featured in the 'Aberlour and Dufftown Trail' (see p.40). Dufftown is 52 miles (one
hour and 20 minutes' drive) from Aberdeen, via the A96 to Huntly and the A920.

ORKNEY TRAIL ▪▬▪▬▪▬▪▬▪▬▪ 🚗

*A long distance trail which takes you to the beautiful Orkney Islands, home to
Scapa and* **Highland Park** *distilleries. While Scapa is not regularly open to the
public, its near neighbour offers a very rewarding and full visitor experience.*

**When travelling by ferry, allow at least three days for a trip to Orkney and
Highland Park. Flights from Aberdeen to Kirkwall take approximately 50
minutes.**

If you are bound for the Orkney Islands and want to avoid the long drive to the
Caithness ferry terminals of Gill's Bay and Scrabster (see Inverness Trail) there is
a limited car ferry service from Aberdeen to Kirkwall, see
www.northlinkferries.co.uk. **Highland Park Distillery** (see p.149) is just a few
minutes' drive from the harbour , via the A961.   Alternatively, regular flights also
connect Aberdeen with Kirkwall in Orkney, providing easy access to Highland
Park.
There are plenty of historical and cultural places of interest on Orkney to
supplement a day or two's visit to the island. Of particular interest are the Stone
Age settlement of Skara Brae and the Ring of Brogar stand stones. For more
information on the Orkney Islands, see www.visitorkney.com.

AROUND ABERLOUR AND DUFFTOWN

The River Spey is the second-longest river in Scotland, after the Tay, having its source in Loch Spey, 350 metres above sea level in the Monadhliath Mountains. It flows for 107 miles in a north-easterly direction until it enters the Moray Firth, north-east of Elgin.

The Spey is one of Scotland's great salmon-fishing rivers, but it is also renowned for its associations with whisky. The Speyside classification of single malt Scotch whiskies embraces around half of the active distilleries in Scotland, and this beautiful area of the north-east, which includes the counties of Moray and Banffshire, is an essential part of any whisky lover's touring agenda.

Set in the heart of Scotland's 'malt whisky country,' the neighbouring villages of Aberlour and Dufftown offer the perfect base for anyone exploring Speyside. Both Aberlour and Dufftown were planned settlements, with the modern layout of 'Charlestown of Aberlour' dating from 1812. In that year the local land owner, Charles Grant of Wester Elchies, established a new village, to the east of the old one, close to the banks of the River Spey, and gave it his own name. Today, however, few people refer to it as anything other than 'Aberlour.'

Dufftown is just six miles east of Aberlour, and stands at the confluence of the rivers Fiddich and Dullan, in the shadow of the Conval hills. Like Aberlour, it was the work of a local laird, in this case James Duff, 4th Earl of Fife. Construction began five years after work started on the building of Aberlour, though there was a settlement in the locality as long ago as 700AD, when Mortlach Church was established.

Today, Aberlour is home to the factory and headquarters of the thriving family firm of Walker's Shortbread Limited. Walkers Shortbread is the largest independent biscuit maker in the Britain, and produces 60 per cent of all shortbread exported from Scotland. At the opposite end of the village's main street to the Walker's complex is Aberlour Distillery (see p.100), while a number of others, such as Glenallachie (see p.193), are in close proximity.

There is an old rhyme that states 'Rome was built on seven stills, Dufftown stands on seven stills,' and the village still plays host to no fewer than six working distilleries, while the silent plants of Convalmore and Parkmore also remain externally intact. The landmark clock tower in Dufftown square dates from 1839 and was built as the local jail. Legend has it that it was also the location for an illicit distillery at some unspecified time! The eye-catching structure now functions as a seasonal tourist information office.

Dufftown is on the Malt Whisky Trail www.maltwhiskytrail.com, which is a 70 miles-long route, linking the seven working distilleries of Benromach, Cardhu, Glen Grant, Glen Moray, Glenfiddich, The Glenlivet, and Strathisla, as well as the silent but preserved Dallas Dhu Distillery (see p.229), and the Speyside Cooperage (see below).

The Speyside Way is an official 'Long Distance Route,' which runs from Aviemore to the Moray coast, generally following the River Spey, and passing through Aberlour and Dufftown. For further information visit www.moray.gov.uk/area/speyway.

SPEYSIDE

GETTING TO ABERLOUR AND DUFFTOWN

Dufftown is 52 miles (one hour and 20 minutes' drive) north-west of Aberdeen, via the A96. It is 57 miles (one hour and 30 minutes' drive) from Inverness via the same A96. Aberlour is six miles from Dufftown, via the A95 and A941 while the village of Craigellachie is mid way between the two.

From the south, take the A9 from Perth, then the A95 after the Aviemore junction to Aberlour. The journey is 117 miles (two hours and 40 minutes' drive).

The nearest train station to Aberlour and Dufftown is **Elgin Station**, Station Road, Elgin, IV30 1QP, **tel. 08457 484950**, which is 14 miles north of Aberlour and 17 miles from Dufftown. Trains running between Inverness and Aberdeen stop at Elgin. Alternatively, **Aviemore Station**, Grampian Road, Aviemore, PH22 1PD, **tel. 08457 484950** is on the Perth to Inverness main line, giving access to the Speyside area by way of local bus or taxi services. See www.nationalrail.co.uk for details of all timetables and fares.

Aberlour and Dufftown bus services. Buses run between Aberlour and Dufftown, linking to Elgin, Grantown-on-Spey and Aviemore, as well as many other local destinations. For details of services see www.moray.gov.uk.

Aberdeen and Inverness Airports. Please see North East & North Highland section.

WHISKY SHOPPING

■ **Gordon & MacPhail Ltd.** 58-60 South Street, Elgin, IV30 1JY, **tel. 01343 545110**, www.gordonandmacphail.com. Gordon & MacPhail are one of Scotland's oldest independent whisky bottlers, owners of Benromach Distillery (see p.104). Elgin is 14 miles (20 minutes' drive) north of Aberlour and 17.5 miles from Dufftown, via the A941.

■ **The Wee Spey Dram Whisky Shop.** 72-74 High Street, Grantown on Spey, PH26 3EL, **tel. 01479 870114**, www.weespeydram.co.uk. Grantown-on-Spey is 21 miles (30 minutes' drive) south-west of Aberlour, by way of the A95.

■ **The Whisky Castle.** 6 Main Street, Tomintoul, Ballindalloch, AB37 9EX, tel. 01807 580213, www.whiskycastle.com. Tomintoul is 19 miles (35 minutes' drive) from Dufftown, via the B9009 and B9008.

■ **The Whisky Shop Dufftown.** 1 Fife Street, Dufftown, AB55 4AL, **tel. 01340 821097**, www.whiskyshopdufftown.co.uk.

RECOMMENDED BARS

■ **The Fiddichside Inn**. Craigellachie, AB38 9RR (on the A95, north-east of the village), tel. 01340 881239.

■ **The Grouse Inn**. Lower Cabrach, AB54 4EL (eight miles south-west of Dufftown, on the A941, open Easter to the end of October), tel. 01466 702200.

■ **The Highlander Inn**. 2 Victoria Street, Craigellachie, AB38 9SR, tel. 01340 881446, www.whiskyinn.com.

■ **The Quaich Bar**. The Craigellachie Hotel, Victoria Street, Craigellachie, AB38 9SR, tel.01340 881204.

■ **The Mash Tun**. 8 Broomfield Square, Aberlour, AB38 9QP, tel. 01340 881 771, www.mashtun-aberlour.com.

PLACES OF INTEREST

Ballindalloch Castle dates from at least the 16th century, and remains the family home of the Macpherson-Grants, although it is also open to the public. Ballindalloch is one of very few privately-owned castles in Scotland to have been occupied continuously by its original family. The rivers Spey and Avon flow through the castle grounds, which also boast a famous herd of pedigree Aberdeen Angus cattle. Ballindalloch Castle, Ballindalloch, AB37 9AX (seven miles from Aberlour, on the A95), **tel. 01807 500205**, www.ballindallochcastle.co.uk.

Baxter's Highland Village is located in the village of Fochabers, on the banks of the River Spey, and serves as a showcase for the family-owned Baxter's Food Group. George Baxter opened his first grocery shop in 1868, and today the four-star rated Highland Village recounts the story of the entrepreneurial Baxter family and offers for sale Baxter's products, other specialist food items, cookware and clothing. There is also a self-service restaurant. Baxter's Highland Village, Fochabers, IV32 7LD, (20 miles from Aberlour, via the A95 and A96), **tel. 01343 820666**, www.baxters.com.

Elgin is the commercial and administrative capital of Moray, and the largest town in the area. It stands close to the River Lossie, 14 miles north of Aberlour, and is first documented in 1190. Elgin, with its Glen Moray Distillery (see p.118), is well worth visiting in its own right, and one of its architectural and historical jewels is **Elgin Cathedral**. Although now in ruins, this is one of Scotland's most beautiful medieval buildings, being founded in 1224 and burnt in 1390 by Alexander Stewart, Earl of Buchan, better known as the 'Wolf of Badenoch.' Elgin Cathedral, Elgin, IV30 1HU, **tel. 01343 547171**, www.historic-scotland.gov.uk.

Johnston's of Elgin is a company specialising in cashmere clothing, and operates from a historic mill in Elgin. The firm was established in 1797 and its mill is the only one in Scotland which transforms cashmere from raw fibre into finished articles. A £1.5 million heritage centre and retail outlet opened in 2008, and includes a coffee shop which boasts Scottish home baking. Newmill, Elgin, IV30 4AF, **tel. 01343 554040**, www.johnstonscashmere.com.

FURTHER GENERAL INFORMATION

Tourist Information Centre, The Clock Tower, The Square, Dufftown, AB55 4AD, **tel. 01343 543451**, www.greaterspeyside.com, www.speyside.moray.org and dwww.dufftown.co.uk.

RECOMMENDED HOTELS

- **Aberlour Hotel.** 87 High Street, Aberlour, AB38 9QB,
  tel. 01340 871287, www.aberlour-hotel.com (STB ★★★) Under £75

- **Archiestown Hotel.** Archiestown, AB38 7QL (six miles from Aberlour,
  via the B9102),
  tel. 01340 810218, www.archiestownhotel.co.uk (STB ★★★ Small Hotel)
  £75-£125

- **Craigellachie Hotel.** Victoria Street, Craigellachie, AB38 9SR,
  tel. 01340 881204, www.oxfordhotelsandinns.com (STB ★★★) £75-£125

- **Dowans Hotel.** Aberlour, AB38 9LS,
  tel. 01340 871488, www.dowanshotel.com (STB ★★★ Small Hotel) Under £75

- **Eastbank Hotel.** 15/17 High Street, Rothes, AB38 7AU (4.5 miles from
  Aberlour, via the A941),
  tel. 01340 831564, www.eastbankhotel.co.uk (STB Commended ★★★)
  Under £75

- **Highlander Inn.** 2 Victoria Street, Craigellachie, AB38 9SR,
  tel. 01340 881446, www.whiskyinn.com Under £75

- **The Mash Tun.** 8 Broomfield Square, Aberlour, AB38 9QP,
  tel. 01340 881 771, www.mashtun-aberlour.com £75-£125

- **Morven** (B&B). The Square, Dufftown, AB55 4AD,
  tel. 01340 820507, www.morverndufftown.co.uk Under £50

- **Tannochbrae Guest House & Restaurant.** 22 Fife Street, Dufftown, AB55 4AL,
  tel. 01340 820541, www.tannochbrae.co.uk (STB ★★★★ Guest House)
  Under £75

RECOMMENDED RESTAURANTS

- **Archiestown Hotel & Bistro.** (Contemporary/ Scottish) Archiestown, AB38 7QL
  (six miles from Aberlour, via the B9102),
  tel. 01340 810218, www.archiestownhotel.co.uk £35+

- **La Faisanderie.** (French/Scottish) 2 Balvenie Street, Dufftown, AB55 4AB,
  tel. 01340 821273. Under £35

- **The Mash Tun.** (Contemporary/Scottish) 8 Broomfield Square, Aberlour,
  AB38 9QP,
  tel. 01340 881 771, www.mashtun-aberlour.com Under £35

- **The Old Pantry.** (British) High Street, Aberlour, AB38 9NY,
  tel. 01340 871617. Under £25

- **Tannochbrae Guest House & Restaurant.** (Contemporary/Scottish)
  22 Fife Street, Dufftown, AB55 4AL,
  tel. 01340 820541, www.tannochbrae.co.uk Under £35

- **A Taste of Speyside.** (Scottish) 10 Balvenie Street, Dufftown, AB55 4AB,
  tel. 01340 820860, www.taste-of-scotland.com £35+

SPEYSIDE TRAIL

There are no fewer than 13 distilleries with visitor facilities within a 20 miles radius of Aberlour and Dufftown. These include:

Benromach Distillery The smallest working distillery in Speyside and the closest to Inverness.

Cardhu Distillery Set in beautiful surroundings, the only malt distillery pioneered by a woman, Elizabeth Cumming.

Cragganmore Distillery Tours, with sampling of whiskies taking place in the 'Cragganmore Club.'

Dallas Dhu Distillery A completely preserved distillery which now serves as a museum.

Glenfiddich Distillery Offering free, budget and connoisseurs' tours, and within walking distance of Dufftown village.

Glenfarclas Distillery One of the few remaining family owned and run distilleries in Scotland.

Glen Grant Distillery Unique stills and a magnificent wooded garden, incorporating Major Grant's heather- thatched dram pavilion.

The Glenlivet Distillery Situated in the scenic heart of Glenlivet and offering free tours.

Glen Moray Distillery 'Elgin's distillery,' with a variety of tour experiences to choose from.

Strathisla Distillery With its double pagoda-topped kiln and intact water wheel, this is one of the most picturesque distilleries on Speyside.

The remaining three distilleries focus on specialist and personal tours, for those who want a more in-depth experience or who wish to sample rarer whiskies:

Aberlour Distillery Offers detailed tours and tasting sessions with the chance to bottle your own single malt.

Balvenie Distillery Presents a lengthy, connoisseurs' tour and an opportunity to hand-bottle Balvenie for purchase.

Macallan Distillery No fewer than 21 small stills operate at The Macallan, and tours include a warehouse visit, where 'The Story of Oak' explores the distillery's famous use of ex-Sherry casks.

It is best not to attempt to tour more than two distilleries per day.

The Speyside Cooperage

Located on the outskirts of the village of Craigellachie, The Speyside Cooperage is the only working establishment in the UK where you can explore the ancient art of coopering. The business was established in 1947, and provides casks for many distilleries in Speyside and far beyond.

Visitors learn about the life cycle of casks, watch skilled coopers at work and even have the opportunity to try their hand at making a mini-cask for themselves. Additionally, there is a gift and coffee shop. The cask-related exhibition and coopering audio-visual presentation are available in English, French, Spanish, German, Japanese and Italian. Dufftown Road, Craigellachie, AB38 9RS, tel. 01340 871108.

Festivals

This area of Speyside is a Mecca for whisky enthusiasts from around the globe at most times of year, but there are also two dedicated, annual whisky festivals, with the Spirit of Speyside Whisky Festival being staged in April/May and the Autumn Speyside Whisky Festival during late September/early October. These allow visitors the chance to tour distilleries not usually open to the public, as well as experiencing talks, tastings, ceilidhs and many other whisky-themed events. For more details visit www.spiritofspeyside.com. The spring festival tends to be the busier of the two events, so forward planning for this festival is strongly recommended.

RIVER SPEY, ABERLOUR

ITINERARIES AND AMENITIES

AROUND INVERNESS

Inverness is widely known as the 'Capital of the Highlands,' and stands among some of the most splendid scenery Scotland has to offer. Now a bustling city, the settlement was originally a modest fort, but it had developed sufficiently by the 12th century to be granted a Royal Burgh charter by King David of Scotland in 1158, while 1307 saw Robert the Bruce seize the first of five castles to have existed in Inverness from English forces.

Over four centuries later, the last battle on British soil took place at nearby Culloden Moor, when the Jacobite army of Charles Edward Stuart (Bonnie Prince Charlie) was defeated by government troops, led by the Duke of Cumberland.

Inverness was formerly home to three distilleries, all of which were active until the 1980s. Today, only remains of Millburn are to be found, incorporated into the 'Auld Distillery Bar & Restaurant' www.theaulddistillery.com on Millburn Road, a mile from the centre of the city. Here, drams of the now rare single malt itself are on sale.

Millburn was actually the oldest of the city's trio of distilleries, being established around 1805/7, and it passed through several sets of hands before ending up in the portfolio of the vast Distillers Company Ltd (DCL) in 1943. Like many distilleries, it also suffered a serious fire, and in the case of Millburn this occurred during April 1922; the conflagration being extinguished with the help of troops from nearby Cameron Barracks

The 1980s saw DCL close more than 20 distilleries due to over-production in the Scotch whisky industry, and Millburn was one casualty, along with its fellow Inverness distilleries of Glen Albyn and Glen Mhor. Glen Albyn had opened in 1844, on the site of a former brewery, close to the Caledonian Canal, and for most of its existence produced single malt almost exclusively for blending purposes.

It was purchased by DCL in 1972, along with the neighbouring Glen Mhor distillery, which dated from 1892. The 'make' of Glen Mhor and was also principally used for blending, although the whisky was also quite widely available as a single malt and enjoyed a good reputation.

Glen Albyn and Glen Mhor were both closed by DCL in 1983 and demolished three years later. The Telford Retail Park (IV 3) now occupies the site of the distilleries, though Glen Albyn and Glen Mhor single malts, along with Millburn, are still available from independent bottlers, notably **Gordon & MacPhail** of Elgin www.gordonandmacphail.com.

INVERNESS CASTLE

HIGHLAND (NORTHERN)

GETTING TO INVERNESS

The main road from Perth to Inverness is the A9, which continues north to Caithness and the principal ferry terminal for the Orkney Islands at Scrabster, near Thurso. The A96 to the east links Inverness to Aberdeen, while to the south-west the A82 leads ultimately to Fort William and to the Isle of Skye, via the A87.

Inverness Station. Station Square, Academy Street, Inverness, IV1 1LF, **tel. 0845 601 5929**.

Inverness enjoys good rail links to every point of the compass – north to Thurso and Wick, east to Nairn and Aberdeen, south via Aviemore to Glasgow, Edinburgh and London, and west to Kyle of Lochalsh and the Isle of Skye. There are direct sleeper services to London. See www.nationalrail.co.uk for details of all timetables and fares.

Farraline Park Bus Station. Inverness, IV1 1NH, **tel. 01463 233371**.

Regular buses link Inverness with other Highland communities, and express coach services run to the main cities of Scotland and the rest of the United Kingdom. For details **tel.08705 505050**, www.citylink.co.uk or **tel. 01463 239 292**, www.stagecoachbus.com.

Inverness Airport. Dalcross, Inverness, IV2 7JB, **tel. 01667 464000**, www.hial.co.uk is located 20 minutes' drive from the city centre and connects Inverness with a wide range of locations, including Birmingham, Dublin, Edinburgh, Manchester and the London airports of Gatwick, Heathrow and Luton. There are also scheduled flights to Kirkwall, on Orkney, allowing the opportunity to visit Highland Park Distillery.

WHISKY SHOPPING

■ **The Whisky Shop**. 17 Bridge Street, Inverness, IV1 1HD, **tel. 01463 710525**, www.whiskyshop.com.

RECOMMENDED BARS

■ **Blackfriars**. 93-95 Academy Street, Inverness, IV1 1LU, tel. 01463 233881, www.blackfriarshighlandpub.co.uk.

■ **Castle Tavern**. 1 View Place, Inverness, IV2 4SA, tel. 01463 718178, www.castletavern.net.

■ **Hootananny Inverness**. 67 Church Street, Inverness, IV1 1QU, tel. 01463 233651.

■ **Johnny Foxes**. 26 Bank Street, Inverness, IV1 1QU, tel. 01463 236577?. The King's Highway. 72-74 Church Street, Inverness, IV1 1EN, tel. 01463 251800.

■ **Number 27**. 27 Castle Street, Inverness, IV2 3DU, tel. 01463 241999.

ITINERARIES AND AMENITIES

PLACES OF INTEREST

Eden Court Theatre is the city's principal venue for drama and entertainment, presenting a varied year-round programme of shows to suit all tastes.
Eden Court, Bishop's Road, Inverness, IV3 5SA, **tel. 01463 234234**, www.eden-court.co.uk.

Inverness Museum & Art Gallery gives visitors the opportunity to explore the art, history and heritage of the Highlands, with particular emphasis on the development of Inverness. The Museum stands close to **Inverness Castle**, which houses a range of administrative and legal services and is largely a neo-Norman structure, dating from the 19th century.
Inverness Museum & Art Gallery. Castle Wynd, Inverness, IV2 3EB,
tel. 01463 237114, www.invernessmuseum.com.

The Caledonian Canal links Inverness to the west coast, and runs for 60 miles along the Great Glen to Corpach, near Fort William. The hugely ambitious construction project, to the design of Thomas Telford, began in 1803, and by the time the canal finally opened in 1822 it had taken 17 years to build and cost £840,000. A second phase of construction was undertaken between 1844 and 1847. The Canal allowed mariners to avoid the long and often hazardous route round the west of Scotland and through the Pentland Firth to the north of the Scottish mainland.

A lengthy section the Caledonian Canal utilises **Loch Ness**, which is over 20 miles long, a mile wide and 700 feet deep in places. It is the largest loch in Scotland by volume and is, in itself, one of Scotland's major tourist attractions, with many people hoping to catch a glimpse of the Loch Ness Monster during their visit! To reach Loch Ness, take the A82 or B862 south from Inverness.

Culloden Battlefield is in the care of the National Trust for Scotland and is situated seven miles south-east of Inverness, via the A82 and B9006. It features a state of the art, yet visually non-intrusive, visitor centre, opened in 2008. This facility helps to tell the story of the final battle of the 1745/46 Jacobite Rising, which attempted to restore the exiled Stuart dynasty to the British throne. Culloden saw the defeat of Charles Edward Stuart (Bonnie Prince Charlie), who spent the rest of his life in exile.
Culloden Moor, Inverness, IV2 5EU, **tel. 0844 493 2159**, www.nts.org.uk.

FURTHER GENERAL INFORMATION

Tourist Information Centre, Castle Wynd, Inverness, IV2 3BJ,
tel. 01845 2255121, www.inverness-scotland.com.

HIGHLAND (NORTHERN)

RECOMMENDED HOTELS

- **Columba Hotel.** 7 Ness Walk, Inverness, IV3 5NF,
  tel. 01463 231391, www.oxfordhotelsandinns.com (STB ★★★) £50-£75

- **Culloden House Hotel.** Culloden, Inverness, IV2 7BZ,
  tel. 01463 790461, www.cullodenhouse.co.uk (STB ★★★★ Country House Hotel)
  £125+

- **Eden House.** Ballifeary Road, Inverness, IV3 5PJ,
  tel. 01463 230278, www.edenhouseinverness.co.uk (STB ★★★★ Guest House)
  Under £50

- **Express by Holiday Inn.** Stoneyfield, Inverness, IV2 7GG,
  tel. 01463 732700, www.hiexpress.com (STB ★★★ Metro Hotel) £50-£75

- **The Ghillie's Lodge.** 16 Island Bank Road, Inverness, IV2 4QS,
  tel. 01463 232137, www.ghillieslodge.com (STB ★★★ B&B) Under £50

- **Glen Mhor Hotel.** Ness Bank, Inverness, IV2 4SG,
  tel. 01463 234308, www.glen-mhor.com (STB ★★★) £75-£125

- **Glenmoriston Town House.** 20 Ness Bank, Inverness, IV2 4SF,
  tel. 01463 223777, www.glenmoristontownhouse.com (STB ★★★★) £125+

- **Ramada Inverness.** Church Street, Inverness, IV1 1DX,
  tel. 0844 815 9006, www.ramadajarvis.co.uk (STB ★★★) £75-£125

- **Rocpool Reserve.** Culduthel Road, Inverness, IV2 4AG,
  tel. 01463 240089, www.rocpool.com (STB ★★★★) £125+

- **Waterside Hotel.** 19 Ness Bank, Inverness, IV2 4SF,
  tel. 01463 233065, www.thewatersideinverness.co.uk (STB ★★★) £75-£125

RECOMMENDED RESTAURANTS

- **Abstract Restaurant.** (French/Scottish) Glenmoriston Town House,
  20 Ness Bank, Inverness, IV2 4SF, tel. 01463 223 777,
  www.glenmoristontownhouse.com £35+

- **Contrast Brasserie.** Glenmoriston Town House, 20 Ness Bank, Inverness,
  IV2 4SF,
  tel. 01463 223 777, www.contrastbraserie.co.uk Under £35

- **The Kitchen Restaurant.** (Eclectic) 15 Huntly Street, Inverness, IV3 5PR,
  tel. 01463 259119, www.kitchenrestaurant.co.uk Under £35

- **The Mustard Seed.** (Eclectic) 16 Fraser Street, Inverness, IV1 1DW,
  tel. 01463 220220, www.themustardseedresturant.co.uk Under £35

- **Riva Restaurant.** (Italian) 4-6 Ness Walk, Inverness, IV3 5NE,
  tel. 01463 237377, www.rivarestaurant.co.uk Under £35

- **The Riverhouse.** (European) 1 Grieg Street, Inverness, IV3 5PT,
  tel. 01463 222033, www.riverhouseinverness.co.uk £35+

ITINERARIES AND AMENITIES

INVERSE-SHIRE TRAIL ▰▰▰▰▰▰▰▰ 🚗

The two closest distilleries to Inverness are **Tomatin** *and* **Glen Ord,** *and either one can be reached by road in 30 minutes. However, one is to the north-west of the city, while the other is to the south-east. Tomatin was once the largest malt whisky distillery in Scotland in terms of capacity, while spirit from the latter makes an important contribution to a number of Diageo's best-known blends.*

Allow a full day to visit both distilleries. Alternatively, either one can be visited on a half-day drive from Inverness.

Tomatin Distillery (see p.142) is situated in dramatic scenery, close to the A9 road, 17 miles (25 minutes' drive) south-east of Inverness. To reach **Glen Ord Distillery** (see p.134), retrace your steps to Inverness, by way of the A9, cross the Kessock Bridge, and take the A832 to Muir of Ord. The distillery is just off the A832, after you pass through the village. Glen Ord is 27 miles (40 minutes' drive) from Tomatin, and 13 miles (20 minutes' drive) from Inverness.

NORTH-EAST HIGHLANDS COASTAL TRAIL ▰▰▰▰▰▰ 🚗

This tour takes in two of the best known distilleries in the Highlands, in the shape of **Dalmore** *and* **Glenmorangie,** *and also gives the visitor an opportunity to see from the outside several other working distilleries which are not open to the public or have restricted access.*

Allow a full day to visit both distilleries. Alternatively, either one can be visited on a half-day drive from Inverness.

Dalmore Distillery (see p.128) is owned by Whyte & Mackay Ltd, and stands next to the shores of the Cromarty Firth, on the outskirts of the town of Alness, 20 miles (30 minutes' drive) north of Inverness. It is accessed from the A9 via the B817 at Alness. The town is also home to Diageo's Teaninich Distillery (see p.217, not open to the public), which is located on the Alness Industrial Estate (IV17 0XB).

Glenmorangie Distillery (see p.132) is a further 15 miles (20 minutes' drive) north on the A9 from Alness, and is located beside the main road which bypasses the neighbouring town of Tain. Glenmorangie is 34 miles (45 minutes' drive) from Inverness.

The pretty **Balblair Distillery** (see p.216) is open to the public by appointment and is to be found in the village of Edderton, just five miles (10 minutes' drive) north-east of Glenmorangie, via the A9 and A836.

The port of Invergordon is four miles from Alness, and home to Whyte & Mackay's Invergordon grain distillery (not open to the public, IV18 0HP). This large, industrial complex was constructed between 1959 and 1961, and can produce up to 27 million litres of grain spirit per annum. From 1965 to 1976 the site also housed a small malt distillery, named Ben Wyvis.

As an alternative to driving, there is a regular coach service by Citylink www.citylink.co.uk, **tel. 08705 505050**) between Inverness and Wick/Thurso, which follows the A9 via Alness and Tain.

FAR NORTH TRAIL ▄▬▄▬▄▬▄▬▄ 🚗

Scotland's two northernmost mainland distilleries, **Clynelish** *and* **Pulteney**, *are within a reasonable drive of Inverness, and the Caithness vehicle ferry terminals at Gill's Bay www.pentlandferries.co.uk and Scrabster www.northlinkferries.co.uk provide access to the Orkney Islands and Highland Park Distillery, close to the island 'capital' of Kirkwall. See www.visitorkney.com and www.highlandpark.com.*

Allow a full day to visit Clynelish, and if travelling on to Pulteney, an overnight stay is recommended in order to get the best out of the trip.

Clynelish Distillery (see p.126) is on the northern outskirts of the East Sutherland coastal town of Brora, 57 miles (one hour and 15 minutes' drive) north of Inverness on the A9. **Pulteney Distillery** (see p.140), in the Pulteneytown area of the fishing port of Wick, is a further 46 miles (one hour's drive) north of Clynelish, and 103 miles (two hours and 15 minutes' drive) from Inverness, via the A9 and A99.

Inverness-Wick/Thurso coaches (see 'Trail 2' above) stop at Brora and Wick, and there is also a regular rail service from Inverness to Wick (see www.nationalrail.co.uk).

Additionally, Inverness serves as a suitable base for exploring the Isle of Skye www.skye.co.uk and visiting **Talisker Distillery** (see p.148).

DUNROBIN CASTLE

ITINERARIES AND AMENITIES

51

AROUND FORT WILLIAM

Fort William is the largest town in the west Highlands of Scotland and the commercial heart of the Lochaber area. It is a major tourist centre, nestling on the shores of Loch Linnhe, with Glencoe to the south and Glenfinnan to the west. It also stands in the shadow of Scotland's highest mountain, Ben Nevis. Glen Nevis forms the valley on the eastern flank of Ben Nevis, and the glen featured in both the *Rob Roy* and *Braveheart* films.

Fort William is located at the northern end of the West Highland Way, a long distance route which runs 95 miles from Milngavie, on the outskirts of Glasgow. Additionally, the town stands at the western end of the Great Glen Way, which links Fort William and Inverness. Given its strategic location and magnificent scenery, it is not surprising that Fort William is marketed as 'The outdoor capital of the UK.'

The town developed as a settlement alongside a stone fortress which was constructed around 1698, and was used to help suppress the Jacobite Risings of 1714/15 and 1745/46, when Charles Edward Stuart ('Bonnie Prince Charlie') led attempts to restore a Stuart monarch to the British throne.

Today, the town is home to Ben Nevis Distillery (see p.124), but there were once three whisky-making facilities in Fort William. From 1878 until 1908 a separate distillery, adjacent to Ben Nevis, operated under the Nevis name. It was built by Donald McDonald of Ben Nevis distillery to help meet burgeoning demand for his Dew of Ben Nevis blended whisky, and the plant was ultimately absorbed into its larger neighbour.

Closer to the centre of town was Glenlochy Distillery, which came on stream in April 1901, just as the great 'whisky bubble' of prosperity was in the process of bursting. The new distillery changed hands several times and suffered periods of closure before being acquired in 1937 by Train & McIntyre Ltd, a company initially owned by National Distillers of America Inc and the Canadian entrepreneur Joseph Hobbs. The colourful, Scots-born millionaire was also proprietor of Ben Nevis distillery from 1941 until his death in 1964.

In 1953, Glenlochy was sold to the Distillers Company Ltd's (DCL) subsidiary Scottish Malt Distillers Ltd, and when DCL undertook a major programme of distillery closures during the 1980s, the small and relatively old-fashioned Glenlochy plant was one of those to fall silent. The last spirit flowed in 1983, and although some of the site was cleared after distilling ceased, a number of buildings survive, including the 'listed' kiln and malt barn, with the latter having been developed into affordable accommodation units. Additionally, a number of former staff cottages have been converted into the Distillery Guest House (see 'Recommended Hotels').

BEN NEVIS

GETTING TO FORT WILLIAM

Fort William is 108 miles (two hours and 30 minutes' drive) north of Glasgow, via the M8, Erskine Bridge and A82. Inverness is 65 miles (one hour and 25 minutes' drive) to the north-east, by way of the A82.

Fort William Station. Tom-na-Faire, Station Square, Fort William, PH33 6TQ, **tel. 0845 601 5929.** Fort William has rail links to Glasgow and Edinburgh and a sleeper service which connects it with various English cities. Additionally, the West Highland Line joins Fort William to the fishing and ferry port of Mallaig on the Atlantic coast. See www.nationalrail.co.uk for details of all timetables and fares. In summer the privately-operated Jacobite Express steam train runs on the Fort William-Mallaig route www.westcoastrailways.co.uk.

Fort William is connected to Oban, Inverness and many other Scottish destinations by **Scottish City Link** coach services. For details see www.citylink.co.uk or **tel. 08705 505050.** Additionally, **Skye-Ways Travel**, www.skyeways.co.uk, **tel. 01599 534328**, operates a Glasgow-Fort William-Skye coach service.

The nearest airports offering scheduled flights are

Inverness Airport. Dalcross, Inverness, IV2 7JB, **tel. 01667 464000**, www.hial.co.uk and

Glasgow International Airport. Paisley, PA3 2ST, **tel. 0141 887 1111**, www.glasgowairport.com.

WHISKY SHOPPING

■ **The Whisky Shop.** 93 High Street, Fort William, PH33 6DH, **tel. 01397 706164**, www.whiskyshop.com.

RECOMMENDED BARS

■ **Ben Nevis Inn.** Claggan, Achintee, Fort William, PH33 6TE, tel. 01397 701227, www.ben-nevis-inn.co.uk.
■ **The Crofter Bar.** High Street, Fort William, PH33 6DH, tel. 01397 704899.
■ **The Drovers.** 141 High Street, Fort William, PH33 6EA, tel. 01397 706413?.
■ **The Grog & Gruel.** 66 High Street, Fort William, PH33 6AE, tel. 01397 705078, www.grogandgruel.co.uk.
■ **Nevisport Bar.** Airds Crossing, High Street, Fort William, PH33 6EU, tel. 01397 704790.
■ **Volunteer Arms.** 47 High Street, Fort William, PH33 6DH, tel. 01397 702344.

PLACES OF INTEREST

The **Ben Nevis Mountain Range Experience** is located north of Ben Nevis. Britain's only mountain gondola transports visitors up to a height of 650 metres, where mountain trails offer panoramic views. There is also a restaurant and bar on site. **Tel. 01397 705825**, www.nevisrange.co.uk.

Treasures of the Earth is Europe's finest collection of crystals, gemstones and fossils, which took more than 500 million years to create. The collection is housed in an atmospheric simulation of caves, caverns and mining scenes. Treasures of the Earth (PH33 7JL) is in the centre of Corpach village, four miles from Fort William via the A830 Mallaig road. **Tel. 01397 772283**, www.treasuresoftheearth.co.uk.

West Highland Folk Museum is located in central Fort William and holds fascinating collections of pictures, photographs, archives and artefacts, including many relating to the Jacobite Risings of the 18th century.

Cameron Square, Fort William, PH33 6AJ, **tel. 01397 702169**, www.westhighlandmuseum.org.uk.

FURTHER GENERAL INFORMATION

Tourist Information Centre, Cameron Centre, Cameron Square, Fort William, PH33 6AJ, **tel. 01845 2255121**, www.visit-fortwilliam.co.uk.

GLENFINNAN MONUMENT

RECOMMENDED HOTELS

- **Alexandra Hotel.** The Parade, Fort William, PH33 6AZ,
  tel. 01397 702241, www.strathmorehotels.com (STB ★★★) £75-£125

- **Aros Ard Bed & Breakfast.** Seafield Gardens, Fort William, PH33 6RJ,
  tel. 01397 704142, www.arosard.com (STB ★★★★ B&B) Under £75

- **Ben Nevis Hotel & Leisure Club.** North Road, Fort William, PH33 6TG,
  tel. 01397 702331, www.strathmorehotels.com (STB ★★ Hotel) £125+

- **Best Western Imperial Hotel.** Fraser Square, Fort William, PH33 6DW,
  tel. 01397 702040, www.bestwestern.co.uk (STB ★★★) Under £75

- **Cruachan Hotel.** Achintore Road, Fort William, PH33 6RQ,
  tel. 01397 702022, www.cruachanhotel.co.uk (STB ★★★) Under £75

- **Distillery Guest House.** Alma Road, Fort William, PH33 6HA,
  tel. 01397 700103, www.stayinfortwilliam.co.uk (STB ★★★★ B & B) Under £50

- **Inverlochy Castle.** Torlundy, Fort William, PH33 6SN,
  tel. 01397 702177, www.inverlochycastlehotel.com (STB ★★★★★ Country House
  Hotel) £125+

- **Moorings Hotel.** Banavie, Fort William, PH33 7LY,
  tel. 01397 772797, www.moorings-fortwilliam.co.uk (STB ★★★) £75-£125

- **Premier Inn Fort William.** Airds Way, Fort William PH33 6FB,
  tel. 01397 703707, www.premierinn.com (STB Budget Hotel) Under £75

- **The Stronlossit Inn.** Roy Bridge, Fort William, PH31 4AG,
  tel. 01397 712253, www.stronlossit.co.uk (STB ★★★ Small Hotel) £75-£125

RECOMMENDED RESTAURANTS

- **Crannog Restaurant.** (Seafood) Town Pier, Fort William, PH33 6DB,
  tel. 01397 705589, www.crannog.net £35+
- **Glen Nevis Restaurant and Lounge Bar.** (Eclectic) Glen Nevis, Fort William,
  PH33 6SX,
  tel. 01397 705459, www.glennevisrestaurant.co.uk Under £35
- **The Indian Garden Restaurant.** (Indian) 88 High Street, Fort William, PH33 6AD,
  tel. 01397 705011. Under £25
- **Inverlochy Castle Restaurant.** (Scottish) Torlundy, Fort William, PH33 6SN,
  tel: 01397 702177, www.inverlochycastlehotel.com £35+
- **The Lime Tree Restaurant.** (Eclectic) The Old Manse, Achintore Road,
  Fort William, PH33 6RQ,
  tel. 01397 701806, www.limetreefortwilliam.co.uk £35+
- **Number 4 The Restaurant.** (Scottish/Eclectic) 4 Cameron Square,
  Fort William, PH33 6AJ,
  tel. 013977 04222?, www.no4-fortwilliam.co.uk Under £35

WEST HIGHLANDS TRAIL

This trail includes the last two surviving 'West Highland' distilleries, namely **Ben Nevis** *and* **Oban**.

Allow half a day to visit each distillery or a full day to visit both.

Ben Nevis Distillery (see p.124) is two miles north-east of Fort William, at the foot of the mountain, beside the A82 Inverness to Fort William road, and close to the junction with the A830 to Mallaig.

    Oban Distillery (see p.138) is situated the popular holiday town and ferry port of the same name, 44 miles (one hour and 20 minutes' drive) south-west of Fort William by way of the A82, A828 and A85. Coaches operate on the Fort William to Oban route under the auspices of Citylink and West Coast Motors **tel. 08705 505050**, www.citylink.co.uk, while trains also connect the two West Highland towns **tel. 0845 601 5929**, www.nationalrail.co.uk. Oban Distillery sits back from the seafront, and is one of few in Scotland to be found in the middle of a town. For further information on Oban **tel. 01631 563122** or visit www.oban.org.uk.

WAVERLEY STEAMER AT OBAN

ISLE OF MULL TRAIL ▬▬▬▬▬▬▬

Although this tour only involves one distillery, **Tobermory,** *(unless visiting Oban en route) the magnificent scenery of Mull and the relatively short and enjoyable ferry crossing from Oban makes it an essential on the itinerary of anyone spending time in the West Highlands.*

Allow a full day to visit Tobermory, and ideally schedule an overnight stay in order to capitalise on your time on Mull.

Tobermory Distillery (see p.150) is similar to Oban in that it is located close to the seafront and within the island capital of Tobermory. Oban is reached from Fort William as in Trail 1 (above), and the Calmac vehicle ferry **tel. 0800 066 5000,** www.calmac.co.uk, takes some 45 minutes to cross from Oban to the ferry terminal at Craignure on Mull. A coach service operates in conjunction with the ferry, transporting passengers on the 45 minutes' trip to Tobermory. If you choose to take your car, follow the A848 and A849 on the 20 miles' journey from Craignure to Tobermory. For further information on Mull **tel. 01680 812377** or visit www.tobermory.co.uk.

Steeped in history and intrinsically interwoven with Scotland's ancient kings and clan lines, Duart Castle on Mull enjoys a most dramatic setting which can be enjoyed by all arriving on the ferry to Craignure. Although requiring an additional day on Mull, a visit to the island of Iona, to see its Abbey, and to Staffa, to experience Fingal's Cave, is highly recommended.

Fort William also makes a good base for a visit to the Isle of Skye and **Talisker Distillery** (see p.148) via the scenic A830 'Road to the Isles' and the Mallaig/Armadale car ferry **tel. 0800 066 5000,** www.calmac.co.uk. An overnight stay on Skye is essential. See www.skye.co.uk for further information about the island.

DUART CASTLE

AROUND ISLAY

If Speyside represents the 'heart' of mainland Scotch whisky distilling, then Islay is Scotland's 'whisky island.' With no fewer than eight working distilleries on an island of just 240 square miles, as well as one on neighbouring Jura, Islay is an essential destination for all serious Scotch whisky devotees.

Islay is the southernmost of the Inner Hebrides, and lies just 25 miles north of the Irish coast. Its 'capital' is Bowmore, which was established by the island's then owner, Daniel Campbell of Shawfield and Islay, in 1768. It was the first 'planned' village in Scotland, and sits on the shores of Loch Indaal. Other principal villages are Port Ellen, to the south of Bowmore, and Port Charlotte, across Loch Indaal to the west.

Along with Port Askaig, Port Ellen is one of two terminals for the car ferry to the mainland, with the latter being founded in 1821 by landowner Walter Frederick Campbell, and named after his wife Ellinor, or Eleanor. Today, Port Ellen is home to a large, modern malting plant, owned by Diageo, which produces peated malt for the company's Caol Ila and Lagavulin distilleries, as well as for a number of other distilleries in different ownership.

The maltings were built in 1972/73 next to Port Ellen distillery, which had been established in 1825. Septimus Fox tested and refined his newly-invented 'spirit safe' there, while both Aeneas Coffey and Robert Stein also carried out research work at Port Ellen, aiding the development of the 'continuous' still, which produced grain whisky.

The distillery was silent between 1930 and 1967, when it was largely rebuilt by owners The Distillers Company Ltd (DCL). However, Port Ellen closed again in 1983, at a time when Islay single malts were nowhere near as popular as they are today and the industry, in general, was plagued by over-production. Today, most of the 1960s distillery has been demolished, and what remains are the two original pagodas, maltings, and some splendid stone warehouses, fronting the sea.

Port Charlotte commemorates the mother of Walter Frederick Campbell, who built the settlement in 1828. The remnants of another 'lost' Islay distillery are to be found here, where the Lochindaal Distillery was first licensed in 1829. Like Port Ellen, Lochindaal was ultimately in the ownership of DCL, who ceased operating it in 1929, when global economic depression and US Prohibition decimated the Scotch whisky industry. Several distillery buildings survive, with some being used by the Islay Youth Hostel and Field Centre. The two stone-built, bonded warehouses on the hill behind the village centre are currently used by nearby Bruichladdich distillery, and there are ongoing plans to equip one of the warehouses with production equipment and make single malt whisky under the Port Charlotte banner.

Although whisky attracts a great number of visitors to Islay, almost as many go to see the rich variety of bird life on the island. The Royal Society for the Protection of Birds www.rspb.org.uk has extensive reserves at Loch Gruinart, north of the A847, between Bridgend and Bruichladdich, and on the Oa peninsula, south-west of Port Ellen. Islay is particularly noted for its large colonies of barnacle geese, which winter on the island.

ISLAY

GETTING TO ISLAY

Ferry Services. The principal ferry route to Islay is operated by Caledonian MacBrayne ferries **tel. 01880 730253,** www.calmac.co.uk from Kennacraig, PA29 6YF, near Tarbert in Argyllshire. The ferry travels to either Port Askaig in the north of the island or Port Ellen in the south. Kennacraig is 106 miles (two hours and 20 minutes' drive) from Glasgow, via the M8, M898 (Erskine Bridge), A82 and A83.

If you are travelling by public transport, there is a regular Citylink coach service **tel. 08705 505050,** www.citylink.co.uk between Glasgow and Campbeltown, which calls at the Kennacraig ferry terminal.

Island Bus Services. A network of local bus services link the main settlements on Islay, including many of the distilleries. They are operated by Islay Coaches, **tel. 01496 840273,** and Royal Mail, **tel. 08457 740740,** www.islayinfo.com.

Islay Airport. Glenegedale, Isle of Islay, PA42 7AS, **tel. 01496 302361,** www.hial.co.uk. The airport is located alongside the A846, between Bowmore and Port Ellen. Scheduled flights operate between Glasgow International Airport, Paisley, PA2 3ST, **tel. 0141 887 1111,** www.glasgowairport.com and Islay.

WHISKY SHOPPING

- **The Islay Whisky Shop.** Shore Street, Bowmore, PA43 7LB, tel. 01496 810689, www.islaywhiskyshop.com.
- **The Bridgend Stores.** Bridgend, PA44 7PQ, tel. 01496 810335.

RECOMMENDED BARS

- **Ardview Inn.** Frederick Crescent, Port Ellen, PA42 7BD, tel. 01496 302014.
- **Ballygrant Inn.** Ballygrant, PA45 7QR, tel. 01496 840277, www.ballygrant-inn.co.uk.
- **Duffies Bar.** Lochside Hotel, Shore Street, Bowmore, PA43 7LB, tel. 01496 810244, www.lochsidehotel.co.uk.
- **Lochindaal Hotel.** 11 Main Street, Port Charlotte, PA48 7TX, tel. 01496 850202.
- **Port Askaig Hotel.** Port Askaig, PA46 7RB, tel. 01496 840245, www.portaskaig.co.uk.
- **Port Charlotte Hotel.** Port Charlotte, PA48 7TU, tel. 01496 85360, www.portcharlottehotel.co.uk.

ITINERARIES AND AMENITIES

PLACES OF INTEREST

Finlaggan. Loch Finlaggan is located a few miles south-west of Port Askaig, and islands in the loch were once home to the chiefs of Clan Donald, the immensely powerful 'Lords of the Isles.' During the Middle Ages, the Lords ruled the islands and some of the west coast Scottish mainland, from Lewis in the north to Kintyre in the south, making Finlaggan a centre of major administrative and symbolic significance in Scottish history. Finlaggan is signposted from the A846, a mile north of Ballygrant, and an information centre (open seasonally) stands close to the loch, at the end of a single-track road. For further details, contact The Finlaggan Trust, The Cottage, Ballygrant, PA45 7QL, **tel. 01496 840644**, www.finlaggan.com.

Islay Ales. Marketing its products as 'Leann an Ile - Ales from the Isle of Malts,' the Islay Ales Co Ltd was set up during 2003/04 in a converted tractor shed on the Islay Estate at Bridgend. The micro-brewery produces cask and bottle-conditioned beers, which are on sale in many bars and hotels on the island. Visitors are welcome to tour the brewery, which also sells bottled ales and a range of branded merchandise. The Brewery, Islay House Square, Bridgend, PA44 7NZ, **tel. 01496 810014**, www.islayales.com.

Kildalton Cross. The High Cross of Kildalton is one of the finest early Christian crosses in Scotland, and dates from the second half of the 8th century. It is located beside the now ruined Old Parish Church of Kildalton, which is thought to have been built in the late 12th or early 13th century. The High Cross of Kildalton and the Old Parish Church are situated some seven miles north-west of Port Ellen, and are reached by following the single-track Ardtalla road beyond the A846 to Ardbeg distillery. A few miles further on is the beautiful, sheltered Claggain Bay, which is also well worth a visit.

In addition to the Old Parish Church of Kildalton, another particularly interesting ecclesiastical building is the idiosyncratic **Round Church** in Bowmore. This eye-catching structure stands at the top of the Main Street, and dates from 1767/69, when it was created for Islay laird Daniel Campbell the Younger. It is claimed that the church was built in the round so that there were no corners for the devil to hide in! The 'A-listed' structure, properly Kilarrow Parish Church, welcomes visitors on a daily basis. See www.theroundchurch.org.uk for further details.

The Museum of Islay Life is housed in a former Free Church in the village of Port Charlotte, having been established in 1976/77. The Museum holds an archive of more than 1,000 books, extensive paper archives and a photographical collection boasting almost 4,000 items. There is also a significant holding of artefacts, ranging from ancient, archaeological items to 19th century crofting life displays and even an illicit still. Islay's distilling heritage, which included many small-scale, farm-based distilleries, is well represented in the Museum. Port Charlotte, PA48 7UA, **tel. 01496 850358**, www.islaymuseum.org.

ISLAY

RECOMMENDED HOTELS

- **Ballygrant Inn & Restaurant.** Ballygrant, PA45 7QR,
  tel. 01496 840277, www.ballygrant-inn.co.uk (STB ★★ Inn) Under £75

- **Bridgend Hotel.** Bridgend, PA44 7PJ,
  tel. 01496 810212, www.bridgend-hotel.com Under £75

- **Bowmore Hotel.** Jamieson Street, Bowmore PA43 7HL,
  tel. 01496 810416, www.bowmorehotel.co.uk Under £75

- **Caladh Sona.** 53 Frederick Crescent, Port Ellen, PA42 7BD,
  tel. 01496 302694. (STB ★★★ B&B) Under £75

- **Harbour Inn.** The Square, Bowmore, PA43 7JR,
  tel. 01496 810330, www.harbour-inn.com (STB ★★★★ Restaurant with Rooms)
  £125+

- **Lochside Hotel.** Shore Street, Bowmore, PA43 7LB,
  tel. 01496 810244, www.lochsidehotel.co.uk £75-£125

- **The Machrie Hotel.** Port Ellen, PA42 7AN,
  tel. 01496 302310, www.machrie.com (STB ★★ Small Hotel) £75-£125

- **Port Askaig Hotel.** Port Askaig, PA46 7RB,
  tel. 01496 840245, www.portaskaig.co.uk **Under £75**

- **Port Charlotte Hotel.** Port Charlotte, PA48 7TU,
  tel. 01496 850360, www.portcharlottehotel.co.uk (STB ★★★★ Small Hotel)
  £75-£125

- **White Hart Hotel.** 1 Charlotte Street, Port Ellen, PA42 7DF,
  tel. 01496 300120, www.whitehearthotelislay.com Under £75

RECOMMENDED RESTAURANTS

- **An Tigh Seinnse.** (Scottish/Seafood) 11 Queen Street, Portnahaven, PA47 7SJ,
  tel. 01496 860224. Under £35
- **Ballygrant Inn & Restaurant.** (Scottish/Contemporary) Ballygrant, PA45 7QR,
  tel. 01496 840277, www.ballygrant-inn.co.uk Under £25
- **Croft Kitchen Restaurant.** (Scottish) Port Charlotte, PA48 7UD,
  tel. 01496 850230. Under £25
- **Harbour Inn.** (Scottish/Contemporary) The Square, Bowmore, PA43 7JR,
  tel. 01496 810330, www.harbour-inn.com £35+
- **Port Charlotte Hotel.** (Scottish/Contemporary) Port Charlotte, PA48 7TU,
  tel. 01496 850360, www.portcharlottehotel.co.uk £35+
- **Taj Mahal Restaurant.** (Indian) 320 Shore Street, Bowmore, PA43 7LB,
  tel. 01496 810033. Under £25

FURTHER GENERAL INFORMATION

Tourist Information Centre, The Square, Bowmore, PA43 7JP, **tel. 08707 200 617**, www.islayinfo.com and www.visitscottishheartlands.com.

ITINERARIES AND AMENITIES

KILDALTON TRAIL

This Trail comprises the three 'Kildalton' area distilleries, located on the southern coast of Islay. The distilleries in question are **Laphroaig, Lagavulin** *and* **Ardbeg**.

Allow a full day to visit the three distilleries, perhaps lunching in the Kiln Cafe at Ardbeg.

Laphroaig Distillery (see p.168) is 1.7 miles (seven minutes' drive) east of Port Ellen on the A846, and 14.7 miles south-east of Bowmore. A scenic, inland alternative to the A846 is the B8016 road, which runs south from near Bridgend – with an unclassified linking road to Bowmore - to join the A846, just north of Port Ellen.

Ardbeg Distillery (see p.152) is 3.5 miles (ten minutes' drive) east of Port Ellen, past Laphroaig and Lagavulin distilleries along the A846. The only one of the three distilleries offering food, it is advisable to plan a visit to Ardbeg around lunchtime.

Lagavulin Distillery (see p.166) is located alongside the A846 road, midway between Ardbeg and Laphroaig.

BOWMORE TRAIL

The Bowmore Trail takes in **Bowmore** *Distillery, the oldest surviving whisky-making operation on Islay, along with either* **Caol Ila** *or* **Bunnahabhain** *Distilleries, to the north-east.*

Allow half a day to visit each distillery.

Bowmore Distillery (see p.154) is situated in the village of the same name, on the shores of Loch Indaal, and just a few yards from the Main Street.

For **Caol Ila** and **Bunnahabhain** Distilleries, see 'North-Eastern Islay Trail, below.

NORTH-EASTERN ISLAY TRAIL

Two of Islay's distilleries are situated in the north-east of the island, and both **Bunnahabhain** *and* **Caol Ila** *enjoy magnificent views across the Sound of Islay to neighbouring Jura.*

Allow a full day to visit both distilleries, lunching at the Port Askaig Hotel near Caol Isla.

Caol Ila Distillery (see p.160), is one mile along a single track road, off the A846 just before it descends to Port Askaig and the ferry terminal. Caol Ila is 11 miles (25 minutes' drive) north-east of Bowmore.

Bunnahabhain Distillery (see p.158) is the most remote of all Islay's distilleries, being situated at the end of a four miles-long, unclassified road. The road is accessed off the A846, just after the hamlet of Keills, and a mile before it reaches Port Askaig. Bunnahabhain is 13.5 miles (35 minutes' drive) north-east of Bowmore.

RHINNS OF ISLAY TRAIL ▰▰▰▰▰▰ 🚗

*The Rhinns of Islay is the area of the island which forms a peninsula to the west of Loch Indaal. It is home to **Bruichladdich** and **Kilchoman** Distilleries.*

As the distilleries are relatively close to each other, they can both be visited within four to five hours. Alternatively, if time permits, they can be spaced out to give a more leisurely full day, based on lunching in the café at Kilchoman Distillery.

Kilchoman Distillery (see p.164) is the only one of the island's eight working distilleries not to front the sea, though it is only a short distance from Machir Bay. The distillery is off the B8018 road, which leads off from the A847 some four miles west of Bridgend, before it reaches Bruichladdich. Kilchoman is 12 miles (35 minutes' drive) north-west of Bowmore. It is well signposted and relatively easy to find.

To get from Kilchoman to **Bruichladdich Distillery** (see p.156), return to the A847 and head south towards Port Charlotte and Portnahaven. Bruichladdich Distillery stands beside the A847 road, overlooking Loch Indaal, two miles north-east of Port Charlotte. It is 6.5 miles (25 minutes' drive) from Kilchoman and 8.5 miles (20 minutes' drive) from Bowmore, via Bridgend.

JURA TRAIL ▰▰▰▰▰▰ 🚗

This Trail involves taking the short car ferry trip from Port Askaig on Islay to neighbouring Jura, in order to visit the Isle of Jura Distillery.

Allow a full day for a trip to Jura.

The island of Jura lies to the north-east of Islay. The southern part of Jura is dominated by three mountains, known as the Paps of Jura, while the main centre of population is the village of Craighouse, situated on the east coast of the island. The **Isle of Jura Distillery** stands beside the main road in Craighouse, which also boasts the Jura Hotel, offering good food and accommodation. Craighouse, Isle of Jura, PA60 7XU, **tel. 01496 820243**, www.jurahotel.co.uk.

The ferry to Jura **tel. 08707 200 617**, www.islayinfo.com runs frequently between Port Askaig, 10.5 miles (20 minutes' drive) north-east of Bowmore by the A846, and Feolin, on Jura. The crossing takes around five minutes and bookings are not necessary.

Festival
Staged in May, the **Islay Festival of Malt and Music** – Feis Ile in Gaelic – is a week-long celebration of the island's whiskies, with each distillery enjoying a dedicated day on which to showcase its products. There are also concerts, ceilidhs, distillery tours, guided walks and numerous other events. See www.feis.stream-linenettrial.co.uk. The festival is a great time to visit Islay and Jura, particularly if you want to soak up the festive atmosphere. However, accommodation becomes difficult to obtain and the distilleries tend to get very busy.

ITINERARIES AND AMENITIES

Age By law, Scotch whisky must be matured in wood for a minimum of three years, but most reputable single malt whiskies are matured for much longer. If a blended whisky carries an age statement, then it must refer to the youngest whisky in the blend.

Angels' share A distillers' term for *maturation* losses. In Scotland, some two per cent of all maturing whisky evaporates through the porous oak casks each year.

Barley The principal raw material used in the whisky-making process in Scotland. See also *Malting*.

Barrel Sometimes used as a generic term for a *cask*, but in the Scotch whisky industry a barrel is specifically a cask with an approximate capacity of 40 gallons (180 litres).

Blend A blended Scotch whisky is one made from a mixture of grain and malt spirit. Theoretically, the higher the malt content the better the blend, although this is not always the case. Much depends on the quality and age of grain and malt whiskies used.

Blended malt Previously known as 'vatted malt,' blended malt is a combination of two or more malt whiskies, and contains no grain spirit.

Brewing The process which follows *malting* in the production of malt whisky, and consists of *mashing* and *fermentation*.

Butt The second largest size of cask regularly used by the whisky industry for maturation purposes. The butt contains approximately 110 gallons or 500 litres, twice the amount of the hogshead.

Cask A generic term for containers of varying capacity in which spirit is stored during maturation.

Cask strength Whisky sold at cask strength has not been diluted to the standard 40% or 43%, but is bottled at the strength at which it leaves the cask. This will vary depending on the age of the whisky, as older whiskies lose considerable strength during extended maturation.

Chill-filtering The process of refrigerating whisky and finely filtering it to ensure it retains its clarity in the bottle and when water is added by the consumer. Many connoisseurs consider that chill- filtration detracts from the character of the whisky in subtle ways, and a number of bottlers now make a virtue of not chill-filtering their products.

Coffey still   Patented in 1830 by former Irish Inspector-General of Excise Aeneas Coffey, this still revolutionised whisky making. Also known as the column, continuous or patent still, it allowed large quantities of spirit to be distilled much more quickly than in the traditional *pot still*, paving the way for the development of blended Scotch whisky. Essentially, the stills used in Scottish grain distilleries are very similar to Coffey's original, consisting of two tall 'columns,' the first being the analyser, which separates the spirit from the wash, while the second, known as the rectifier, concentrates the spirit to a greater degree.

Cutting   During distillation, the stillman, or stillhouse computer programme, 'cuts' from collecting *foreshots* to the *middle cut* or *heart of the run*, before then cutting back to collect *feints*. 'Cut points' are crucial to the character of the spirit produced, and every distillery has its own formula for them, based on alcoholic strength and/or timescale.

Dark grains   Cubes or pellets of high protein animal feed produced by treating *pot ale* with dried *draff*. Pot ale evaporates into dark brown syrup, hence the name.

Distillation   Distillation follows the process of *fermentation* in whisky making, and is characteristic of all spirit production. During distillation the alcohol is separated from the *wash* by heating it in stills. Alcohol boils at a lower temperature than water and is driven off as vapour, leaving behind the water. It is subsequently condensed back into liquid form.

Draff   The spent *grist* left behind in the *mash tun* after the *mashing* process has been completed. Being high in protein it makes excellent cattle food, and is either sold off to farmers in its 'raw' state or converted into *dark grains*.

Dram   A measure of Scotch whisky of unspecified size, although in some Scottish bars a 'dram' is taken to mean a large or double whisky. 'Dramming' in distilleries was the semi-official practice of offering employees amounts of spirit at regular intervals during the working day. The advent of drink driving laws and 'health and safety' legislation finally ended the custom.

Dunnage   Traditional warehousing for whisky *maturation*, which consists of a stone or brick building, ideally with an ash and earth-covered floor. Casks are stacked no more than three high on wooden runners. Most experts believe such warehousing creates the optimum maturation conditions for malt Scotch whisky.

Feints	The final flow of distillation, produced after the *middle cut* has been collected. The feints consist of the heavier compounds and less volatile components of the *low wines*, such as fusel oil. Although not desirable in large quantities, a small amount of feints contributes to the overall character of the whisky being made.
Fermentation	Along with *mashing*, fermentation is part of the *brewing* process of whisky production. Yeast is added to the *wort* in the *washbacks* and the result is wash. This is the first time during whisky-making that alcohol has been produced.
Fillings	*New make* spirit, once filled into casks.
Finish	The practice of 'finishing' whisky is a relatively new phenomena. Essentially, after a substantial period of maturation in its original cask, the whisky is transferred into a different one, which has previously held another alcoholic drink, for a period of finishing. This provides variations on 'house' style. The most common finishes feature various styles of Sherry, but others include rum, Madeira, Burgundy and port.
Foreshots	The initial flow of distillation, produced before the *middle cut* is collected. It contains an excess of acids, aldehydes and esters, but, like *feints*, a small quantity of foreshots contributes to the character of the whisky. As with feints, the amount present depends on the distillery's 'cut points.'
Grain	In Scotland grain whisky is distilled principally from wheat or corn in *continuous* stills. Although a number of single and blended grain whiskies are available, the vast majority of grain whisky distilled is used for blending.
Green malt	At the point when germination is halted during malting, the barley is referred to as green malt.
Grist	Ground, malted barley ready for mashing.
Heart of the run	See *Middle cut*
Hogshead	Often colloquially referred to as a 'hoggie,' the hogshead is a common size of whisky *cask*, having an approximate capacity of 55 gallons (250 litres.)
Kiln	During *malting* the *green malt* is dried in a kiln in order to prevent germination proceeding too far and using up the starch essential for the production of alcohol. During kilning, *peat* smoke may be introduced to flavour the malt, though the principal fuel used in the kiln is coke.

A-Z GLOSSARY

Low wines   In the *pot still* whisky-making process, low wines are the product of the first distillation in the *wash still*. They are impure and weak, and a second distillation in the *spirit* or low wines still is subsequently necessary.

Lyne arm/pipe   Also known as a lye arm or lye pipe, this is the pipe connecting the head of the still to the condenser or *worm*. The angle of the lyne arm has a significant effect on the style of spirit produced. See also *Reflux*.

Malt   Barley prepared for whisky-making by steeping, germinating and kiln-drying. The purpose of malting is to break down the cell walls of the cereal to release the starch and begin the process of converting that into sugars which will subsequently produce alcohol.

Mash   *Malt* mixed with hot water to form *wort*. Mashing follows malting and precedes fermentation in the whisky-making process, and the mash of *grist* and hot water is mixed in a large, circular vessel, known as a mash tun. Mashing extracts soluble sugars from the malted grain.

Maturation   The practice of storing whisky in casks in order to achieve a more mellow and well-rounded spirit. Many countries specify a legal minimum maturation period. During maturation the porous casks allow the whisky to interact with the external atmosphere, and the spirit takes colour and flavour from the wood. At the same time, some of the higher alcohols are transformed into esters and other compounds with attractive aroma profiles.

Middle cut   The most pure and desirable spirit collected during distillation. Also known as the *Heart of the run*. See *Cutting*.

New make   Freshly-distilled whisky. See *Fillings*.

Nose   The aroma or bouquet of a whisky. Along with colour, body, palate and finish, the 'nose' is used to quantify and describe a whisky. Most whisky professionals, particularly blenders, use their noses as the principal means of analysing whiskies.

Peat   Peat has an important influence on whisky character when it is used to flavour *malt* in the *kiln*, but much of the process water used in Scottish distilleries flows over peat and this also plays a minor part in influencing the finished product.

Piece   The term applied to a quantity of germinating *barley* while it is on the malting floor.

Pot ale   The high protein waste liquor left in the low wines still after the first distillation has taken place.

Pot still   A copper distillation vessel. The size and shape of pot stills varies from distillery to distillery, and pot still variables play an important part in determining the character of spirit produced.

Proof   Measurement of the strength of spirits, expressed in degrees, calculated using a hydrometer. Although still employed in the USA, the proof system has now been superseded in Europe by a measurement of alcohol strength as a percentage of alcohol by volume.

Reflux   During distillation some of the heavier flavours with comparatively high boiling points condense from vapour back into liquid form before leaving the still and are redistilled. This is known as reflux, and the greater the degree of reflux the lighter and 'cleaner' the spirit produced. Short, squat stills produce little reflux, compared to tall, slender stills. The angle at which the *lyne arm* is attached also affects the levels of reflux.

Run   The flow of spirit from a still during a specific period of distillation.

Scotch   Whisky distilled and matured in Scotland, but usually with the colloquial implication of blended whisky.

Silent   Just as a closed theatre is said to be 'dark,' so a closed, though potentially productive, distillery is described as 'silent.'

Single   A single malt whisky is the product of one distillery, not vatted or blended with any others.

Single cask   Most bottles of single malt will contain spirit from between 100 and 150 casks, vatted to give consistency, but a single cask bottling comes from one individual cask. It is frequently sold at cask strength and is prized for its individuality.

Spirit   Until it has been matured for three years in its country of origin, Scotch whisky is officially known as spirit. It is produced in a spirit *still*, monitored and separated in a *spirit safe*, and collected in a spirit receiver.

Spirit safe   A secure, brass and glass box within which *cutting* takes place without the stillman being able to have direct physical contact with the spirit.

Still   Whether a pot or continuous still, operation is on the principal that alcohol boils at a lower temperature than water and is driven off as vapour, leaving behind the water. It is subsequently condensed back into liquid form.

Switcher

A mechanism consisting of rotating arms which is fitted to a *washback* to reduce excessive frothing during *fermentation*.

Triple distillation

The practice of distilling whisky three times rather than the usual twice in order to achieve a light, pure style of spirit. Triple distillation is a traditional characteristic of Irish whiskey, and also of Scottish Lowland whisky-making.

Tun

A large vessel in which *mashing* takes place, usually known as a *mashtun*. However, in a distillery the 'tun room' is home to the *washbacks*.

Vatting

The process of mixing or blending components in a vat. Regarding Scotch whisky, the term was formerly most often applied to 'vatted malts,' that is more than one malt vatted together prior to bottling. The term has now been dropped by the Scotch Whisky Association and most distillers in favour of the expression 'blended malt,' which is thought to be less confusing for consumers.

Wash

The liquid at the end of the *fermentation* process, ready for distillation.

Washback

The vessel in which fermentation takes place, traditionally constructed of wood, but now often made of stainless steel, which is easier to keep clean.

Water

One of the key components of whisky production. Water is necessary for steeping during the malting process, for mashing and for cooling the vapour from the stills back into liquid form. As a source of reliable, pure water is crucial to distilling, most distillery sites have been chosen with this in mind.

Worm

A long, coiled copper tube, attached to the *lyne arm* of the *pot still*, and fitted into a large wooden vat filled with cold water, known as a worm tub. Before the introduction of 'shell and tube' condensers, the worm tub was the only means of condensing alcohol vapour back into liquid form. A number of distilleries continue to use worm tubs, as experts insist that the character of whisky made using a worm tub differs significantly from that cooled in a modern condenser.

Wort

Essentially unfermented beer, wort is produced in the *mashtun*. See *mash*.

DISTILLERIES WITH FULL VISITOR FACILITIES

Just as every distillery is different from the outside, so they also vary significantly on the inside. If the distillery is old, it may well have been extensively re-modelled and re-equipped, and in many distilleries computers control processes formerly carried out by individual members of staff. Look out for rare, traditional features such as open, cast iron mash tuns, and for stills with sections which are riveted rather than welded.

Distillery guides are always knowledgeable, and should be able to answer most questions, but nothing beats talking to the people who actually make the whisky, so if you get the chance, do stop and say hello. Speaking to a mashman or a stillman can enrich a distillery visit immeasurably.

POINT OF NOTE

Virtually all distilleries have a 'silent season;' the part of the year when the plant closes down for annual maintenance and repair work and for many members of staff to take holidays. Traditionally, the silent season takes place during the drier, summer months when there was often a shortage of water for production processes. Modern silent seasons tend to be much shorter than was usually the case in days gone by, but if planning distillery visits during the summer it may be worth checking that the site is operational if you wish to get the most out of your time there. Usually, the visitor centre and shop remains open and tours continue to be offered, but they lack the atmosphere generated when whisky-making is in full flow. Many distilleries also close over the Christmas and New Year period, so again, it is worth checking before making your journey.

Some distilleries become very busy at peak times, while others may close early during quieter months, so if a visit to a specific distillery is a priority, then it is advisable to book in advance. Please remember that the distilleries are places of work and that production must come before tourism.

Disabled access is usually good for visitor centres, cafes and shops, but almost always very limited in actual production areas. If in doubt, check before visiting.

SYMBOLS
T Timing of distillery tours, whether set or flexible
C Catering options for visitors
S Shopping facilities, indicating whether whisky is sold and scale of the shop

---

BENRINNES DISTILLERY

SECTION INDEX

LISTED ALPHABETICALLY WITHIN WHISKY REGIONS

Each page in this section is colour coded in the top corner to reflect the whisky region. See the map on the inside front and back covers for the distillery location.

ABBREVIATIONS

PRINCIPAL SINGLE MALT The primary expressions of malt whisky widely available.

PRINCIPAL BLENDS The main blends to which the distillery's spirit contributes.

STILLS The number of stills with which a distillery is equipped. However, this is not necessarily an indication of volume output, as still sizes vary considerably.

CAPACITY The output of each distillery is given in thousands or millions (m) of litres per annum.

MALT Indicates the level of peat influence in the malting process.

CASK Most Scotch whisky is matured in American Oak casks which formerly held Bourbon whiskey, produced in the USA . European Oak casks which previously contained Sherry are used to a lesser degree due to their comparatively high cost.

AUCHENTOSHAN

Meaning of name and pronunciation guide
'Corner of the field'
– OGH-en-TOSH-an

Owner
Morrison Bowmore Distillers Ltd (Suntory Ltd)

House style
Light, subtle, delicate, floral and fruity.

Principal single malts
Auchentoshan Classic, 12 and 18-year-old, Three Wood.

Principal blends
Rob Roy, Islay Legend.

Getting technical
Stills: one wash, one intermediate, one spirit

Capacity: 1.8m litres

Malt: unpeated

Casks: ex-Bourbon and ex-Sherry

Water: Loch Katrine

HISTORY

The distillery was first licensed in 1823, though there is evidence that distilling had already been taking place on the site since around 1800.

Auchentoshan passed through a number of hands, being rebuilt in 1875, and during much of the 20th century was in the ownership of various brewing interests, most notably the famous Glasgow firm of J&R Tennent.

It was extensively damaged during the Second World War by German bombers raiding the nearby ship-building centre of Clydebank. In 1969 Auchentoshan was purchased from Bass Charrington by Eadie Cairns Ltd, who carried out a substantial modernisation programme.

The distillery then passed to Stanley P Morrison in 1984, joining Bowmore (see p 154) and Glengarioch (see p 94). A decade later, Morrison Bowmore was acquired by the giant Japanese distilling concern of Suntory Ltd. Subsequent investment in the distillery and in the Auchentoshan brand has seen a number of new expressions appear on the market.n developed along with the new visitor facilities.

POINTS OF SPECIAL INTEREST

Auchentoshan is the only distillery in Scotland which still practices full triple distillation for its entire output. Triple distillation was once a hallmark of Lowland distilling enterprises, and is a process which produces a lighter-bodied spirit.

LOWLAND

VISITOR EXPERIENCE

Auchentoshan is a comparatively new recruit to the ranks of distilleries open to the public, having only developed a dedicated reception centre and shop in 2004.

Today, after significant further investment, the site boasts conference facilities and an attractive retail area, with a range of quality giftware in addition to whisky. Bottles may be personalised and visitors can also hand-fill their own bottle of Auchentoshan from a selected cask.

The standard tour includes an audio-visual presentation about the distillery and its history, followed by a distillery tour and a complementary dram. The 'Auchentoshan Experience' lasts for one and a half hours and includes a comparative tasting of Auchentoshan and single malt from the owners' other distilleries of Bowmore and Glen Garioch.

Most extensive is the 'Ultimate Auchentoshan Experience,' which includes a tasting session in the warehouse and a sensory awareness masterclass of mature and cask strength whiskies.

Distillery tours are available in English and Spanish and there are also written guides in French, Italian and German.

Contacts
Tel: 01389 878561
E-mail: info@morrison
bowmore.co.uk

Website
www.auchentoshan.com

Admission
£ Standard Tour:
  £5.00
  Auchentoshan
£ Experience: £23.00
  Ultimate
  Auchentoshan
£ Experience: £45.00

Advance booking required for premium tours.

T Set times
C Hot and cold drinks
S Whisky and some gift and book items

LOCATION

Dalmuir, Clydebank, Dunbartonshire G81 4SJ
The distillery is situated 10 miles from Glasgow, off the A82, just south of the Erskine Bridge. Only accessible via the north-bound carriageway, drivers from the north or via the Erskine Bridge need to take the first left turn after the bridge then double back for 500 yards (200m).

🕐 All year except Christmas and New Year
Monday to Sunday 9:30 to 17:00

Personal notes relating to visit:

Whiskies tasted notes/opinions:

Manager/guide signature:

Date visited:

SECTION INDEX ON PAGE 71

BLADNOCH

Meaning of name and pronunciation guide
'Place of small splinters'
– BLAD-noch

Owner
Co-ordinated Development Services Ltd

House style
Light-bodied, fresh, floral, quite dry, grassy, fruity.

Principal single malts
Bladnoch 7-year-old (lightly peated), 8, 16, 18 and 19-year-old.

Principal blends
N/A

Getting technical
Stills: one pair

Capacity: 100,000 litres

Malt: usually unpeated

Casks: ex-Bourbon and ex-Sherry

Water: River Bladnoch

HISTORY

Bladnoch was established in 1817 by brothers John and Thomas McClelland, gaining its first licence in 1825. It subsequently changed hands several times and experienced a number of periods of closure, being owned by the Belfast distiller Dunville & Co Ltd between the two world wars. It was purchased by Arthur Bell & Sons Ltd of Perth in 1983, but Bell's was taken over by Guinness two years later, and Bladnoch subsequently found itself absorbed into the United Distillers empire. In 1993, 'UD' closed Bladnoch, along with fellow Lowland distillery Rosebank, at Falkirk, Pittyvaich in Dufftown, and Balmenach, near Grantown-on-Spey.

This seemed to spell the end of whisky-making at Bladnoch, but then the charismatic and energetic Northern Irish entrepreneur Raymond Armstrong acquired the site in October 1994, initially with no intention of recommencing distilling. However, an agreement was reached with United Distillers in 2000, whereby Armstrong was allowed to distil a maximum of 100,000 litres of whisky a year at Bladnoch, and the distillery was re-equipped, with the first spirit flowing in December 2000.

POINTS OF SPECIAL INTEREST

Currently, the most southerly working distillery in Scotland, Bladnoch also hosts occasional 'Whisky Schools' where participants get their hands dirty, undertaking the various processes of spirit production for themselves. See www.whiskyschool.co.uk

LOWLAND

VISITOR EXPERIENCE

Despite the comparative isolation of Bladnoch, deep in south-west Scotland, the distillery attracts not far short of 30,000 visitors per year. Admission includes a tour of the plant plus a complementary dram, and the shop is one of the most extensive distillery outlets in the country. The distillery also offers regular live music sessions, and serves as a popular local venue for a wide variety of functions, including weddings.

For those with time on their hands and a yearning to make whisky, Bladnoch runs an occasional three-day Whisky School. Cask of whisky can also be purchased and matured on site.

Printed tour guides are available in Dutch, French, German, Italian, Japanese, Portuguese, Spanish and Swedish.

LOCATION

Bladnoch, Dumfries & Galloway DG8 9AB
Some 55 miles from Dumfries. Take the A75 to Newton Stewart, then the A714 towards Wigtown and on to the small village of Bladnoch.

🕐 All year except Christmas to New Year
Monday to Friday 9:00 to 17:00
plus Saturday 11:00 to 17:00 and Sunday 12:00 to 17:00
(July, August and Bank Holidays)

Contacts
Tel: 01988 402605
E-mail: enquiries@
bladnoch.co.uk

Website
www.bladnoch.co.uk

Admission
£ Standard Tour:
£3.00

T Flexible
C Light meals
S Whisky and a good range of gifts and books

Personal notes relating to visit:

Whiskies tasted notes/opinions:

Manager/guide signature:

Date visited:

SECTION INDEX ON PAGE 71

GLENKINCHIE

Meaning of name and pronunciation guide
'Glen de Quincey'
– glen-KIN-chee

Owner
Diageo plc

House style
Light, comparatively sweet, delicate, malty and fruity.

Principal single malts
Glenkinchie 12-year-old, Glenkinchie Distillers Edition.

Principal blends
Haig, Johnnie Walker.

Getting technical
Stills: one pair

Capacity: 2m litres

Malt: lightly peated

Casks: ex-Bourbon

Water: an on-site well

HISTORY

Glenkinchie was established as Milton distillery in 1825 by the farming brothers John and George Rate, with the Glenkinchie name being adopted in 1837. After a period operating as a saw mill from 1853 until 1879, Glenkinchie returned to distilling under the auspices of a consortium of Edinburgh businessmen, and in 1890 the Glenkinchie Distillery Company Ltd was formed.

Major refurbishment work subsequently took place, and in 1914 Glenkinchie was one of five Lowland distilleries (along with Clydesdale, Grange, Rosebank and St Magdalene) which merged to form Scotttish Malt Distillers (SMD). Membership of SMD probably helped Glenkinchie survive the difficult trading years of the First World War and its aftermath. In 1925 SMD was acquired by the Distillers Company Ltd.

In 1986 Glenkinchie was chosen as the Lowland representative in the original Classic Malts line up. This was in preference to Rosebank, which presented a far less visitor-friendly location than the rolling East Lothian farmland around Glenkinchie, just a few miles from Edinburgh.

POINTS OF SPECIAL INTEREST

The wash still is the largest operating in the Scotch whisky industry, and the worm tubs used for condensing the spirit are constructed from cast iron rather than the usual timber.

MODEL STILLS

LOWLAND

VISITOR EXPERIENCE

In addition to the excellent distillery tour and audio-visual presentation, Glenkinchie has more to offer the committed visitor than most other Scottish distilleries.

The former maltings has been a museum since 1969, and is now officially the Museum of Malt Whisky Production, housing a fascinating range of distilling plant and memorabilia, including a scale model distillery built for the 1924 British Empire Exhibition.

The standard tour offers the opportunity to sample two malts, but for an extra payment, four malts may be sampled on the Upgrade Tour.

Written guides are available in Dutch, French, German, Dutch, Italian, Mandarin, Russian, Spanish and Swedish.

LOCATION

Peastonbank, Pencaitland, East Lothian EH34 5ET
Some 18 miles south-east of Edinburgh, the distillery is located south of the village of Pencaitland. From the outskirts of Edinburgh, follow the A1 and exit for Tranent on the A199. Then take the B355 to Pencaitland, going through the village, following the distillery signs along unclassified roads for 1.7 miles.

🕐 April – October
Monday to Saturday 10:00 to 16:00
plus Sunday 12:00 to 17:00
🕐 November – March
Monday to Friday 12:00 to 15:00
plus Saturday, Sunday 12:00 to 17:00 (November)

Contacts
Tel: 01875 342004
Email: glenkinchie.distillery@diageo.com

Website
www.discovering-distilleries.com

Admission
£ Standard Tour: £5.00
£ Upgrade Tour: £7.00

T Flexible
C No
S Whisky and a good range of gifts and books

Personal notes relating to visit:

Whiskies tasted notes/opinions:

Manager/guide signature:

Date visited:

SECTION INDEX ON PAGE 71

ABERFELDY

Meaning of name and pronunciation guide
'Mouth of the Pheallaidh Burn' - aber-FELL-dee

Owner
John Dewar & Sons Ltd (Bacardi Limited)

House style
Medium-bodied, with honey and spice, sweet, malty, nutty and fruity.

Principal single malts
Aberfeldy 12 and 21-year-old single malt.

Principal blends
Dewar's White Label, 12-year old, 18-year-old and Signature.

Getting technical
Stills: two pairs

Capacity: 3.5m litres

Malt: unpeated

Casks: ex-Bourbon and ex-Sherry

Water: Pitilie Burn

HISTORY

Aberfeldy distillery was established during the height of the great Victorian 'whisky boom' of the late 19th century, with the first spirit flowing in 1898. It was built by the successful Perth family firm of John Dewar & Sons to provide malt for its increasingly popular blends. The White Label blend – now the bestseller in the USA - first appeared on the market the year after the distillery came on stream. The distillery was constructed close to the site of the former Pitilie distillery, which closed in 1867.

When Dewar's merged with the Distillers Company Ltd (DCL) in 1925, Aberfeldy became part of the largest whisky-making concern in Scotland. When the next 'whisky boom' arrived during the 1960s and early '70s, Aberfeldy was expanded to increase its capacity, with a new tun room and still house doubling the number of stills from two to four. The still house was constructed in characteristic 'DCL' style for the time, with large windows enabling passers by to see the gleaming copper stills in all their glory.

In 1998 Aberfeldy was one of four distilleries sold by DCL's successor company, Diageo, to John Dewar & Sons, itself owned by Bermuda-based Bacardi Limited.

POINTS OF SPECIAL INTEREST

Aberfeldy was constructed close to the Aberfeldy-Perth railway line to allow for the easy transport of coal, barley and empty casks to the distillery. Full casks would then be transported by train south to Dewar's vast blending and bonding facility in Perth. Today, Aberfeldy displays an old shunting or 'puggie' engine, which once saw service at Dailuaine distillery on Speyside.

HIGHLAND (SOUTHERN)

VISITOR EXPERIENCE

Aberfeldy is home to 'Dewar's World of Whisky,' one of the most innovative distillery visitor facilities in Scotland. Opened in 2000, Dewar's 'World of Whisky' is a state-of-the-art visitor and retail centre, based in the former distillery maltings. Hand-held audio-guides, touch screen interactive displays and an e-mail booth make this a very modern visitor experience, though there is also plenty for the less technologically-minded to get to grips with, including a painstaking reconstruction of Dewar's blending room in Perth and an absorbing collection of promotional material. Latest addition is a 'Brand Family Room,' where visitors are able to gauge their olfactory ability on a large-scale blender's nosing wheel. Regular tours of the distillery itself are also undertaken.

In addition to the 'standard tour,' there is the option of a Cask Tour, which includes the opportunity to sample single malts from the cask in the warehouse, and a Deluxe Tour, which embraces an in-depth tasting session, featuring Aberfeldy 12 and 21-year-olds, Dewar's 12-year-old blended whisky, and a 'guest' whisky. A complementary tasting glass is also presented.

The ultimate experience is the Connoisseur Tour, which allows participants to taste whiskies direct from the cask, along with the 18-year-old cask strength expression, launched in 2010, and the exclusive Dewar's Signature blended whisky.

Printed distillery tour guides are available in Chinese, Dutch, French, German, Greek, Italian, Japanese, Russian and Spanish, while visitor centre audio-guides are programmed in the same range of languages.

LOCATION

Aberfeldy, Perthshire PH15 2EB
31 miles from Perth, via the A9, then the A827 at Ballinluig. The distillery can be found on the eastern outskirts of the village of Aberfeldy.

🕐 April – October
Monday to Saturday 10:00 to 18:00
Sunday 12:00 to 16:00

🕐 November - March
Monday to Saturday 10:00 to 18:00

Contacts
Tel: 01887 822010
E-mail: world of whisky@dewars.com

Website
www.dewars.com

Admission
£ Standard Tour: £6.50
£ Cask Tour: £12.00
£ Deluxe Tour: £18.00
£ Connoisseur Tour: £30.00

The three more in-depth tours should be booked in advance.

T Flexible
C Light meals
S Whisky and a good range of gifts and books

Personal notes relating to visit:

Whiskies tasted notes/opinions:

Manager/guide signature:

Date visited:

BLAIR ATHOL

Meaning of name and pronunciation guide
'Plain of the New Ireland'
- blair ATH-oll

Owner
Diageo plc

House style
Aromatic, honeyed, fruity, nutty, spicy and sweet.

Principal single malts
Blair Athol 12-year-old (Flora & Fauna Series).

Principal blends
Bell's.

Getting technical
Stills: two pairs

Capacity: 3m litres

Malt: unpeated

Casks: ex-Bourbon plus some ex-Sherry

Water: Allt Dour Burn (Burn of the Otter)

HISTORY

Blair Athol is one of Scotland's few surviving distilleries to have its origins in the 18th century. The distillery was established by John Stewart and Robert Robertson, and had several owners before being acquired in 1932 by Arthur Bell & Sons Ltd, as part of the Dufftown-Glenlivet Distillery Co Ltd.

Bell's did not use the distillery until 1949, when it was substantially rebuilt, being extended from two to four stills in 1973, at a time when sales of the Bell's blend were increasing dramatically. Following the takeover of Bell's by Guinness plc in 1985, Blair Athol subsequently became part of United Distillers, and is now in the hands of successor company Diageo.

POINTS OF SPECIAL INTEREST

Somewhat confusingly, Blair Athol distillery is located in the popular holiday town of Pitlochry, rather than the village of Blair Atholl (with an extra 'l'), which lies seven miles to the north.

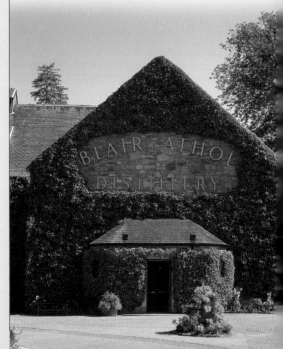

VISITOR EXPERIENCE

Visually, Blair Athol is a treat, with its courtyard dotted with flowers and surrounded by ivy-clad stone buildings. The town of Pitlochry is notably popular with holidaymakers, and the distillery is kept busy with visitors.

A typically professional and informative Diageo distillery tour is on offer, plus complementary dram and well presented shop. The distillery has a long association with Bell's blended whisky, with some 95 per cent of output destined for their blending vats, and Blair Athol serves as something of a 'brand home' for Bell's.

In addition to the standard tour, there are two private tours available. For groups of three to 18 people there is the 'Flora and Fauna Tour,' and for two to eight people there is the 'Allt Dour Deluxe Tour.' The latter includes tasting drams from the distillery's 'Whisky Treasure Trove,' and pre- booking is essential.

Tours are available in a variety of languages but these vary annually depending on staffing. There are written guides in Chinese, Dutch, French, German, Italian, Japanese, Russian, Spanish and Swedish.

Contacts
Tel: 01796 482003
Email: blair.athol.
distillery@diageo.com

Website
www.discovering-
distilleries.com

Admission
- **£** Standard Tour: £5.00 (including a voucher part redeemable on 70cl bottles purchased in the shop)
- **£** Flora & Fauna Tour: £10.00
- **£** Allt Dour Deluxe Tour: £22.00

Pre booking is essential for non-standard tours.

T Flexible during summer months, set at other times of year
C No
S Whisky and some gift and book items

Personal notes relating to visit:

LOCATION

Perth Road, Pitlochry, Perthshire PH16 5LY
The distillery is situated beside the A924 on the southern outskirts of Pitlochry, off the A9 Perth to Inverness road, 26 miles north of Perth.

🕐 Easter – October
Monday to Saturday 9:30 to 17:00
plus Sunday 10:00 to 17:00 (July and August)
🕐 November – Easter
Monday to Friday 10:00 to 16:00

Whiskies tasted notes/opinions:

Manager/guide signature:

Date visited:

COOPERAGE TOOLS

SECTION INDEX ON PAGE 71

EDRADOUR

Meaning of name and pronunciation guide
'Between two waters' - 'edra-DOWER'

Owner
Signatory Vintage Scotch Whisky Co Ltd

House style
Medium bodied, sweet and honeyed, spicy, malty and nutty, with a suggestion of smoke.

Principal single malts
Edradour 10-year-old, 'Straight from the Cask' range, Ballechin (heavily peated), Caledonia 12-year-old.

Principal blends
N/A

Getting technical
Stills : one pair

Capacity: 96,000 litres

Malt: unpeated for Edradour, peated to 50ppm+ for Ballechin

Casks: ex-Sherry for Edradour, ex-Bourbon for Ballechin

Water: springs on Moulin Moor

HISTORY

Edradour is the last surviving example of the once numerous Perthshire 'farm distilleries,' and received its first official mention in 1837, though a farmer's distilling co-operative had been founded in 1825. The farming partners formed John MacGlashan & Co in 1841 to formalise the whisky-making operation.

In 1922 William Whiteley & Co Ltd, a subsidiary of American distiller JG Turney & Sons, purchased Edradour to provide malt for its blends, including King's Ransom and House of Lords. Interestingly, Whiteley renamed the distillery Glenforres-Glenlivet, despite its distance from the famous distilling glen!

During the prohibition years, Whiteley's blends were distributed in the USA by Frank Costello, of Mafia fame, and on whom the Godfather films were supposedly based. There is strong evidence to suggest that Costello indirectly owned Edradour for a time from the late 1930s, through his associate Irving Haim, via JG Turney & Sons.

In 1982 Edradour was acquired by Pernod Ricard subsidiary Campbell Distilleries, They introduced The Edradour as a 10-year-old bottling in 1986, and maintained output at full production through their tenure to support the House of Lords blend. However, following their acquisition of Seagram's Scotch whisky operations, they declared Edradour surplus to requirements in 2002.

The independent bottler Signatory Vintage then purchased the distillery, with the range of Edradour products being significantly expanded. Since late 2007 the whisky has been bottled on site in Signatory's new, purpose-built bottling facility.

POINTS OF SPECIAL INTEREST

Long renowned as the smallest distillery in Scotland, Edradour produces in a year what an average Speyside distillery turns out in a week. If the spirit still was any smaller it would be illegal.

VISITOR EXPERIENCE

The small, traditional and extremely compact nature of Edradour makes it the perfect place to gain a clear understanding of the processes of malt whisky production. The distillery is also notably picturesque and enjoys a beautiful setting. Not surprisingly, it attracts a large number of visitors, averaging 90,000 per annum, making it the third most visited distillery in Scotland after Tullibardine and Glenturret.

Admission includes a complementary dram and an excellent video presentation in a converted malt barn.

An attractive shop contains souvenir items and the full line up of Edradour whiskies, including rare limited and 'finished' editions. As Edradour is owned by the independent bottlers Signatory, there is also a wide range of their bottlings from other distilleries. A tasting bar on site offers in excess of 70 whiskies.

A VIP facility is due to open in late 2010, offering private tours and tutored tastings, including the option to tour the new cask warehouse complex.

The video has subtitle options in French, German, Japanese and Spanish.

LOCATION

Balnauld, Pitlochry, Perthshire PH16 5JP
Nestled just behind Pitlochry, along the A924, then an unclassified road, 27 miles north of Perth.

🕐 May - October
Monday to Saturday 9:30 to 17:00 (except May and October when distillery opens at 10:00)
Sunday 12:00 to 17:00
🕐 November – April
Monday to Saturday 10:00 to 16:00
Sunday 12:00 to 16:00 (except Jan and Feb)

Contacts
Tel: 01796 472095

Website
www.edradour.com

Admission
£ Standard Tour:
£5.00

T Flexible
C Hot and cold drinks
S Whisky and some gift and book items

Personal notes relating to visit:

Whiskies tasted notes/opinions:

Manager/guide signature:

Date visited:

SECTION INDEX ON PAGE 71

GLENGOYNE

Meaning of name and pronunciation guide
'Glen of the wild geese'
– glen-GOYN

Owner
Ian Macleod
Distillers Ltd

House style
Medium-bodied, sweet, floral and malty, with notes of vanilla.

Principal single malts
Glengoyne 10, 12, 17 and 21-year-old.

Principal blends
Cutty Sark, Famous Grouse, Lang's Supreme.

Getting technical
Stills: one wash and two spirit

Capacity: 1.1m litres

Malt: unpeated

Casks: ex-Bourbon and ex-Sherry

Water: Loch Carron

HISTORY

Glengoyne was first licensed to George Connell in 1833 as Burnfoot distillery, and stands in an area that was once a hotbed of illicit distilling. In 1886 local historian Guthrie Smith wrote that in the early years of the 19th century, "the smoke of 13 illicit stills" was visible in the Blane valley.

Lang Brothers Ltd began a long association with Glengoyne when they purchased it in 1876, changing the name from Burnfoot to Glenguin. The present name was adopted in 1905, and six decades later Lang Brothers was taken over by a fellow Glasgow company, Robertson & Baxter Ltd, which ultimately became The Edrington Group.

Edrington sold Glengoyne distillery, a significant quantity of stock and the Lang's blended whisky brand to Ian Macleod Distillers Ltd in 2003, and the Broxburn-based blenders and bottlers have subsequently doubled the distillery's output and introduced a wide range of new Glengoyne expressions and limited edition releases.

POINTS OF SPECIAL INTEREST

The theoretical 'Highland Line' that divides Highland and Lowland single malts runs through the distillery site, meaning that although the spirit is distilled in the Highlands it is matured in the Lowlands, as Glengoyne's warehouses are 'below' the line!

HIGHLAND (SOUTHERN)

VISITOR EXPERIENCE

Glengoyne offers the most extensive visitor menu of any distillery in Scotland and attracts some 40,000 people per year. The 'standard' Glengoyne Tour comprises an audio-visual presentation, distillery tour and complementary dram of 10-year-old Glengoyne.

The Wee Tasting Tour includes an additional glass of 17-year-old, while the Tasting Tour comprises samples of the 10, 12, 17 and 21-year-old expressions in the luxurious Glengoyne Club Room.

New for 2010 is 'Cask Idol,' which entails sampling three single cask bottled expressions and three straight from the cask, one of which you will be helping to choose for a future special release.

For the dedicated enthusiast, there is the Master Blender Session, where guests spend time in the dedicated Sample Room, tasting Lang's Select blend and Glengoyne 17-year-old whilst learning about the art of the Master Blender. Guests will then have the opportunity to create their own blend which will be bottled in a 100ml sample bottle to take away.

The ultimate experience is the Masterclass, which claims to offer the most in-depth and comprehensive distillery tour in Scotland. Highlights include a tasting of Glengoyne 17-year-old whisky at the foot of Glengoyne waterfall, presentations on new make spirit and the maturation process, nosing of two grain whiskies plus a presentation on grain whisky and a hands-on whisky blending session in the Sample Room. At the end of the visit, guests are presented with a 200ml bottle of their created blend with a certificate and cellar book.

Tours are available in French and German, while brochures and DVD presentations are offered in a wide range of languages.

Contacts
Tel: 01360 550254
E-mail: reception@glengoyne.com

Website
www.glengoyne.com

Admission
- £ Glengoyne Tour: £6.50
- £ Wee Tasting Tour: £8.50
- £ Tasting Tour: £15.00
- £ Cask Idol: £70.00
- £ Master Blender Session: £30.00 Masterclass: £100.00

The Cask Tasting and Master Tours should be booked in advance.

T Set times
C Dining available for groups of 12 or more, booked in advance
S Whisky and a good range of gifts and books

Personal notes relating to visit:

Whiskies tasted notes/opinions:

Manager/guide signature:

Date visited:

LOCATION

Dumgoyne, Stirlingshire G63 9LB
The distillery is located beside the A81 Glasgow to Aberfoyle road, 15 miles north of Glasgow, and well signposted, just south-east of Loch Lomond.

All year except Christmas and New Year
Monday to Sunday 10:00 to 17:00
Closing at 16:30 (December – February)

GLENTURRET

Meaning of name and pronunciation guide
'Glen of the small, dry stream'
– glen-TURRET

Owner
The Edrington Group

www.famousgrouse.com

House style
Medium-bodied, sweet and smooth, with honey and vanilla.

Principal single malts
The Glenturret 10-year-old.

Principal blends
The Famous Grouse.

Getting technical
Stills: one pair

Capacity: 340,000 litres

Malt: lightly peated

Casks: ex-Bourbon and ex-Sherry

Water: Loch Turret

HISTORY

Glenturret has a strong claim to be the oldest working distillery in Scotland, with illicit distilling taking place there in 1775. The Turret Burn was notably popular with illicit distillers, who were operating in the area by 1717.

Glenturret was first licensed to John Drummond, under the name Hosh, in 1818, with the Glenturret name being adopted in 1875. Another distillery in the vicinity had previously used the Glenturret name from 1826 until 1852.

In 1921 distilling ceased, and eight years later, the distillery was dismantled, subsequently being used for agricultural storage. The distillery remained silent until businessman James Fairlie acquired the premises in 1957 and proceeded to re-equip it for distilling, with production recommencing two years later. Ownership passed to Remy Cointreau in 1981, then in 1990 it came under the auspices of Highland Distillers, now part of the Edrington Group.

Today, Glenturret serves as a 'brand home' for The Famous Grouse.

POINTS OF SPECIAL INTEREST

One of the more bizarre records in the Scotch whisky industry belongs to Towser, the late, lamented Glenturret distillery cat, who earned herself a place in the *Guinness Book of Records* by dispatching no fewer than 28,899 mice during her 24 years at the Perthshire distillery. The tortoiseshell terror is now immortalised in a statue close to the visitor centre.

VISITOR EXPERIENCE

Glenturret distillery and its visitor centre were re-branded as 'The Famous Grouse Experience' in 2002, and the site now attracts some 100,000 visitors annually. Distillery tours embrace 'The Flight of the Grouse,' - a state-of-the-art, BAFTA award-winning interactive show, which was significantly upgraded during 2009.

Anyone wanting a more in-depth experience than that provided by the 'standard' distillery tour can take part in the Experience Tour, which includes two complementary drams and information on blending The Famous Grouse. Alternatively, the Malt Tasting Tour boasts a tutored tasting of malt whiskies, while the Stillman's Choice Tour includes the sampling of five different expressions.

For the real connoisseur, there is 'Warehouse No.9,' which involves participating in a sampling of the Famous Grouse malt range in one of the maturation warehouses at the end of the regular distillery tour.

A Whisky School and a Cook School (cooking with whisky) are run by the production manager and the restaurant chef. Further details can be found on the distillery website.

There is also a stylish 'nosing and tasting bar' where visitors can find out just how good their noses are. The excellent Famous Grouse Experience Restaurant and adjoining bar are situated on the first floor of the visitor centre. Exclusive, gourmet food and whisky matching dinners, named Fasan Ur, may be booked in advance by groups.

Distillery tours are available in 10 languages, all printed on translation sheets, and there are also written guides in Chinese, Dutch, French, English, German, Italian, Japanese, Russian, Spanish and Swedish.

LOCATION

The Hosh, Crieff, Perthshire PH7 4HA
The distillery is located just over a mile to the north of Crieff, off the A85 Crieff to Oban road. .

🕐 March - December
   Monday to Sunday 9:00 to 18:00
🕐 January - February
   Monday to Sunday 10:00 to 16:30

Contacts
Tel: 01764 656565

Website
www.thefamousgrouse
.com

Admission
£ Standard Tour:
  £6.95
£ Experience Tour:
  £8.50
£ Malt Tasting Tour:
  £10.95
£ Stillman's Choice
  Tour: £18.50
£ Warehouse No.9:
  £40.00 (Booking
  essential)

Under 12s Free

T Flexible
C Full meals
S Whisky and a good
range of gifts and
books

**Personal notes
relating to visit:**

**Whiskies tasted
notes/opinions:**

**Manager/guide
signature:**

Date visited:

SECTION INDEX ON PAGE 71

TULLIBARDINE

Meaning of name and pronunciation guide
'Hill of warning'
- tully-BAR-din

Owner
Tullibardine Distillery Ltd

House style
Sweet and creamy, with vanilla, fruit, nuts and spice.

Principal single malts
Tullibardine Aged Oak, 1993, 1992, 1988 and some 1960s bottlings, plus a range of wood finish expressions.

Principal blends
N/A

Getting technical
Stills: two pairs

Capacity: 2.7m litres

Malt: unpeated

Casks: ex-Bourbon and ex-Sherry

Water: Danny Burn

HISTORY

Although the present distillery was only built in 1949, a distillery had operated under the Tullibardine name in this part of Perthshire during the late 18th and early 19th centuries. The 1949 distillery was designed by William Delmé-Evans, who went on to create Jura and Glenallachie distilleries. It was operated by Brodie Hepburn Ltd from 1953 until that company's takeover by Invergordon Distillers Ltd in 1971.

Under the control of Invergordon, capacity was increased by the installation of a second pair of stills in 1973, but when Invergordon was acquired by Whyte & Mackay Distillers Ltd in 1993, Tullibardine was deemed surplus to requirements, being mothballed the following year.

Production resumed in 2003 when a consortium of businessmen purchased Tullibardine from Whyte & Mackay for £1.1 million. The distillery site was substantially developed for retail usage and much of it was sold on to a property development company.

A notable feature of the consortium's ownership of Tullibardine has been the wide range of cask finishes offered to the consumer, along with vintage bottlings which feature the year of distillation rather than an age statement.

POINTS OF SPECIAL INTEREST

Tullibardine was built on the site of what is said to the first public brewery in Scotland. Certainly, it is recorded as supplying ale to King James IV in the year of his coronation at Scone Palace, near Perth. The year in question was 1488.

VISITOR EXPERIENCE

Since Tullibardine re-opened in December 2003, visitor interaction has been a crucial element of the operation. The visitor centre is open all year round, offering tours of the distillery, as well as access to the '1488' shop, which features a wide range of quality giftware as well as whisky, and the licensed, 'Café 1488,' which boasts locally-sourced food and home-baking, plus Starbucks coffee and free WiFi.

In addition to the Tullibardine distillery facilities on site, there are a number of adjacent retail units, including a large Baxter's store, selling the company's wide range of Scottish-made produce and much more besides.

The 'standard' distillery tour last approximately 45 minutes and features a nosing session, with samples of two Tullibardine single malts. Those visitors wishing to delve a little deeper, may like to opt for the Tutored Tasting, which includes sampling three expressions of Tullibardine whiskies in the Tasting Room, or the Bonded Tour. According to the distillers, this "...gives you the full experience of the skill and effort that goes into creating The Tullibardine single malt whisky. The tour will end in our tasting room, where you will nose and sample three of our Tullibardine whiskies."

The ultimate visitor experience is the Connoisseur Tour, which is a "...more in-depth tour for the aficionado, and takes around two hours. We will take you around the distillery and into the bonded warehouse where our guide will pull a whisky (or two) straight from a cask for nosing. Afterwards, you will be taken to the tasting room for a tutored tasting of the Tullibardine range."

Printed tour guides are available in English, French, German, Italian and Spanish.

LOCATION

Stirling Street, Blackford, Perthshire PH4 1QG
Situated beside the A9, 16 miles north-east of Stirling or 18 miles south-west of Perth.

All year except Christmas and New Year
Monday to Sunday 10:00 to 17:00

Contacts
Tel: 01764 682252
Email:
info@tullibardine.com

Website
www.tullibardine.com

Admission
£ Standard Tour:
   £5.00
£ Tutored Tasting:
   £7.50
£ Bonded Tour:
   £15.00
£ Connoisseur Tour:
   £25.00

T Flexible
C Light meals
S Whisky and a good range of gifts and books

Personal notes relating to visit:

Whiskies tasted notes/opinions:

Manager/guide signature:

Date visited:

FETTERCAIRN

Meaning of name and pronunciation guide
'Wooded slope'
– FETTER-cairn

Owner
Whyte & Mackay Ltd

House style
Comparatively light in body, reasonably sweet, malty, nutty and spicy, with notes of vanilla and honey.

Principal single malts
Fettercairn 1824 12-year-old.

Principal blends
Whyte & Mackay Special.

Getting technical
Stills: two pairs

Capacity: 2m litres

Malt: lightly peated

Casks: ex-Bourbon and ex-Sherry

Water: springs in the Grampians

HISTORY

Fettercairn was converted from a former corn mill into a distillery in 1824 by local landowner Sir Alexander Ramsay, and was first licensed to James Stewart & Co the following year. In 1830, Ramsay sold his Estate and the distillery, to Sir John Gladstone, father of the future Prime Minister, William Ewart Gladstone.

The distillery effectively remained in the Gladstone family until its closure in 1926, though between 1890 and 1912 there were also a number of other owners. After falling silent, the distillery came close to being dismantled, before being purchased by Ben Nevis owner Joseph Hobbs' Associated Scottish Distillers Ltd in 1939.

In 1966 the number of stills was increased from two to four, with Hay & McLeod & Co and W&S Strong Ltd taking over control under the auspices of the Tomintoul-Glenlivet Distillery Co Ltd in 1971. Two years later, that company was acquired by Whyte & Mackay Ltd, who have run Fettercairn ever since. In 2007, Whyte & Mackay became part of the Indian-owned United Breweries Group.

POINTS OF SPECIAL INTEREST

Prior to the establishment of Fettercairn distillery in 1824, a whisky-making facility of the same name operated without benefit of licence a couple of miles away on the remote slopes of Cairn O'Mount, an area popular with illicit distillers.

HIGHLAND (EASTERN)

VISITOR EXPERIENCE

Fettercairn is one of the lower profile distilleries in the Highlands, both in terms of its single malt and its status as a visitor attraction. Yet, Fettercairn is a most attractive, traditional distillery, blessed with a beautiful setting in the foothills of the Cairngorm Mountains. It is surrounded by fertile farmland, capable of growing high quality malting barley.

Fettercairn has operated a visitor centre and shop since 1989, and though not on an obvious tourist trail, the distillery is definitely worth seeking out.

The video presentation is first class, the tours low-key and friendly, and the unique, self-cooling spirit stills with water flowing down them are worth the visit alone.

Additionally, single cask, cask-strength bottlings of Fettercairn are exclusively available at the distillery visitor centre.

Contacts
Tel: 01561 340205

Website
www.whyteandmackay
.com

Admission
£ Standard Tour:
£2.00

T Flexible
C No
S Whisky and some
gift and book items

LOCATION

Distillery Road, Fettercairn, Laurencekirk, Kincardineshire AB30 1YE
The distillery is located off the B966, five miles from the A90 Dundee to Aberdeen road, on the outskirts of the village.

🕐 May – September
Monday to Saturday 10:00 to 14:30

Personal notes relating to visit:

Whiskies tasted notes/opinions:

Manager/guide signature:

Date visited:

FETTERCAIRN DISTILLERY Co.

SECTION INDEX ON PAGE 71

GLENDRONACH

Meaning of name and pronunciation guide
'Valley of the brambles'
– glen-DRON-ach

Owner
The BenRiach-GlenDronach Distilleries Co Ltd

House style
Full-bodied, richly Sherried, with vanilla, malt, spice, nut and fruit notes.

Principal single malts
Glendronach 12, 15 and 18-year-old.

Principal blends
Ballantine's, Teacher's.

Getting technical
Stills: two pairs

Capacity: 1.3m litres

Malt: unpeated

Casks: ex-Bourbon and ex-Sherry

Water: The Dronach Burn

HISTORY

One of many distilleries to date from the years immediately after the passing of the 1823 Excise Act, Glendronach was built 1826 by a consortium of local farmers and businessmen, headed by James Allardice, in an area previously noted for illicit distilling.

In 1852 it was taken over by Walter Scott, formerly manager of Teaninich distillery, proceeding to expand the operation. On his death in 1887 the distillery was acquired by a Leith partnership which ran it until 1920, when Charles Grant, son of Glenfiddich founder William Grant, purchased it for the sum of £9,000.

In 1960 William Teacher & Sons Ltd bought Glendronach, doubling the number of stills to four in 1966/67. The distillery passed with the rest of Teacher's assets to Allied Breweries Ltd in 1976, and it remained in the Allied fold until 2005, when acquired by Pernod Ricard subsidiary Chivas Brothers. The plant was mothballed between 1996 and 2002, and in July 2008 it was acquired by the BenRiach Distillery Company. Subsequently, an ambitious programme of releases, including a number of single cask bottlings, was embarked upon.

POINTS OF SPECIAL INTEREST

Until 2005 Glendronach remained the last distillery in Scotland to heat its stills with coal. In that year the stills were converted to steam heating.

VISITOR EXPERIENCE

GlenDronach was comparatively early in creating a visitor centre, first opening in 1976. New visitor facilities were unveiled in 2009, complete with a shop and video presentation.

A small distillery with disused malting floors still in place, GlenDronach offers a charming and traditional tour experience.

In addition to the 'standard' Discovery Tour, there is a 'Connoisseurs Experience,' which includes an in-depth distillery tour, followed by a tutored tasting in the company of former distillery manager Frank Massie.

LOCATION

Forgue, Huntly, Aberdeenshire AB54 6DB
The distillery stands beside the B9024, close to its junction with the B9001, nine miles from Huntly, off the A97 Huntly to Banff road.

All year except Christmas and New Year
Monday to Saturday 10:00 to 16:30
Sunday 12:00 to 16:00

Connoisseurs' Experience: Monday and Wednesday only

Contacts
Tel: 01466 730202
Email: info@glendronachdistillery.co.uk

Website
www.glendronachdistillery.co.uk

Admission
£ Standard Tour: £3.00
£ Connoisseurs' Experience: £20.00 (pre-booking is essential)

T Flexible
C No
S Whisky and some gift and book items

Personal notes relating to visit:

Whiskies tasted notes/opinions:

Manager/guide signature:

Date visited:

GLENGARIOCH

Meaning of name and pronunciation guide
'Glen of the rough ground'
– glen-GEE-rie

Owner
Morrison Bowmore Distillers Ltd
(Suntory Ltd)

House style
Honey sweetness, hints of heather and a touch of spice.

Principal single malts
Glen Garioch 1797 Founder's Reserve and 12 Years Old, plus annual vintages.

Principal blends
N/A

Getting technical
Stills: one wash and two spirit

Capacity: 1.5m litres

Malt: unpeated, with the exception of the 1978 vintage

Casks: ex-Bourbon and ex-Sherry

Water: The Silent Spring of Coutens Farm

HISTORY

Glengarioch distillery is one of Scotland's oldest surviving distilleries, having been established in 1797 by John Manson. It remained in his ownership until 1884, when it was bought by a firm of Leith-based wine and spirits merchants. They were soon joined by William Sanderson, who had recently developed his Vat 69 brand, and much of the Glengarioch 'make' subsequently went into that blend.

Ultimately, Glengarioch became part of the Distillers Company Ltd when DCL acquired the distillery's then proprietors Booth's Distilleries Ltd in 1937. DCL closed Glengarioch in 1968, claiming there was insufficient water available for distillation, but two years later Stanley P Morrison Ltd purchased the distillery and proceeded to dig a new well in a nearby field, thereby solving the problem.

Morrison's increased the number of stills to three in 1972, and added a fourth the following year, though this was subsequently decommissioned. The company continued to use its floor maltings until 1993, producing a relatively peaty single malt. Two years later the distillery fell silent until 1997

In 2004 a 1958 expression of Glen Garioch appeared - the oldest bottling of the whisky ever released.

POINTS OF SPECIAL INTEREST

In 1982 Glengarioch became the first Scottish distillery to use North Sea gas for heating purposes. The distillery also experimented with a tomato-growing greenhouse enterprise at one time, using waste heat and carbon dioxide from the fermentation and distillation processes.

Curiously, the single malt produced by Glengarioch distillery has long been marketed as Glen Garioch.

HIGHLAND (EASTERN)

VISITOR EXPERIENCE

One of Scotland's oldest distilleries, Glengarioch visitor centre opened in October 2005, and is located in the distillery's former maltings. An audio-visual presentation preceeds the distillery tour, which ends with a complementary dram. A tastefully stocked shop ensures you can buy samples to take home.

Tours are available in English and German, and there are also written guides in French, German, Italian, Japanese, Russian, Spanish and Swedish.

LOCATION

Distillery Road, Oldmeldrum, Aberdeenshire
AB51 OES
Gelengarioch is located within a residential area in the north of Oldmeldrum, some 14 miles from the outskirts of Aberdeen. Oldmeldrum can be reached via the A947 from Aberdeen or the A96 and B9170 if travelling from the west. Follow the A947 through the village until Distillery Road on the left.

All year except Christmas to New Year
Monday to Friday 10:00 to 16:30
plus Saturday in high season

Contacts
Tel: 01651 873450
Email: info@morrison
bowmore.co.uk

Website
www.glengarioch.com

Admission
£ Standard tour:
£4.00

VIP tours can be arranged by prior appointment.

T Set times
C No
S Whisky and some gift and book items

Personal notes relating to visit:

Whiskies tasted notes/opinions:

Manager/guide signature:

Date visited:

SECTION INDEX ON PAGE 71

GLENGLASSAUGH

HISTORY

Glenglassaugh was constructed between 1873 and 1875 by the Glenglassaugh Distillery Company. Within 15 years the distillery was renovated and upgraded, with new stills being installed, and in 1892 it was sold to the Glasgow blending concern of Robertson & Baxter Ltd, who had previously been a customer for Glenglassaugh spirit.

Robertson & Baxter bought the distillery and passed it on to its 'sister' company Highland Distilleries Ltd, now part of The Edrington Group. This set the way for a history of intermittent spells of operation, interspersed by lengthy periods of closure. Though some sources note that distilling took place during the 1930s, records suggest that the distillery remained silent for half a century.

The bulk of the current buildings date from a radical reconstruction programme, conducted between 1957 and 1959, and only the warehousing and malt barns survive from the original 19th century distillery.

In 1986 Glenglassaugh was mothballed in the face of growing whisky stocks, and also because of the expensive process of treating the hard water available on site in order to make it closer in composition to that of The Glenrothes, which was favoured stylistically by the mutual owners for use in its Famous Grouse blend.

Glenglassaugh was rescued from silence in 2008, when a Dutch-based consortium, the Scaent Group, acquired it for £5 million and proceeded to restore it to full operational order.

POINTS OF SPECIAL INTEREST

As well as releasing vintage expressions of Glenglassaugh, the new owners have also bottled an innovative 'single mash' variant of new make spirit as 'The Spirit drink that dare not speak its name.'

Meaning of name and pronunciation guide
'Glen of the grey-green place'
- glen-GLASS-och

Owner
Glenglassaugh
Distillery Co Ltd
(The Scaent Group)

House style
Medium-bodied, quite sweet and fruity, with spice and smoke.

Principal single malts
Glenglassaugh 21, 30 and 40-year-old.

Principal blends
N/A

Getting technical
Stills: one pair

Capacity: 1m litres

Malt: unpeated

Casks: ex-Bourbon and ex-Sherry

Water: Glassaugh Spring

HIGHLAND (EASTERN)

VISITOR EXPERIENCE

A fascinating chance to see a distillery getting back on its feet having been closed for so long. Informal and extremely well informed 'Spirit Drink' tours of the distillery are conducted by members of the production staff and include a sample of Glenglassaugh 'new make,' newly distilled spirit before it becomes whisky.

There is also a weekly, in-depth 'Behind the Scenes' tour, which involves a tutored tasting of the 21 and 30-year-old expressions which takes place on Friday mornings.

LOCATION

Portsoy, Banffshire AB45 2SQ
The distillery stands by the Moray Firth coast, off the A98, two miles west of the village of Portsoy. Some 70 miles from Aberdeen and 25 miles from Elgin.

🕐 All year except Christmas to New Year
Monday to Friday 10:00 set tour time
plus other times by prior arrangement

Contacts
Tel: 01261 842367
Email: info@
glenglassaugh.com

Website
www.glenglassaugh.
com

Admission
£ 'Spirit Drink' Tour:
  £5.00
£ 'Behind the Scenes'
  Tour: £25.00
  (pre-booking
  recommended)

T Flexible
C No
S No

Personal notes
relating to visit:

Whiskies tasted
notes/opinions:

Manager/guide
signature:

Date visited:

SECTION INDEX ON PAGE 71

ROYAL LOCHNAGAR

HISTORY

The present Lochnagar distillery dates from 1845, when it was built by John Begg. Two previous legal distilling ventures in the area had been burnt down, in 1823 and 1841, probably by irate illicit distillers who resented their presence, though the latter distillery was rebuilt and survived until 1860.

Begg's distillery was known as 'New Lochnagar,' and soon came to prominence as a result of obtaining a Royal Warrant from the occupant of nearby Balmoral Castle in 1848, after which the name 'Royal Lochnagar' was proudly used.

Lochanagar remained in the Begg family until 1916, when it was sold to John Dewar & Sons Ltd, having been substantially rebuilt a decade earlier.

When Dewar's became part of the Distillers Company Ltd in 1925, Lochnagar joined the great DCL empire, subsequently being transferred to its Scottish Malt Distillers (SMD) operating subsidiary.

1963 saw a major reconstruction project take place, while a visitor centre was added in 1990.

POINTS OF SPECIAL INTEREST

The smallest operational distillery owned by Diageo plc, Lochnagar earned its 'royal' prefix as a result of a visit by Queen Victoria and her family while staying at neighbouring Balmoral Castle in 1848.

Meaning of name and pronunciation guide
'Little loch of the noisy summit'
- LOCH-na-GAR

Owner
Diageo plc

House style
Medium to full-bodied, quite sweet, with Sherry, fruit, nuts, spice and a whiff of smoke.

Principal single malts
Royal Lochnagar 12-year-old, Royal Lochnagar Selected Reserve, Royal Lochnagar Distiller's Edition.

Principal blends
Johnnie Walker Blue Label.

Getting technical
Stills: one pair

Capacity: 450,000 litres

Malt: lightly peated

Casks: American and European oak

Water: Scarnock Springs from the foothills of Lochnagar

HIGHLAND (EASTERN)

VISITOR EXPERIENCE

Royal Lochnagar enjoys a notably scenic location, close to the Royal Family's Balmoral Castle summer retreat and in the shadow of the mountain that gives the distillery its name.

It is a pretty, traditional distillery, which boasts an open mash tun, wooden washbacks, condensing worm tubs, unusually dumpy stills and on-site cask-filling.

The visitor centre is attractive and inviting, while distillery tours are professional, well-informed and intimate. In addition to the 'standard' tour, a Royal Lochnagar Whisky Family Tour is also available. This includes the opportunity to experience the three principal Royal Lochnagar single malt expressions. Specialist tours with tutored tastings may also be arranged by contacting the distillery.

Written guides are available in Danish, Dutch, French, German, Italian, Japanese, Mandarin, Russian, Spanish and Swedish.

LOCATION

Balmoral, Crathie, Ballater, Aberdeenshire AB35 5TB
Mid-way between Braemar and Ballater and just past Balmoral Castle, the distillery is accessed along an unclassified road off the B976, just beyond its junction with the A93 and the turning for the castle.

🕐 January – February
Monday to Friday 10:00 to 16:00
🕐 April – October
Monday to Saturday 10:00 to 17:00
Sunday 12:00 to 17:00
🕐 November, December and March
Monday to Saturday 10:00 to 16:0

Contacts
Tel: 01339 742700
Email: royal.lochnagar.
distillery@diageo.com

Website
www.discovering-
distilleries.com

Admission
£ Standard Tour:
£5.00
£ Royal Lochnagar
Whisky Family Tour:
£10.00

Both tours include a voucher redeemable on 70cl bottles purchased in the shop.

T Flexible from April to October, set times during winter months
C No
S Whisky and some gift and book items

Personal notes relating to visit:

Whiskies tasted notes/opinions:

Manager/guide signature:

Date visited:

SECTION INDEX ON PAGE 71

SPEYSIDE

ABERLOUR

Meaning of name and pronunciation guide
'Mouth of the chattering burn' – aber-LOUR

Owner
Chivas Bros Ltd (Pernod Ricard)

House style
Medium-bodied, comparatively sweet, with honey, sherry, spices, malt and fruit notes.

Principal single malts
Aberlour 10 and 15-year-old single malt, Aberlour a'bunadh.

Principal blends
Clan Campbell, House of Lords.

Getting technical
Stills: two pairs

Capacity: 3.5m litres

Malt: peated to 2ppm

Casks: ex-Bourbon and ex-Sherry

Water: a spring on Ben Rinnes

HISTORY

Aberlour was one of many new distilleries to be established in the wake of the revolutionary 1823 Excise Act, which did much to stimulate legal, commercial whisky distilling in the Scottish Highlands.

The distillery was founded by Peter Weir and James Gordon in 1826, but a new distillery was built in 1879 after a serious fire destroyed the original. Some of the present structure dates from 1898, when the plant was rebuilt after a second major fire. It was designed by the legendary distillery architect Charles Doig.

Aberlour was acquired by the French company Pernod Ricard in 1974, a year after the distillery had been significantly upgraded and extended, with its capacity being doubled by the addition of two new stills.

Today, Aberlour trades as part of Pernod's Chivas Brothers subsidiary, and Aberlour single malt enjoys notably strong sales in France. Indeed, a significant percentage of the Aberlour 'make' is bottled as single malt, with only around 50 per cent of the distillery's output finding its way into blended whiskies.

POINTS OF SPECIAL INTEREST

The original water source for the distillery was St Drostan's Well, situated in the present grounds and used by the Pictish Saint Drostan (or Dunston) for Christian baptisms more than a thousand years ago. Drostan eventually became Archbishop of Canterbury.

SPEYSIDE

VISITOR EXPERIENCE

Until 2002 Aberlour was not open to the public, but the Aberlour Distillery Experience now offers an in-depth and detailed distillery tour and tasting session which lasts for around one hour and 45 minutes and is aimed principally at the more serious and informed whisky aficionado. It includes an audio-visual presentation, a tour of the plant and a tutored nosing and tasting of five mature Aberlour expressions and 'new make' spirit in No 1 Warehouse.

For an additional payment, participants may bottle their own malt from a specially selected cask.

The Founder's Tour was inaugurated in 2010 and focuses initially on the heritage of Aberlour distillery in a presentation made in the Fleming Rooms; not usually open to the public. A distillery tour is followed by the extremely rare opportunity to sample a range of different 'cuts' of spirit, after which there is a whisky and speciality chocolate matching session, all rounded off with a dram straight from a Sherry butt in No 6 Warehouse. This is served in a presentation tasting glass which visitors may then take home with them.

There are printed guides in French, German, Italian and Spanish.

Contacts
Tel: 01340 881249
Email: aberlour.admin
@chivas.com

Website
www.aberlour.co.uk
or www.maltwhisky
distilleries.com

Admission
£ Standard Tour:
  £10.00
£ Founder's Tour:
  £25.00

All tours must be booked in advance.

T Set times
C No
S Whisky and some gift and book items

LOCATION

Aberlour, Banffshire AB38 9PJ
The distillery stands back from the main A95, at the south-western end of Aberlour's main street.

🕐 April - October
Monday to Sunday 9:00 to 17:00
🕐 November - March (exc 19th Dec - 4th Jan)
Monday to Friday 09:00 to 17:00

Standard Tour: 10:00 and 14:00 daily
Founder's Tour: 10:30 Wednesday and Thursday

Personal notes relating to visit:

Whiskies tasted notes/opinions:

Manager/guide signature:

Date visited:

BALVENIE

Meaning of name and pronunciation guide
'Beathan's Farm'
– bal-VEN-ee

Owner
William Grant & Sons Ltd

House style
Medium to full bodied, rich, sweet, malty and spicy.

Principal single malts
Signature 12 Year Old, Doublewood 12 Year Old, Portwood 1991, Single Barrel 15 Year Old, Portwood 21 Year Old, Balvenie Thirty.

Principal blends
William Grant's Family Reserve.

Getting technical
Stills: five wash and six spirit

Capacity: 6.4m litres

Malt: very lightly peated

Casks: ex-Bourbon and ex-Sherry

Water: The Balvenie Springs

HISTORY

Balvenie was William Grant's second distillery, built just four years after its neighbour, Glenfiddich. The first spirit began to flow in May 1893. Adopting the same sense of thrift that had enabled Glenfiddich to be constructed and equipped comparatively cheaply; Grant incorporated the old mansion of Balvenie New House into the structure as part of the maltings and purchased second-hand stills from Lagavulin on Islay and Glen Albyn in Inverness.

The distillery was upgraded and capacity was increased during the 1950s and '60s, with new stills being added in 1957, 1965 and 1971, taking the complement up to eight. Balvenie was first officially bottled in 1973, and currently occupies 10th place in the list of global best-selling single malts.

POINTS OF SPECIAL INTEREST

Balvenie is one of just six Scottish distilleries which still operates its own floor maltings, and malt made there accounts for some 10 per cent of the total requirement.

The Balvenie website (www.thebalvenie.com) features a unique facility that enables visitors to assemble an online 'Whisky Shelf,' 'at Warehouse 24' - the members' area, named after one the distillery's oldest warehouses. Here members may list and rate thousands of different single malt whiskies and compare notes with other members and experts who have already created their own Whisky Shelves.

SPEYSIDE

VISITOR EXPERIENCE

Since 2005 Balvenie has offered a 'connoisseurs'' tour, designed to complement the more mainstream visitor attractions of their sister distillery, Glenfiddich. Each tour lasts for approximately three hours and is limited to a maximum of eight people. Participants begin with a cup of coffee in the Distillery Office, where the tour manager outlines the distillery's history before setting off to explore the site.

This presents the rare opportunity to see working floor maltings, a traditional warehouse and a cooperage in action, before sampling a range of Balvenie whiskies, from 'new make' spirit to the Balvenie Thirty.

There is also the chance to 'bottle your own' Balvenie, with a choice of three different casks on offer. Bottling is only available as part of the tour.

Contacts
Tel: 01340 820373

Website
www.thebalvenie.com

Admission
£ Tour: £25.00

Advance booking essential.

T Set times
C Light meals at neighbouring Glenfiddich Distillery
S Whisky and gift at neighbouring Glenfiddich Distillery

LOCATION

Dufftown, Banffshire AB55 4BB
The distillery is situated just off the A941, on the northern outskirts of Dufftown, four miles from the A95 junction at Craigellachie and 16 miles from Elgin. Balvenie sits behind Glenfiddich distillery and tours start from the Glenfiddich visitor centre.

🕐 All year except Christmas to New Year
Monday to Thursday 10:00 and 14:00 set tour times
Friday 10:00 only

Personal notes relating to visit:

Whiskies tasted notes/opinions:

Manager/guide signature:

Date visited:

SECTION INDEX ON PAGE 71

BENROMACH

Meaning of name and pronunciation guide
'Shaggy mountain'
– ben RO-mac

Owner
Gordon & MacPhail

House style
Medium-bodied, floral, fruity, spicy and malty.

Principal single malts
Benromach Traditional
Benromach Organic,
Benromach Peat
Smoke, Benromach 10,
21 and 25-year-old.

Principal blends
N/A

Getting technical
Stills: one pair

Capacity: 500,000 litres

Malt: mostly peated to around 10/12ppm

Casks: ex-Bourbon and ex-Sherry

Water: Chapleton Spring

HISTORY

Benromach was constructed at the height of the 1890s whisky boom to the design of prolific local architect Charles Doig. Production commenced in May 1900, and Benromach passed through a number of hands before eventually being acquired by the Distillers Company Ltd in 1953.

In 1983 Benromach was one of nine distilleries closed by DCL, but it was saved from oblivion by the internationally renowned Elgin-based independent bottler, wholesaler and retailer Gordon & MacPhail, who purchased the site in 1993 and set about reviving the distillery. The completed project was subsequently unveiled by HRH the Prince of Wales in 1999.

Although technically a reopened distillery, Benromach is, in essence, a new distillery constructed within the shell of an old one, with only half the original production space now in use. The new stills installed at Benromach were considerably smaller than the originals, and were designed with comparatively broad necks to catch the heavier flavours created during the first distillation. The aim is to produce a spirit that is quite quick to mature, but also has enough character, body and depth to last in cask for 20 or 30 years.

POINTS OF SPECIAL INTEREST

Benromach is the smallest working distillery on Speyside, and is run by just two men, including the manager.

SPEYSIDE

VISITOR EXPERIENCE

In terms of output, Benromach is one of Scotland's smaller distilleries, and is a traditional operation boasting the world first fully certified 'organic' single malt. A DVD presentation features a history not only of the distillery but also its owners, Gordon & MacPhail, who have been buying casks and blending and bottling whisky for over 100 years.

There is a dedicated visitor centre, opened in 1988, housing a shop, dramming area and the DVD viewing facilities. The distillery tour provides an excellent opportunity to grasp the essentials of whisky-making due to the compact nature of the revived operation, with all the production processes taking place in one area. Visitors may also fill and purchase their own bottle of Benromach from an exclusive cask selected by the manager. Tutored tastings are also available.

Written guides are available in English, French, German, Italian, Japanese and Polish.

LOCATION

Invererne Road, Forres, Morayshire IV36 3EB
Benromach is located 28 miles from Inverness, just off the A96 Inverness to Aberdeen road, on the eastern outskirts of Forres.

🕐 May - September
Monday to Saturday 9:30 to 17:00
Sunday 12:00 to 16:00 (June - August only)
🕐 October - April (except Christmas and January)
Monday to Fri 10:00 to 14:00

Contacts
Tel: 01309 675968
E-mail: info@benromach.com

Website
www.benromach.com

Admission
£ Standard Tour: £3.50 (£2.50 redeemable on purchases over £25.00)

T Flexible
C No
S Whisky and some gift and book items

Personal notes relating to visit:

Whiskies tasted notes/opinions:

Manager/guide signature:

Date visited:

SECTION INDEX ON PAGE 71

CARDHU

HISTORY

John Cumming took out a licence for Cardhu (or Cardow as it was originally called) in 1824, following the groundbreaking Excise Act of the previous year. However, he had been distilling there without benefit of a licence since taking the lease on Cardhu farm in 1811, and had numerous convictions to prove it.

After John's death in 1846, his son, Lewis, and daughter-in-law, Elizabeth, took over the distillery, but following Lewis's death in 1872, Elizabeth adopted the role of principal distiller. She completely rebuilt the distillery on nearby land in 1884 and subsequently sold off some of the old plant, including a pair of very thin and patched pot stills, to a certain William Grant, who was then in the process of setting up Glenfiddich distillery. Cardhu was subsequently extended in 1887.

In 1893 Cardhu was acquired by John Walker & Sons of Kilmarnock for £20,500, becoming part of the Distillers Company Ltd in 1925. In 1960/61 the distillery was largely rebuilt, with the number of stills being increased from four to six.

POINTS OF SPECIAL INTEREST

The spiritual home of Johnnie Walker, the world's best selling blended Scotch whisky.

SPEYSIDE

VISITOR EXPERIENCE

One of eight Speyside distilleries on the official Malt
Whisky Trail, Cardhu is a hidden gem, nestling beneath
the Mannoch hill, close to the village of Knockando.
Steeped in history, it is the only distillery to have been
pioneered by a woman. The welcome is warm and the
atmosphere relaxed, and the tour highly professional.

In addition to the 'standard' tour, there is also the
Classic Tour and an 'Aromas & Flavours Tour.' The
latter presents a unique opportunity to sample three
single malts and one award-winning Johnnie Walker
blend which have been carefully selected and paired
with various foods.

*Written guides are available in Dutch, French,
German, Italian, Japanese, Russian, Spanish and
Swedish.*

LOCATION

Knockando, Morayshire AB38 7RY
Eight miles south-west of Aberlour, the distillery
is situated off the B9102 Grantown-on-Spey to
Craigellachie road, reached via an unclassified
road off the A95 south of Aberlour.

🕐 Easter – September
Monday to Friday 10:00 to 17:00
plus Saturday 10:00 to 17:00 (July - September)
and Sunday 12:00 to 16:00 (July - September)

🕐 October – Easter
Monday to Friday 11:00 to 15:00

Contacts
Tel: 01479 874635
Email: cardhu.distillery
@diageo.com

Website
www.discovering-
distilleries.com

Admission
£ Standard Tour:
£4.00
£ Classic Tour: £6.00
(both include a
£3.00 voucher
redeemable on 70cl
bottles purchased
in the shop)
£ Aromas & Flavours
Tour: £8.00, (with
£5 redeemable
voucher)

Aromas & Flavours
Tour must be booked
in advance.

T Flexible
C No
S Whisky and some
gift and book items

**Personal notes
relating to visit:**

**Whiskies tasted
notes/opinions:**

**Manager/guide
signature:**

Date visited:

SECTION INDEX ON PAGE 71

CRAGGANMORE

Meaning of name and pronunciation guide
'The big rock'
– crag-an-MORE

Owner
Diageo plc

House style
Medium-bodied, complex, quite sweet, spicy and notably floral.

Principal single malts
Cragganmore 12-year-old, Cragganmore Distillers Edition.

Principal blends
Haig, Old Parr, White Horse and Johnnie Walker Green Label.

Getting technical
Stills: two pairs

Capacity: 1.6m litres

Malt: unpeated

Casks: ex-Bourbon

Water: Corries Springs

HISTORY

John Smith had an impressive distilling record by the time he obtained a lease to create Cragganmore distillery at Ayeon Farm on the Ballindalloch Estate in 1869. Smith had previously managed Macallan, Glenfarclas, Wishaw and Glenlivet, and is thought to have been the illegitimate son of Glenlivet founder George Smith.

Cragganmore was designed by the Speyside distillery architect Charles Doig, and in 1901 Doig was again called on to modernise the distillery. The Smith family's control lapsed in 1923, and four years later 50 per cent of Cragganmore came into the ownership of the Distillers Company Ltd, with the other half belonging to Sir George Macpherson-Grant of Ballindalloch Estate. DCL acquired the remaining 50 per cent of the distillery in 1965, a year after the plant's capacity had been doubled with the installation of a new pair of stills.

Cragganmore has long enjoyed a reputation as a leading Speyside single malt, as well as a top class blending whisky, and in 1998 it was chosen by DCL's predecessor United Distillers to be the Speyside representative in the newly-formed Classic Malts line up.

POINTS OF SPECIAL INTEREST

One of the reasons why Smith chose the Cragganmore location in which to build his distillery was the close proximity of the Great Highland Railway line. Smith was a keen advocate of railway transport, both for business and for personal travel, but he weighed 22 stones, and as his bulk could not fit through carriage doorways he always had to travel in the guard's van! Smith died in 1886, and the following year the first of many 'Whisky Special' goods trains left Ballindalloch station with a cargo consisting exclusively of 16,000 gallons of whisky.

SPEYSIDE

VISITOR EXPERIENCE

Now with extended opening to meet growing demand to explore this beautifully located Speyside distillery, Cragganmore offers a classic Diageo visitor experience, featuring a warm welcome and knowledgeable guides.

Also available is a Premium Tour, which includes admission to the exclusive Cragganmore Clubroom where visitors can watch a video while enjoying coffee and shortbread. This is followed by a distillery tour and a taste of Cragganmore 12-year-old and Craggnmore Distillers Edition. The Clubroom is not usually open to the public, and features a fascinating array of historical Cragganmore-related memorabilia.

The Connoisseurs' Tour boasts all the features of the Premium Tour, along with a tutored nosing and tasting.

Written guides are available in Dutch, French, German, Japanese, Russian, Spanish and Swedish.

LOCATION

Ballindalloch, Banffshire AB37 9AB
Nine miles south of Aberlour, the distillery is located along a farm road, off the A95 Grantown-on-Spey to Elgin road, just west of Bridge of Avon.

🕐 April – October
Monday to Friday 10:00 to 16:00

Contacts
Tel: 01479 874700
Email: cragganmore.distillery@dageo.com

Website
www.discovering-distilleries.com

Admission
£ Standard Tour: £4.00 (including a £3.00 voucher as below)
£ Premium Tour: £8.00 (including a £5.00 voucher)
£ Connoisseurs' Tour: £16.00, (including an £8.00 voucher)

Vouchers are redeemable against a 70cl bottle from the distillery shop.

T Flexible
C No
S Whisky and some gift and book items

Personal notes relating to visit:

Whiskies tasted notes/opinions:

Manager/guide signature:

Date visited:

GLENFARCLAS

HISTORY

Founded in 1836 by Robert Hay, Glenfarclas was in turn acquired by John Grant and his son George in 1865. Leased for five years by John Smith until he left to establish nearby Cragganmore, Glenfarclas has remained in the Grant family ever since. George Grant, son of current chairman, John, represents the sixth generation of the family to have been involved in running the business.

The distillery was modernised in 1896/97, with the number of stills being increased from two to four in 1960, and from four to six in 1976. Widely considered to be one of the Speyside 'greats,' much of the spirit currently being produced is filled into oloroso Sherry casks, despite the fact that they can cost as much as ten times more than their ex-Bourbon counterparts.

Glenfarclas offers a unique range of single cask bottlings under the 'Family Casks' label, each of which represents a year from 1952 to 1994.

POINTS OF SPECIAL INTEREST

Glenfarclas is one of very few Scotch whisky distilleries to remain in family ownership, and operates the biggest mash tun and the largest stills on Speyside. Unusually, they are direct-fired by gas, rather than heated by steam.

Meaning of name and pronunciation guide
'Valley of the Green Grass'
– glen-FAR-class

Owner
J&G Grant

House style
Big-bodied, complex and Sherried, nutty, malty and comparatively sweet. An after-dinner dram.

Principal single malts
Glenfarclas 10, 12, 15, 21, 25 and 30-year-old, Glenfarclas 105 (cask strength).

Principal blends
Isle of Skye.

Getting technical
Stills: three pairs

Capacity: 3m litres

Malt: lightly peated

Casks: ex-Sherry

Water: Green Burns

SPEYSIDE

VISITOR EXPERIENCE

Glenfarclas was one of the first distilleries to create a purpose-built visitor centre, which opened in 1973. The 'Ship's Room,' in which visitors enjoy their complementary dram, boasts wood panelling from the liner *Empress of Australia*, along with the original ship's bar. There is a well-stocked shop and informative, friendly tours of the distillery itself.

In-depth Ambassador's Tour and Tasting events are staged on Fridays during July and August.

Tours are available in French, Spanish and Italian by prior appointment. Brochures are available in French, German and Spanish.

LOCATION

Ballindalloch, Banffshire AB37 9BD
The distillery is located just off the A95 Grantown-on-Spey to Aberlour road, five miles south of Aberlour.

🕐 April – September
Monday to Friday 10:00 to 17:00
plus Saturday 10:00 to 16:00 (July – September)
🕐 October – March
Monday to Friday 10:00 to 16:00

Contacts
Tel: 01807 500345
E-mail: info@glenfarclas.co.uk

Website
www.glenfarclas.co.uk

Admission
£ Standard Tour: £3.50
£ Ambassador's Tour: £15.00 (bookable in advance for Friday PM, July and August only)

T Flexible
C No
S Whisky and some gift and book items

Personal notes relating to visit:

Whiskies tasted notes/opinions:

Manager/guide signature:

Date visited:

SECTION INDEX ON PAGE 71

GLENFIDDICH

HISTORY

After Mortlach, Glenfiddich was only the second distillery to be built in Dufftown, with construction commencing in 1886, and the first spirit flowing on Christmas Day 1887. The distillery was the creation of former Mortlach manager William Grant and his family, who acquired second-hand stills and other plant from Cardhu to equip the fledgling distillery.

The business prospered to the extent that the Grants built neighbouring Balvenie distillery (see p 102) in 1892, though the collapse of the high profile blending firm of Pattisons Ltd in 1898 was potentially damaging, since Pattison Ltd was Grant's best customer. However, the demise of the Leith-based blending company led Grant to develop the Standfast blend (now renamed Family Reserve), though it took 503 visits to potential customers before a single order was secured!

Today, Glenfiddich remains in the hands of William Grant & Sons Ltd, and is one of just four Scottish distilleries where whisky is châteaux-bottled' on site, though some bottling is also now undertaken at the company's premises, near Glasgow. In 1992 a third Grant's distillery, named Kininvie, was built, principally to serve the firm's needs for yet more blending malt.

POINTS OF SPECIAL INTEREST

Glenfiddich operates more stills than any other distillery in Scotland.

Glenfiddich is the world's best-selling single malt whisky, with annual sales of around 10 million bottles.

Meaning of name and pronunciation guide
'Valley of the Deer'
– glen-FID-ik

Owner
William Grant & Sons Ltd

House style
Light-bodied, sweet, fragrant and floral, with malt and citric notes.

Principal single malts
Glenfiddich Special Reserve 12-year-old, Caoran Reserve 12-year-old, 15, 18, 21 and 30-year-old.

Principal blends
Grant's Family Reserve.

Getting technical
Stills: 10 wash and 18 spirit

Capacity: 11.4m litres

Malt: unpeated

Casks: ex-Bourbon and ex-Sherry

Water: Robbie Dhu Spring

SPEYSIDE

VISITOR EXPERIENCE

Glenfiddich was the first Scottish distillery to open its doors to the public on a regular basis, back in 1969, and since then more than three million visitors have sampled its delights. The distillery now attracts some 80,000 members of the public per annum and runs a very slick and professional tour. £1.8 million has been spent in recent years in order to create a new brand /visitor centre, coffee shop and bar.

In addition to the 'regular' distillery tours, a two and a half hour Connoisseurs' Tour, with a tutored nosing and tasting and a visit to the unique Solera warehouse, runs three times daily.

Tours are available in most European languages during the summer months and there are also written guides in French, German, Italian, Japanese, Mandarin, Russian and Spanish. Audio-visual presentations are also available in eight languages.

Contacts
Tel: 01340 820373
E-mail:
info@glenfiddich.com

Website
www.glenfiddich.com

Admission
£ Standard Tour:
free
£ Connoisseur Tour:
£20.00

Advance booking for the Connoisseur Tour is recommended.

T Flexible
C Light meals
S Whisky and gifts

LOCATION

Dufftown, Banffshire AB55 4DH
The distillery is situated just off the A941 on the northern outskirts of Dufftown, four miles from the A95 junction at Craigellachie and 16 miles from Elgin.

🕐 All year except Christmas to New Year
Monday to Saturday 9:30 to 16:30
Sunday 12:00 to 16:30

Personal notes relating to visit:

Whiskies tasted notes/opinions:

Manager/guide signature:

Date visited:

SECTION INDEX ON PAGE 71

GLEN GRANT

Meaning of name and pronunciation guide
The only distillery in Scotland to be named after its owners, John and James Grant
– glen-GRANT

Owner
Davide Campari-Milano SpA

House style
Light-bodied, dry, nutty, herbal and slightly spirity in younger expressions.

Principal single malts
Glen Grant (no age statement), 5 and 10-year-old.

Principal blends
Chivas Regal, Old Smuggler Braemar.

Getting technical
Stills: four pairs

Capacity: 5.9m litres

Malt: unpeated

Casks: ex-Bourbon plus some ex-Sherry

Water: Back Burn and Tobar-Dhomhnaich Well

HISTORY

Glen Grant was the first distillery to be constructed in the Speyside town of Rothes. It was built by brothers John and James Grant, commencing production in 1840. Such was the success of Glen Grant that James' son, Major James Grant, built a second distillery on the opposite side of the main street in 1898, connected to the original plant by a 'whisky pipe' that ran above the road. The new distillery was christened Glen Grant No 2, though it was later changed to Caperdonich.

In 1953, J&J Grant, Glen Grant Ltd merged with George & JG Smith of Glenlivet to form Glenlivet & Glen Grant Distillers Ltd, and in 1972 the company joined Hill Thompson & Co Ltd and Longmorn-Glenlivet Distilleries Ltd to create The Glenlivet Distillers Ltd. This company was acquired by Seagram of Canada in 1977.

The number of stills was increased from four to six in 1973, and from six to ten in 1977, though today only eight are in operation. In 2001 Glen Grant was acquired by Pernod Ricard subsidiary Chivas Bros, and in 2006 the distillery was sold on to the Italian drinks company Campari. Glen Grant has long enjoyed strong sales in Italy, and the five-year-old is the country's leading single malt Scotch whisky. It is also the second best-selling single malt in the world.

POINTS OF SPECIAL INTEREST

During a visit to Matabeleland in Africa in 1898, Major Grant's hunting party discovered an abandoned child whom he duly brought back to Rothes and educated. Biawa Makalanga – known to locals as 'Byeway' – became Grant's butler, and after the major's death in 1931, Biawa lived on in Glen Grant House until he died in 1972.

SPEYSIDE

VISITOR EXPERIENCE

Glen Grant is on Scotland's Malt Whisky Trail and an impressive new visitor centre opened in 2008, based in the former Coachman's House.

Visitors experience an audio-visual presentation in a recreation of Major James Grant's study, a distillery tour, and access to the magnificently restored 22-acre Victorian garden created by the major, complete with a heather-thatched 'dram pavilion.' Grant also had a safe, containing a whisky bottle, fitted into the rock face beside the burn which flows through the garden in order to be able to supply visitors with a dram of his whisky as they took a stroll.

Tours are available in French, Italian and Spanish, while written boards describing the processes in all sections of the plant are in French, German, Italian and Spanish.

LOCATION

Elgin Road, Rothes, Morayshire AB38 7BS
The distillery is situated just off the A941 roundabout at the north end of Rothes, 10 miles south of Elgin.

🕐 Mid-January - mid-December
Monday to Saturday 9:30 to 17:00
plus Sunday 9:30 to -17:00 (May - October)

Contacts
Tel: 01340 832118
E-mail: visitorcentre@glengrant.com

Website
www.glengrant.com

Admission
£ Standard Tour: £3.50 (including a voucher part redeemable on 70cl bottles purchases in the distillery shop)

T Flexible
C Snacks
S Whisky and a good range of gifts and books

Personal notes relating to visit:

Whiskies tasted notes/opinions:

Manager/guide signature:

Date visited:

SECTION INDEX ON PAGE 71

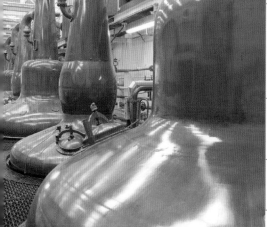

GLENLIVET

Meaning of name and pronunciation guide
'Glen of the smooth place'
– glen-LIV-it

Owner
Chivas Bros Ltd
(Pernod Ricard)

House style
Elegant yet quite robust, floral, fruity, sweet, gently Sherried, spicy and slightly smoky.

Principal single malts
The Glenlivet 12, 15, 18, 21 and 25-year-olds.

Principal blends
Chivas Regal, Royal Salute.

Getting technical
Stills: seven pairs

Capacity: 10m litres

Malt: unpeated

Casks: ex-Bourbon and ex-Sherry

Water: Josie's Well

HISTORY

Probably the most famous distillery in the world, The Glenlivet was the first to be granted a licence in the wake of the 1823 Excise Act, which paved the way for the large-scale, legal Scotch whisky distilling industry we know today. The owner and licensee was George Smith, whose family had been distilling whisky on his farm at Upper Drumin, just over a mile from the present Glenlivet distillery, since 1774.

In 1840 George Smith leased the Cairngorm distillery at Delnabo, near Tomintoul and his son, William, took charge of the distillery at Upper Drumin. However, demand for Smith's whisky outstripped supply, and in 1858 a new, large distillery named Glenlivet was established on the present Minmore site, with Upper Drumin and Cairngorm closing the following year.

Family ownership continued for almost a century, with George & J G Smith Ltd merging with J&J Grant, Glen Grant Ltd to form Glenlivet & Glen Grant Distillers Ltd in 1953. In 1972 the company joined Hill Thompson & Co Ltd and Longmorn-Glenlivet Distilleries Ltd to create The Glenlivet Distillers Ltd.

Seagram of Canada acquired The Glenlivet Distillers Ltd in 1977 and in 2001 The Glenlivet was purchased by Pernod Ricard subsidiary Chivas Bros.

During 2008/09, a new production area was developed, housing a mash tun, eight washbacks and six new stills, virtually doubling the distillery's potential capacity.

The Glenlivet is currently the best-selling single malt Scotch whisky in the USA.

POINTS OF SPECIAL INTEREST

In the latter part of the 19th century, many distilleries tried to capitalise on the fame and reputation of The Glenlivet resulting in the area jokingly being referred to as 'the longest glen in Scotland.' In 1880 legal action by John Gordon Smith resulted in only his Glenlivet distillery being allowed to use the definite article in front of its name. All other distillers had to use 'Glenlivet' as a hyphenated prefix or suffix.

SPEYSIDE

VISITOR EXPERIENCE

The Glenlivet visitor centre started life in 1859 as the distillery's maltings, and visitors are able to tour the distillery and see inside one of its traditional bonded warehouses before sampling one of a selection of single malts from The Glenlivet range in the Dram Room. A 'brand exhibition' is both entertaining and informative.

New from 2010 is the Ambassador's Tour, a once a week in-depth tour and tasting of some exclusive expressions led by one of the Brand Ambassador.

The Glenlivet also offer The Guardians Whisky School which is a three day course at a cost of £250. In addition to learning about distilling, students sample rare expression, visit the hallowed No 1 warehouse and spend time at the Speyside Cooperage gaining an in-depth knowledge of cask production. Exploring the historic Smuggler's Trails and enjoying a traditional Scottish dinner make this a full and memorable three days.

Headphone information is available in French, German, Italian, Spanish and Swedish.

Contacts
Tel: 01340 821720
E-mail: theglenlivet.
admin@chivas.com

Website
www.theglenlivet.com

Admission
£ Standard Tour:
  free
£ Ambassador's Tour:
  £25.00 (each Friday
  morning and must
  be booked in
  advance. Limited to
  10 people per tour)

T Flexible
C Light meals
S Whisky and a good
range of gifts and
books

LOCATION

Ballindalloch, Banffshire AB37 9DB
Although rather remote the distillery is well signposted. Situated either 13 miles along the A95, then B9008 from Aberlour, or 14 miles, via the B9009 and B9008, from Dufftown.

Easter – October
Monday to Saturday 9.30 to 16:00
Sunday 12:00 to 16:00

Personal notes relating to visit:

Whiskies tasted notes/opinions:

Manager/guide signature:

Date visited:

SECTION INDEX ON PAGE 71

GLEN MORAY

Meaning of name and pronunciation guide
'The glen of the sea settlement'
– glen-MURRAY

Owner
La Martiniquaise

House style
Quite light-bodied, sweet, with floral, vanilla, nut and spice notes.

Principal single malts
Glen Moray Classic (no age statement), 12 and 16-year-old.

Principal blends
Label 5.

Getting technical
Stills: two pairs

Capacity: 2.2m litres

Malt: unpeated

Casks: ex-Bourbon

Water: a well by the River Lossie

HISTORY

Glen Moray distillery was founded in 1897, when Speyside was in the grip of the great, late Victorian whisky boom. Like Glenmorangie, it was based on a former brewery, in this case the West Brewery of Henry Arnot & Co. The new distillery traded as the Glen Moray Glenlivet Distillery Co Ltd.

Difficult financial times caused the distillery to close in 1910, and apart from a brief revival two years later, Glen Moray was silent until 1923, when it recommenced operations under new owners Macdonald & Muir Ltd. The story goes that the Leith blenders had the opportunity to purchase either Aberlour or Glen Moray, and left the decision up to their Glenmorangie manager, who opted for the latter.

Reconstruction work took place in 1958, when the floor maltings were replaced by Saladin boxes, though on-site malting ended in 1978. In 1979, the number of stills was increased from two to four. Macdonald & Muir changed its name to Glenmorangie plc in 1996, and in 2004 the company was acquired by Louis Vuitton Moet Hennessy.

During 2008 the Glen Moray distillery and single malt brand was sold to French drinks company and present owners La Martiniquaise.

POINTS OF SPECIAL INTEREST

La Martiniquaise is best known for its Glen Turner blended malt and single malt whiskies, which are top sellers in the French market.

The change of ownership has seen an increase in production and a greater emphasis placed on the Glen Moray brand.

SPIRIT SAFE

SPEYSIDE

VISITOR EXPERIENCE

Acclaimed as "the sunniest distillery in Scotland," Glen Moray joined the Malt Whisky Trail in 2004. At that time a new visitor centre and gift shop was established, incorporating a coffee shop and whisky tasting area. New in 2008 was a 'Bottle your Own' option, which allows visitors to bottle whisky straight from a cask for purchase.

A 'Fifth Chapter' in-depth, connoisseurs' tour is also available, during which Glen Moray whisky from the last five decades can be sampled with distillery manager Graham Coull.

Foreign language cards in French, German, Italian and Spanish can also be provided as an aid during tours.

Contacts
Tel: 01343 550900

Website
www.glenmoray.com

Admission
£ Standard Tour:
£3.00
£ 'Fifth Chapter' Tour:
£15.00 (pre-booking is essential)

T Set times
C Snacks
S Whisky and a good range of gifts and books

LOCATION

Bruceland Road, Elgin, Morayshire IV30 1YE
The distillery is located off the A96 Aberdeen to Inverness road, just to the south-west of Elgin. Tucked away behind housing, directions are well signposted.

🕐 All Year except Christmas and New Year
Monday to Friday 9:00 to 17:00
plus Saturday 10:00 to 16:30 (May - September)

Personal notes relating to visit:

Whiskies tasted notes/opinions:

Manager/guide signature:

Date visited:

THE MACALLAN

Meaning of name and pronunciation guide
derived from two Gaelic words: 'magh,' meaning 'fertile strip of ground,' and 'Ellen,' from 'St Fillan,' an early 8th century missionary
- ma-CALLAN

Owner
The Edrington Group

House style
Big-bodied, Sherried, spicy and fruity, with oak and some smoke.

Principal single malts
The Macallan 10-year-old and various aged expressions up to a 30-year-old. Additionally, a 'Fine Oak' range aged from 10 to 30-year-old.

Principal blends
Famous Grouse, Cutty Sark.

Getting technical
Stills: Seven wash and fourteen spirit

Capacity: 8m litres

Malt: unpeated

Casks: ex-Sherry and ex- Bourbon

Water: boreholes by the River Spey

HISTORY

The Macallan is one of the great names in Scotch whisky, with the Speyside distillery being officially established the year after the 1823 Excise Act made legal distilling considerably more lucrative.

Having initially been licensed to Alexander Reid, The Macallan distillery passed through several hands before being purchased by Roderick Kemp in 1892. A trust and then a limited company subsequently operated The Macallan, until 1986 when the Japanese distilling giant Suntory acquired 25 per cent of the stocks in what was now Macallan-Glenlivet plc. A decade later Highland Distilleries Ltd bought the rest of the stocks, and the Kemp family's involvement came to an end.

In 1999 a partnership of The Edrington Group and William Grant & Sons Ltd purchased Highland Distilleries, going on to form the 1887 Company, with Edrington owning the majority shareholding.

As early as 1965, The Macallan's capacity had been doubled by adding six new stills, and by 1975 the total number of stills stood at 21.

In 2008/9 a dormant stillhouse, containing six stills, was re-commissioned, giving the distillery a projected 30 per cent increase in capacity. Two new, state-of-the-art warehouses were also constructed.

POINTS OF SPECIAL INTEREST

The Macallan is renowned for its continuing use of ex-Sherry casks to mature the majority of its whisky, despite the considerably higher cost than that of former Bourbon barrels. However, in 2004 a Fine Oak range was introduced for those consumers whose preference is for less heavily-Sherried malts.

The Macallan's spirit stills are the smallest on Speyside.

SPEYSIDE

VISITOR EXPERIENCE

The Gardener's Cottage visitor centre opened in 2001, and offers an informative and well-produced audio-visual presentation and retail facilities. A mouth-watering array of rare Macallan bottlings is on display, and many expressions from the vast range of currently available Macallans are on sale.

The Macallan offers two types of tour with an emphasis on a personal experience. The 'Experience' tour lasts one-and-a-quarter hours and takes in the full production process, The Macallan's Mastery of Spirit presentation and the 'Warehouse 7' exhibition, where staff explore 'The Story of Oak.'

The 'Precious Tour,' is an extended, two-and-a-quarter hours visit, which includes the full production process, 'Warehouse 7' and 'The Story of Oak,' ending with a tutored nosing and tasting presentation in the Visitor Centre Nosing Room across a range of The Macallan whiskies.

LOCATION

Easter Elchies, Craigellachie, Aberlour, Banffshire AB38 9RX
The distillery is situated off the B9102, shortly after it leaves the A941 Aberlour to Elgin road. Just north of Craigellachie and the cast-iron bridge.

🕐 Easter – August
Monday to Saturday 9:30 to 16:30
🕐 September – October
Monday to Friday 9:30 to 16:30
🕐 November – Easter
Monday to Friday 11:00 to 15:00

Contacts
Tel: 01340 872280
Email: mgray@edrington.co.uk

Website
www.themacallan.com

Admission
£ Standard Tour: £8.00
£ Precious Tour: £20.00

Advance booking is advised, as there is a limit of 10 people per tour.

T Flexible
C No
S Whisky and some gift and book items

Personal notes relating to visit:

Whiskies tasted notes/opinions:

Manager/guide signature:

Date visited:

SECTION INDEX ON PAGE 71

STRATHISLA

Meaning of name and pronunciation guide
'Valley of the River Isla.'
- strath-EYE-la

Owner
Chivas Bros Ltd
(Pernod Ricard)

House style
Medium-bodied, sweet, fruity, nutty, malty and spicy.

Principal single malts
Strathisla 12-year-old.

Principal blends
Chivas Regal.

Getting technical
Stills: two pairs

Capacity: 2.4m litres

Malt: lightly peated

Casks: ex-Bourbon and ex-Sherry

Water: Fons Bulliens Well

HISTORY

Strathisla was established by George Taylor and Alexander Milne in 1786, initially using the name Milltown. In 1825 it officially became known as Milton, when it was purchased by McDonald Ingram & Co. Several owners later, the name Strathisla was briefly adopted, but two years later this was changed again to Milton-Keith.

William Longmore & Co had a long involvement in ownership of the distillery, dating back to William Longmore's purchase of it in 1830, but in 1940 London financier George Pomeroy acquired a majority interest in the Longmore Company. Pomeroy was subsequently found guilty of tax evasion in 1949, and the business was made bankrupt.

The following year, the distillery was sold to the Seagram Company's newly-acquired Chivas Bros subsidiary at auction for £71,000 and a programme of restoration and upgrading was instigated. The name reverted to Strathisla in 1951 and in 1965 the number of stills was doubled to four.

2001 saw Strathisla distillery, along with Seagram's other spirits assets, purchased by Pernod Ricard.

POINTS OF SPECIAL INTEREST

Arguably the oldest distillery in the Scottish Highlands, and certainly one of the most picturesque.

SPEYSIDE

VISITOR EXPERIENCE

Although due attention is paid to Strathisla single malt, the distillery is principally promoted as 'The home of Chivas Regal.' Visitors are served a glass of 12-year-old Chivas Regal while watching a short DVD presentation, after which they are taken on a tour of the distillery and a traditional warehouse.

The current visitor centre was developed in 1995 and the 'Dram Room' is a relaxing and consciously old-fashioned delight of leather sofas and wood panelling. A dram of Chivas Regal 18-year-old or Strathisla 12-year-old single malt is served there after the tour. Personal labelling of Chivas Regal 12 or 18-year-old purchased in the shop is also an option.

Information leaflets are available in Dutch, French, German, Italian and Spanish.

LOCATION

Seafield Avenue, Keith, Banffshire AB55 5BS
Located off the B9116 and A95/96 Aberdeen to Inverness road, some 17 miles south-east of Elgin and alongside the River Isla in the centre of Keith.

🕐 Easter – October
Monday to Saturday 9:30 to 16:00
Sunday 12:00 to 16:00
🕐 November – December
Monday to Friday 9:30 to 12:30, 13:30 to 16:00

Contacts
Tel: 01542 783044
E-mail: strathisla.
admin@chivas.com

Website
www.maltwhisky
distilleries.com

Admission
£ Standard Tour:
  £5.00

T Flexible
C No
S Whisky and some
gift and book items

**Personal notes
relating to visit:**

**Whiskies tasted
notes/opinions:**

**Manager/guide
signature:**

Date visited:

123

BEN NEVIS

Meaning of name and pronunciation guide
'Mountain water'
– ben NEV-is

Owner
Ben Nevis Distillery (Fort William) Ltd (Nikka Whisky Distilling Co Ltd/Asahi Breweries Ltd)

House style
Quite full-bodied, oily, spicy and smoky, malty, nutty and fruity.

Principal single malts
Ben Nevis 10-year-old plus occasional vintages.

Principal blends
Dew of Ben Nevis, Glencoe (blended malt).

Getting technical
Stills: two pairs

Capacity: 2m litres

Malt: unpeated

Casks: ex-Bourbon and ex-Sherry

Water: Allt a'Mhuilinn (on Ben Nevis)

HISTORY

Ben Nevis distillery was established in the shadow of the famous mountain of the same name in 1825 by 'Long John' Macdonald, who stood six feet for inches tall. His whisky was marketed as 'Long John's Dew of Ben Nevis,' and the 'Long John' name ultimately appeared on a popular blend. Such was the demand for the Ben Nevis make that in 1878 a second distillery, called Glen Nevis, was built close to the existing plant. This functioned as a separate entity for 30 years before becoming an integral part of the Ben Nevis operation.

In 1955 Ben Nevis was acquired by the colourful entrepreneur Joseph Hobbs, a Scot who had migrated to Canada to make his fortune and later returned to his homeland. Hobbs operated a number of distilleries at various times, including Benromach, Bruichladdich, Fettercairn, Glenesk, Glenlochy, Glenury Royal and Lochside, in addition to Ben Nevis.

Alas, the distillery fell silent in 1964, when Joseph Hobbs died, and in 1981 was sold by the Hobbs family to Long John International Ltd, part of the brewing giant Whitbread & Co Ltd. After a £2 million investment programme, Ben Nevis recommenced production three years later, but the revival was short lived, and in 1986 the plant closed once again. It was bought from Whitbread by Japanese distillers Nikka Whisky Distilling Co Ltd (now a subsidiary of Asahi Breweries Ltd) in 1989, and reopened the following year.

POINTS OF SPECIAL INTEREST

Joseph Hobbs installed a Coffey still at Ben Nevis, in order to produce grain whisky for blending purposes on the premises. The Coffey still was removed in 1981.

HIGHLAND (WESTERN)

VISITOR EXPERIENCE

With Scotland's highest mountain towering above, the 'Legend of the Dew of Ben Nevis Visitor Centre' is housed in a former warehouse, which dates from 1862. An audio-visual presentation introduces the mythical giant Hector McDram, and a tour of the distillery is followed by a complementary dram. There is also a coffee shop within the visitor centre.

Children are permitted to take part in the tour provided they are accompanied by an adult.

Tours are usually available during the summer months in French, German and Italian, and there are also written guides in English, French, German, Italian, Japanese and Spanish.

LOCATION

Lochy Bridge, Fort William, Inverness-shire PH33 6TJ
Two miles north-east of Fort William, the distillery is located beside the A82 just beyond the junction with the A830 to Mallaig road. Inverness is 63 miles to the north.

🕐 All year except Christmas and New Year
Monday to Friday 9:00 to 17:00
plus Saturday 10:00 to 16:00 (Easter - September)
plus Sunday 12:00 to 16:00 and weekdays until 18:00 (July and August)

From October to Easter, weekend and evening opening may be possible by arrangement.

Contacts
Tel: 01397 700200
E-mail: colin@
bennevisdistillery.com

Website
www.bennevis
distillery.com

Admission
£ Standard Tour:
£5.00

T Set times
C Snacks
S Whisky and a good range of gifts and books

Personal notes relating to visit:

Whiskies tasted notes/opinions:

Manager/guide signature:

Date visited:

SECTION INDEX ON PAGE 71

CLYNELISH

Meaning of name and pronunciation guide
'Sloped garden'
– KLINE-leesh

Owner
Diageo plc

House style
Medium-bodied, oily, floral, malty and fruity, with lots of spice and hints of peat, seaweed and smoke.

Principal single malts
Clynelish 14-year-old, Clynelish Distillers Edition.

Principal blends
Johnnie Walker.

Getting technical
Stills: three pairs

Capacity: 4.2m litres

Malt: unpeated

Casks: ex-Bourbon plus some ex-Sherry

Water: Clynemilton Burn

HISTORY

Clynelish was established in 1819 by the Marquis of Stafford, later the Duke of Sutherland, to provide an outlet for barley grown by his tenants. Fuel was provided by the local Brora coal mine, which had been in use since the 16th century. The distillery came into the hands of the Distillers Company Ltd in 1925 and finally closed for good in 1983.

The distillery which bears the name Clynelish today dates from 1967/68, and was built alongside the old plant, which was subsequently re-named Brora and distilled whisky using heavily peated malt for a time.

The 'new' Clynelish distillery was constructed in characteristically bold 1960s DCL style, with a glass-fronted still house, along the same lines as Aberfeldy, Caol Ila, Craigellachie, Glen Ord, Teaninich and others.

The installation of a new pair of stainless steel washbacks during 2008 increased potential annual output at the distillery by some 25 per cent.

POINTS OF SPECIAL INTEREST

One of just a few distilleries to be equipped with spirit stills which are larger than the wash stills.

CLYNELISH AND BRORA DISTILLERIES

VISITOR EXPERIENCE

Clynelish distillery is a notable landmark in the quiet countryside near the small Sutherland town of Brora, and is easily visible from the A9 road. Close up, there is a fascinating contrast between the conspicuous, somewhat functional style of the modern distillery, and the neighbouring stone-built, 19th century Brora structures.

Clynelish sits among wild, moorland scenery, close to the East Sutherland coast, and it offers a professional Diageo distillery tour and a small shop. The shop is the only outlet for an exclusive bottling of Clynelish Cask Strength single malt.

Written guides are available in multiple languages.

LOCATION

Clynelish Road, Brora, Sutherland KW9 6LR
The distillery is situated off the A9 Inverness to Scrabster road, just north of Brora.

🕐 April – September
   Monday to Friday 10:00 to 17:00
   plus Saturday 10:00 to 17:00 (June and September)
🕐 October
   Monday to Friday 10:00 to 16:00
🕐 November – March
   by prior appointment only

Contacts
Tel: 01408 623000
Email: clynelish.
distillery@diageo.com

Website
www.discovering-distilleries.com

Admission
£ Standard Tour: £5.00 (including a voucher part redeemable on 70cl bottles purchased in the shop).

T Flexible during summer months, set at other times of year
C No
S Whisky and some gift and book items

Personal notes relating to visit:

Whiskies tasted notes/opinions:

Manager/guide signature:

Date visited:

SECTION INDEX ON PAGE 71

DALMORE

Meaning of name and pronunciation guide
'Big meadowland'
– dal-MORE

Owner
Whyte & Mackay Ltd

House style
Full bodied, with Sherry, malt, spices, nuts and oranges.

Principal single malts
Dalmore 12-year-old, Gran Reserva, 15-year-old, 18-year-old, King Alexander III.

Principal blends
Whyte & Mackay Special.

Getting technical
Stills: four pairs

Capacity: 3.5m litres

Malt: very lightly peated

Casks: ex-Bourbon and ex-Sherry

Water: River Alness

HISTORY

The distillery was established in 1839 by Alexander Matheson, who had made a fortune in the opium trade. Matheson did not operate the distillery himself, but put it in the control of various tenants of his estate. In 1867 he handed over the running of the distillery to the Mackenzie family, headed by Andrew, who eventually bought Dalmore from the Matheson family in 1891. By that time, the number of stills had been doubled to four, and Dalmore had become the first Scotch malt whisky to be exported to Australia (in 1870).

During the First World War the distillery was used by the Admiralty as a mine-making facility, and it was not until 1922 that production resumed, due to damage caused by an explosion during the war years.

The distillery remained in the Mackenzie family until 1960, when Mackenzie Brothers (Dalmore) Ltd merged with the Glasgow firm of Whyte & Mackay Ltd, who had long been customers of Dalmore single malt for their blending requirements. In 1966, with Scotch whisky booming, another four stills were installed to double capacity. 2007 saw Dalmore become part of the United Breweries Group, when that Indian company acquired Whyte & Mackay Ltd.

POINTS OF SPECIAL INTEREST

In 2002 a bottle of 62-year-old Dalmore changed hands for £25,877.50, setting a record for the world's most expensive bottle of whisky sold at auction. In May 2005 a customer at the Pennyhill Park Hotel in Surrey paid £32,000 for a bottle, which he promptly opened and shared with friends.

Subsequently, a bottle of 52-year-old Dalmore Oculus sold at auction in November 2009 for £27,600.

VISITOR EXPERIENCE

Dalmore distillery enjoys a picturesque location overlooking the waters of the Cromarty Firth, yet close to the bustling town of Alness. It is also just a couple of miles from owner Whyte & Mackay's Invergordon grain distillery.

In 2004 Dalmore opened a new visitor centre, complete with exhibition, video presentation, shop and dramming bar. The distillery tour allows the visitor to see one of the most idiosyncratic still houses in Scotland, complete with differing size stills, flat topped stills and a copper water jacket on 'number two spirit still' which dates back to 1874.

LOCATION

Alness, Ross & Cromarty IV17 0UT
The distillery is located beside the B817 Alness to Invergordon road, just off the A9, beside the Cromarty Firth. 20 miles north of Inverness.

🕐 March - October
    Monday to Friday 11:00 to 16:45
    plus Saturday 11:00 to 16:00 (July - September)
🕐 November - February
    Monday to Friday 11:00 to 15:00

Contacts
Tel: 01349 882362
E-mail: enquiries@the
dalmore.com

Website
www.thedalmore.com

Admission
Please contact the distillery for details

T Flexible
C No
S Whisky and some gift and book items

Personal notes relating to visit:

Whiskies tasted notes/opinions:

Manager/guide signature:

Date visited:

SECTION INDEX ON PAGE 71

129

DALWHINNIE

HISTORY

Dalwhinnie was constructed in 1897/98, and was originally named Strathspey. However, the distillery came on stream just as the Scotch whisky industry was about to move from 'boom' to 'bust', and the name only lasted for a matter of months before the founders encountered financial difficulties and sold it. The new owners re-christened the plant Dalwhinnie.

In 1905 Dalwhinnie became the first Scottish distillery to be acquired by an American company, when Cook & Bernheimer spent £1,250 purchasing it at auction. In 1919 Dalwhinnie changed hands again, this time being bought by Macdonald Greenlees & Williams Ltd, which was absorbed by the Distillers Company Ltd in 1926. Four years later, Dalwhinnie was transferred to the DCL subsidiary Scottish Malt Distillers, and in February 1934 a serious fire closed the distillery for four years.

In 1987 Dalwhinnie 15-year-old was chosen as part of the Classic Malts range, and today Dalwhinnie is one of comparatively few Scottish distilleries still equipped with worm tubs for condensing purposes. An earlier pair of worm tubs was replaced in 1986 by 'shell and tube' condensers, but these were found to have a negative effect on the character of the spirit, and were subsequently replaced with the worm tubs currently in place.

POINTS OF SPECIAL INTEREST

After Braeval, Dalwhinnie is the second-highest working distillery in Scotland at 1,073 feet (327m). It also boasts an on-site meteorological station, and is one of Diageo's smallest distilleries.

Meaning of name and pronunciation guide
'Meeting place'
– dal-WHIN-ee

Owner
Diageo plc

House style
Medium bodied, comparatively sweet and honeyed, with fruit, spices and a hint of peat smoke.

Principal single malts
Dalwhinnie 15-year-old, Dalwhinnie Distillers Edition.

Principal blends
Black & White, Buchanan's.

Getting technical
Stills: one pair

Capacity: 2m litres

Malt: lightly peated

Casks: ex-Bourbon

Water: Allt an t'Sluic Burn

HIGHLAND (WESTERN)

VISITOR EXPERIENCE

With easy access from the A9, and in a stunning
Highland setting, it is not surprising that Dalwhinnie is
one of Diageo's most visited distilleries. The visitor
centre dates from 1991, and the usual informative,
professional Diageo 'Classic Malts' tour is on offer,
along with a post-tour complementary dram. The
visitor also gets to see Dalwhinnie's pair of traditional
wooden 'worm tubs' at close quarters.

The 'standard' tour, called the 'Flavours Experience,'
builds on the increasing focus placed by distillers on
whisky flavours. This tour examines the development
of flavour through the whisky-making process,
culminating in 'new make' spirit and ultimately
matured whisky.

*Written guides are available in Dutch, French,
German, Italian, Japanese, Spanish and Swedish.*

Contacts
Tel: 01540 672219
Email: dalwhinnie.
distillery@diageo.com

Website
www.discovering-
distilleries.com

Admission
£ Standard Tour:
 £6.00 (including a
 £3.00 voucher
 redeemable on 70cl
 bottles purchased
 in the shop)

T Set times from
November to Easter,
on demand during
high seasor
C No
S Whisky and some
gift and book items

LOCATION

Dalwhinnie, Inverness-shire PH19 1AB
The distillery stands proudly within sight of the
A9 Perth to Inverness road, in the village of
Dalwhinnie. Approximately 55 miles north of
Perth and 55 miles south of Inverness. Look out
for the exit roads several miles either side of the
village and distillery.

🕐 Easter – September
Monday to Friday 9:30 to 17:00
plus Saturday 9:30 to 17:00 (May - September)
and Sunday 11:00 to 16:00 (July - August)

🕐 October
Monday to Saturday 10:00 to 17:00

🕐 November - Easter
Monday to Friday 11:00 to 14:00

**Personal notes
relating to visit:**

**Whiskies tasted
notes/opinions:**

**Manager/guide
signature:**

Date visited:

SECTION INDEX ON PAGE 71

GLENMORANGIE

Meaning of name and pronunciation guide
'Glen of tranquillity' or 'glen of the large meadows'
 – glen-MOR-angie

Owner
The Glenmorangie Co (Louis Vuitton Moët Hennessy)

House style
Comparatively light-bodied and sweet, with vanilla, floral, malty, spicy and nutty notes.

Principal single malts
Glenmorangie Original (10-year-old), 18 and 25-year-old, Lasanta, Quinta Ruban, Nectar D'or.

Principal blends
Bailie Nicol Jarvie, Highland Queen.

Getting technical
Stills: six pairs

Capacity: 6m litres

Malt: very lightly peated

Casks: ex-Bourbon

Water: Tarlogie Spring

HISTORY

Glenmorangie was established in 1843 by William Matheson, using the remnants of McKenzie & Gallie's Morangie Brewery, which had existed since 1738. However, production did not begin until November 1849. The Glenmorangie Distillery Co Ltd was formed in 1887 when the plant was entirely rebuilt, and at that time Glenmorangie became the first distillery in Scotland to use steam to heat its stills.

In 1918 the whisky blenders Macdonald & Muir Ltd, of Highland Queen fame, acquired 60 per cent of the company, later going on to purchase the other 40 per cent. Glenmorangie was silent from 1931 to 1936, due to world recession and US prohibition, but its post-war record has been one of ever-growing success.

The distillery was internally reconstructed in 1979, when the number of stills was increased from two to four, and a decade later capacity was again doubled with the installation of another four stills.

Glenmorangie is Scotland's best-selling single malt, and the UK number two after Glenfiddich.

During 2008/09 a major, £4.5 million expansion programme took place, involving the installation of a supplementary mash tun, four washbacks and four stills. This development increased potential capacity from four million litres per annum to six million litres.

POINTS OF SPECIAL INTEREST

Standing nearly 17 feet tall, Glenmorangie's stills are the tallest in Scotland, and are based on the design of the original ex-gin stills from London, installed when the distillery first opened. Their height and unusual narrowness contribute to the light, fruity, floral character of the single malt.

Glenmorangie pioneered the use of 'finishing' whiskies in a wide range of casks that have previously held the likes of Burgundy, Madeira, Port and Sherry.

HIGHLAND (NORTHERN)

VISITOR EXPERIENCE

Being equipped with notably tall and elegant stills, Glenmorangie's stunning stillhouse is almost worth the visit alone, though the rest of the distillery is equally fascinating and its location extremely scenic.

The former stillhouse is now a very well-appointed visitor centre and museum, featuring a 130-year-old steam engine. There is also an audio-visual presentation and shop.

Information leaflets are available in French, German, Italian, Japanese, Spanish and Swedish.

Contacts
Tel: 01862 892477
E-mail: tain-shop@
glenmorangie.co.uk

Website
www.glenmorangie.com

Admission
£ Standard Tour:
£2.50 (redeemable against purchases of £16 or over in the Distillery Shop

T Set times
C No
S Whisky and some gift and book items

LOCATION

Tain, Ross-shire IV19 1PZ
The distillery stands beside the A9, on the outskirts of Tain, 30 miles north of Inverness, close to the shores of the Dornoch Firth.

🕐 All year excluding Christmas to New Year
Monday to Friday 10:00 to 17:00
plus Saturday 10:00 to 16:00 (June – August)
and Sunday 12:00 to 16:00 (June – August)

Personal notes relating to visit:

Whiskies tasted notes/opinions:

Manager/guide signature:

Date visited:

SECTION INDEX ON PAGE 71

GLEN ORD

Meaning of name and
pronunciation guide
'Glen of the round-
topped hill'
– glen-ORD

Owner
Diageo plc

House style
Soft and rich, fruity,
sherry and spicy, with
vanilla and toffee
notes.

Principal single malts
Singleton of Glen Ord.

Principal blends
Johnnie Walker.

Getting technical
Stills: three pairs

Capacity: 3m litres

Malt: lightly peated

Casks: ex-Bourbon
and ex-Sherry

Water: Allt Fionnaidh
(the Fair Burn)

HISTORY

The only survivor of nine legal distilleries that were
operating in the Muir of Ord area during the 19th
century, Ord was established in 1838 by Thomas
Mackenzie in the fertile 'Black Isle,' north of Inverness.

The distillery passed through a number of hands
before being purchased in 1896 by the Dundee
blending firm of James Watson & Co Ltd for £15,800.
In 1923 it was sold on to John Dewar & Sons Ltd, who
changed the name of the single malt produced there
from Glen Oran to Glen Ord.

Dewar's became part of The Distillers Company Ltd
in 1925, and Glen Ord was subsequently transferred to
the DCL malt distilling subsidiary Scottish Malt
Distillers (SMD), later becoming part of United
Distillers and ultimately Diageo. The distillery was
largely rebuilt during the 1960s, when the number of
stills was increased from two to six. The whisky
produced at Glen Ord has been marketed under a
number of names over the years, including Glenordie,
Ordie, Ord and Glen Oran.

POINTS OF SPECIAL INTEREST

The Black Isle is noted for its barley production, so it
is not surprising that a maltings plant is located
alongside Ord distillery. Drum maltings were
established there in 1968 and in addition to Glen Ord,
they supply malt to a number of other Diageo
distilleries.

VISITOR EXPERIENCE

At first sight, Glen Ord Distillery appears to be a very traditional establishment, constructed of local stone, and roofed with slate, but a closer encounter reveals a contrasting style of stillhouse and other production buildings, dating from the 1960s. These share design features with fellow Diageo-owned, Northern Highland distilleries Teaninich and Clynelish, and with a number of other former DCL distilleries which were expanded or reconstructed during the post-war period of progressive, global growth in the popularity of Scotch whisky.

Glen Ord attracts some 20,000 visitors per year, and a dedicated visitor centre and shop opened in 1994, based in a converted warehouse. An interesting exhibition is devoted to the heritage of the local area and there is an audio-visual presentation relating to the distillery and its whisky.

Written tour guides are available in Chinese, Czech, Dutch, French, German, Hungarian, Italian, Polish, Spanish and Swedish.

Contacts
Tel: 01463 872004
Email: glen.ord.
distillery@diageo.com

Website
www.discovering-
distilleries.com

Admission
£ Standard Tour:
£5.00 (including
a voucher part
redeemable on 70cl
bottles purchased
in the shop)

T Set times
C No
S Whisky and some
gift and book items

LOCATION

Muir of Ord, Ross-shire IV6 7UJ
Located 15 miles from Inverness, along the A9, then the A832 to Muir of Ord. The distillery is three-quarters of a mile north-west of the village.

April – September
Monday to Friday 10:00 to 17:00
Saturday 11:00 to 17:00
plus Sunday 12:00 to 16:00 (July - September)
October – March
Monday to Friday 11:00 to 16:00

Personal notes relating to visit:

Whiskies tasted notes/opinions:

Manager/guide signature:

Date visited:

SECTION INDEX ON PAGE 71

LOCH EWE

Meaning of name and pronunciation guide
Loch of the yew trees - Loch-YOU

Owner
John Clotworthy

House style
Sweet and fruity, with mild honey and gentle smoke.

Principal single malts
Spirit of Loch Ewe, Uisge Beatha, Loch Ewe Whisky.

Principal blends
N/A

Getting technical
Stills: two (each approximately 120 litres)

Capacity: 1,000 litres

Malt: lightly peated

Casks: Spanish ex-Sherry and second fill rum and port (from one to five gallons)

Water: mains supply

HISTORY

Loch Ewe Distillery was established in the remote North-West Highlands of Scotland in 2004 by Frances Oates, proprietor of Drumchork Lodge Hotel, and John Clotworthy.

Although Wester Ross has a lengthy heritage of illicit whisky-making, Loch Ewe Distillery is the first distillery in the area to boast a licence and it re-creates the type of distilling carried out locally in caves and forests. Loch Ewe Distillery 'cave' and waterfall were developed in a garage, adjacent to the hotel. The distillery is unique as it is, effectively, a legal 'illicit still.' Distilling embraces the illicit methods pertaining to the Gaelic-speaking people of Wester Ross.

'Uisge Beatha' produced at Loch Ewe Distillery is sold or consumed straight from the still or matured in small casks to become 'Spirit of Loch Ewe.' This is a single malt which must, by law, be referred to as a 'spirit drink.' Small quantities of Loch Ewe Whisky will be available in the future, but it will never be the main output of the distillery, as such a product is not traditional illicit whisky.

John Clotworthy gained practical experience of large scale whisky-making at the Bladnoch Whisky School in south-west Scotland, and blended it with knowledge of the illicit distilling methods passed down through generations of local families around Loch Ewe.

POINTS OF SPECIAL INTEREST

Loch Ewe is the smallest legal distillery in Scotland and the first to be granted a 'private licence' in 190 years. The licence had to be approved, due to a loophole in the law, but immediately after it had been issued, the loophole was closed to prevent anyone else from creating their own Scottish, illicit-sized distillery! Loch Ewe is the only distillery which makes whisky using 18th century methods.

HIGHLAND (WESTERN)

VISITOR EXPERIENCE

An intimate distillery tour and insight into how whisky would have been distilled centuries ago followed by a Spirit of Loch Ewe tastings in the Uisge Beatha Lounge of the Drumchork Lodge Hotel.

Also available is a 'Whisky Experience Stay' – which lasts five days and includes dinner, bed and breakfast. It offers a hands-on chance to learn the art of whisky-making with an illicit-sized still.

The package includes an excursion to local caves where illicit distilling is believed to have taken place, an opportunity to distill using 18th century methods plus a whisky tasting session with the Drumchork Whisky Panel. At the end of the stay, participants receive a distilling certificate and a five litres cask of Wester Ross Uisge Beatha.

The award-winning Drumchork Lodge Hotel boasts an array of more than 700 single malts, as well as an open cask of Spirit of Loch Ewe.

Distillery tours are available in French.

LOCATION

Drumchork Estate, Aultbea, Wester Ross IV22 2HU
The distillery is situated close to Aultbea village, beside Drumchork Lodge Hotel. Aultbea is on the A832 road, off the A835 Inverness to Ullapool route, 70 miles from Inverness.

🕐 All year except Christmas and New Year
Monday to Sunday 9:00 to 17:00

Contacts
Tel: 01445 731242
Email: info@lochewe distillery.co.uk

Website
www.lochewedistillery.co.uk

Admission
£ Standard Tour: £5.00

T Flexible
C Snacks/ full meals (in Drumchork Lodge Hotel)
S No

Personal notes relating to visit:

Whiskies tasted notes/opinions:

Manager/guide signature:

Date visited:

SECTION INDEX ON PAGE 71

OBAN

Meaning of name and pronunciation guide
'Little ban'
- OH-bun

Owner
Diageo plc

House style
Quite sweet and malty, with fruit, spice, nuts and some smoke. Medium-bodied, with a tang of salt.

Principal single malts
Oban 14-year-old, Oban Distiller's Edition.

Principal blends
N/A

Getting technical
Stills: one pair

Capacity: 735,000 litres

Malt: lightly peated

Casks: ex-Bourbon

Water: Loch Gleann a'Bhearraidh

HISTORY

Oban is one of Scotland's oldest working distilleries, having been established in 1794 by John and Hugh Stevenson, who were also largely responsible for the creation of the town of Oban itself.

In 1866 the distillery passed out of Stevenson family ownership, being acquired first by Peter Cumstie and in 1883 by James Walter Higgen, who rebuilt the distillery between 1890 and 1894, while continuing production, such was the demand for Oban spirit.

1898 saw another change of ownership, with the Oban Distillery Company Ltd, owned by Buchanan-Dewar, gaining control in 1923. Buchanan-Dewar was absorbed into the Distillers' Company Ltd (DCL) two years later. In common with many distilleries, Oban was silent for several years during the 1930s, and closed again between 1968 and 1972, when a major programme of refurbishment was undertaken.

When DCL's successor company, United Distillers, launched its 'Classic Malts' selection in 1988, Oban was selected to represent the Western Highlands.

POINTS OF SPECIAL INTEREST

Oban is one of very few surviving Scottish distilleries to be located in the centre of a town.

While many of the single malts available today have been introduced in comparatively recent times, Oban has been sold as a single malt since the 1880s.

HIGHLAND (WESTERN)

VISITOR EXPERIENCE

In classic Diageo style, Oban offers well-informed and professional distillery tours and boasts a well-appointed visitor centre and shop in the former maltings. The 'tour collection' area contains a fascinating visual history of Oban and the distillery's founding family.

In 2008 a new 'Sensory and Flavour Finding Tour' was introduced, enabling visitors to explore exactly how Oban single malt's unique character is created. Together with a knowledgeable guide, visitors explore each part of the whisky making process, to discover which flavours come from which parts of the process.

According to Diageo, "During the tour visitors are able to nose the new make spirit, and are given the opportunity to try some cask strength Oban straight from the cask. Visitors are also invited to try Oban 14-year-old West Highland malt along with a piece of crystallised ginger, a true taste sensation! Guests are given a small memento from the distillery to remind them of their visit."

Tours can be conducted in German, depending on availability of guides, and there are also written guides in Dutch, French, German, Italian, Japanese and Spanish.

Contacts
Tel: 01631 572004
Email: oban.distillery
@diageo.com

Website
www.discovering-distilleries.com

Admission
- **£** Sensory and Flavour Finding
- **£** Tour: £6.00 (including a voucher part redeemable on 70cl bottles purchased in the shop)

T Flexible
C No
S Whisky and some gift and book items

Personal notes relating to visit:

Whiskies tasted notes/opinions:

Manager/guide signature:

Date visited:

LOCATION

Stafford Street, Oban, Argyllshire PA34 5NH
The distillery is situated in the centre of the west coast port of Oban, opposite the bay.

🕐 February & December
Monday to Friday 12:30 to 16:00

🕐 March – Easter & November
Monday to Friday 10:00 to 17:00

🕐 Easter – June & October
Monday to Saturday 9:30 to 17:00

🕐 July – September
Monday to Friday 9:30 to 19:30
Saturday & Sunday 9:30 to 17:00

SECTION INDEX ON PAGE 71

PULTENEY

Meaning of name and pronunciation guide
Named after Sir William Pulteney, governor of the British Fisheries Society - PULT-nay

Owner
Inver House Distillers Ltd (Thai Beverage plc)

House style
Medium-bodied, floral and fruity, with nuts, vanilla and a hint of salt.

Principal single malts
Old Pulteney 12, 17, 21 and 30-year-old.

Principal blends
N/A

Getting technical
Stills: one pair

Capacity: 1.7m litres

Malt: unpeated

Casks: ex-Bourbon

Water: Hempriggs Loch

HISTORY

Pulteney distillery was established in 1826 by Caithness distiller James Henderson, ultimately coming into the ownership of the Dundee firm of James Watson & Co Ltd in 1920.

Five years later, Watson's became part of the Distillers Company Ltd, and in 1930 production ceased. It did not recommence until 1951, by which time Pulteney was in the hands of Banff lawyer Robert Cumming, who also owned Balblair distillery.

In 1955 Cumming sold the distillery to Hiram Walker & Sons (Scotland) Ltd, who undertook a comprehensive rebuilding programme in 1958/59.

Allied Breweries Ltd then acquired Pulteney in 1961, and it remained in their control until successor company Allied Domecq sold it to Inver House Distillers Ltd in 1995. Inver House has presided over a high-profile maritime-themed marketing strategy which has seen sales of Old Pulteney grow significantly during the past decade.

POINTS OF SPECIAL INTEREST

Pulteney is Scotland's northernmost mainland distillery, and along with Glen Grant (see p 114) is the only Scotch whisky distillery to be named after an individual.

UNIQUE SHAPED STILLS AT PULTENEY

VISITOR EXPERIENCE

Pulteney offers visitors a warm and personal welcome, with friendly, knowledgeable guides. The well appointed visitor centre opened in 2000 in the former cooperage and maltings, and offers a fascinating glimpse into the maritime history of Wick, once the most important herring port in Europe, as well as the distillery itself.

It is worth the trip to Wick just to see Pulteney's unique spirit still, which has no real head and swan neck, like most other stills. According to distillery legend, this is because the still was found to be too tall to fit into the stillhouse when it was delivered. The manager at the time instructed the coppersmith to cut the top off the still in order for it to be accommodated, thus creating the unique shape.

Visitors have the opportunity to fill and label their own bottle of an exclusive expression of Old Pulteney from the cask.

Contacts
Tel: 01955 602371
E-mail: enquiries@
inverhouse.com

Website
www.oldpulteney.com

Admission
£ Standard Tour:
£4.00 (including a discount voucher redeemable on purchases of 70cl bottle of Old Pulteney)

T Flexible
C No
S Whisky and some gift and book items

LOCATION

Huddart Street, Wick, Caithness KW1 5BA
The distillery is situated in the Pulteney town area of Wick, off the A99 Inverness to John O'Groats road. Hidden away within a largely residential area of the town. From the A99 follow Northcote Street or Harrow Road to Rutherford Street, then Huddart Street.

🕐 All year except Christmas and New Year
Monday to Friday 10:00 to 13:00, 14:00 to 16:00
plus Saturday 10:00 to 16:00 (April – September)

Personal notes relating to visit:

Whiskies tasted notes/opinions:

Manager/guide signature:

Date visited:

TOMATIN

HISTORY

Tomatin dates from the fruitful distilling years of the last decade of the 19th century, being established in 1897 as the Tomatin Spey Distillery Company.

Production continued with only comparatively short breaks for the next 60 years, and then in 1956 the first phase of expansion took place, when a second pair of stills was added. Expansion continued apace, with another pair of stills being installed two years later, followed by four more in 1961. By 1974 the total number of stills had reached a remarkable 23, but its very scale was to prove Tomatin's undoing.

As the Scotch whisky industry began to tighten its belt in the early 1980s, the distillery owners first closed down the 'number two side' of the stillhouse and ultimately went into receivership in 1985.

However, the following year, the Japanese schochu distiller Takara Shuzo Co and hotel group Okara & Co Ltd combined to purchase Tomatin under the name of Tomatin Distillery Company Ltd.

Okara & Co subsequently sold its 20 per cent share in the venture to its partner during 1998, and the current shareholders are Takara Shuzo (81%), Marubeni (14%) and Kokubu Co Ltd (5%). In 2002, 11 of the stills were removed, leaving the present dozen in production.

POINTS OF SPECIAL INTEREST

Tomatin was the first distillery in Scotland to become wholly Japanese owned, and in the mid-1970s it had the largest capacity of any Scottish distillery, with its 23 stills able to turn out a theoretical 12 million litres of alcohol per year.

Meaning of name and pronunciation guide
'Hill of the juniper bush'
- tom-AH-tin

Owner
Tomatin Distillery Company Ltd

House style
Sweet, malty, medium-bodied, with honey, spice and delicate smoke.

Principal single malts
Tomatin 12, 15, 18 and 25-year-old.

Principal blends
Antiquary, Big T, The Talisman.

Getting technical
Stills: six pairs

Capacity: 5m litres

Malt: unpeated

Casks: ex-Bourbon, plus some ex-Sherry

Water: Allt-na-Frithe – the Free Burn

HIGHLAND (NORTHERN)

VISITOR EXPERIENCE

Tomatin is a designated 'four star' visitor attraction, and though far from being the prettiest distillery in Scotland, the surrounding scenery is beautiful and the welcome is warm.

The distillery tour is accompanied by a DVD presentation and a complementary dram, while the attractive shop stocks whisky and other gift items.

For those seeking a more in-depth experience, there is the 'Tomatin Whisky Presentation and Tasting Tour,' which is hosted by a manager and embraces a detailed site tour, with a visit to Tomatin's own cooperage and a bonded warehouse. Also included is a nosing and tasting session across the range of Tomatin whiskies.

There are written tour guides in French, German and Italian, and DVD options of French, German, Japanese and Swedish.

LOCATION

Tomatin, Inverness-shire IV13 7YT
The distillery is situated off the A9 Perth to Inverness road, 16 miles south-east of Inverness and the same distance north-west of Aviemore.

🕐 All year except Christmas and New Year
Monday to Saturday 10:00 to 17:00
Sunday 12:00 to 16:30

Contacts
Tel: 01463 248144
Email: info@tomatin.co.uk

Website
www.tomatin.com

Admission
£ Standard Tour: £3.00
£ Whisky Presentation and Tasting Tour: £30.00 (contact the distillery for further details)

T Flexible
C No
S Whisky and some gift and book items

Personal notes relating to visit:

Whiskies tasted notes/opinions:

Manager/guide signature:

Date visited:

SECTION INDEX ON PAGE 71

ARRAN

Meaning of name and pronunciation guide
'Place of peeked hills' – arr-en

Owner
Isle of Arran Distillers Ltd

House style
Light to medium-bodied, sweet, fruity and floral.

Principal single malts
Arran 10-year-old, 14-year-old, Robert Burns Single Malt and single cask bottlings.

Principal blends
Lochranza and Robert Burns.

Getting technical
Stills: one pair

Capacity: 750,000 litres

Malt: usually unpeated

Casks: ex-Bourbon and ex-Sherry

Water: Loch na Davie

HISTORY

Arran distillery was the brainchild of former Chivas managing director Harold Currie, who established the distillery in 1993, with production commencing two years later. It has been said that during the 19th century there were some 50 distillers on the Isle of Arran, most of them operating without licences, and Currie was keen to restore the old craft of whisky-making to the island. The venture was partly funded by the sale of 2,000 bonds, each of which entitled the bondholder to an amount of whisky once the distillery was in operation.

Arran is a small-scale distillery, and was designed from the outset to be aesthetically pleasing, with mock pagodas and whitewashed buildings which blend well with the island's older architecture. Although no longer owned by the Currie family, the distillery remains in independent hands.

POINTS OF SPECIAL INTEREST

Arran was the first legal distillery to be constructed on the island since a whisky-making operation at Lagg closed in 1837.

ISLAND (SOUTHERN)

VISITOR EXPERIENCE

Because Arran distillery was built with visitors in mind, rather than as a 'whisky factory,' like so many of its forebears, access is good and the processes of whisky-making are easy to follow. There is an informative exhibition and a short video presentation within a recreated Crofters Inn, explaining distillation past and present. Following this is the actual distillery tour and complementary dram.

There is a popular licensed cafe within the complex, and it is not unknown for visitors to catch a glimpse of a golden eagle in the skies around Glen Chalmadale.

The distillery may open outside of the stated times if staff are available.

Tours are usually available in French and Spanish, and there are also printed guides in Dutch, French, German, Italian, Japanese, Portuguese and Spanish.

Contacts
Tel: 01770 830264
E-mail: visitorcentre @arranwhisky.com

Website
www.arranwhisky.com

Admission
£ Standard Tour: £5.00

T Set times
C Light meals
S Whisky and a good range of gifts and books

LOCATION

Shore Road, Lochranza, Isle of Arran KA27 8HJ
Beside the A841, 13 miles north of Brodick and just south of Lochranza.

🕐 Mid March – October
  Monday to Saturday 10:00 to 18:00
  Sunday 11:00 to 18:00
🕐 November – February
  Monday, Wednesday and Saturday 10:00 to 16:00
  Sunday 11:00 to 16:00

Personal notes relating to visit:

Whiskies tasted notes/opinions:

Manager/guide signature:

Date visited:

SECTION INDEX ON PAGE 71

HIGHLAND PARK

Meaning of name and pronunciation guide
The distillery was built on High Park common land
- high-land PARK

Owner
The Edrington Group

House style
Medium-bodied, quite sweet, with floral, toffee and fudge notes, plus distinctive peat.

Principal single malts
Highland Park 12, 18 and 25-year-old.

Principal blends
The Famous Grouse, Cutty Sark.

Getting technical
Stills: two pairs

Capacity: 2.5m litres

Malt: malt from the floor maltings is peated to 20ppm, while the remainder is unpeated

Casks: ex-Bourbon (for spirit to be blended) and ex-Sherry (for single malt bottlings)

Water: Crantit Spring

HISTORY

One of Scotland's oldest distilleries, Highland Park was established in 1798 by David Robertson. It was constructed on the site where local church officer Magnus Eunson had previously operated an illicit still, hiding kegs of his whisky beneath the church pulpit!

From 1826, various members of the Borthwick family ran Highland Park, and in 1895 James Grant, owner of Glenlivet, purchased the distillery. Three years later he doubled capacity by adding a second pair of stills.

In 1937 Highland Distilleries acquired Highland Park, and from 1979 onwards, the company made substantial investments in marketing the single malt, ultimately leading to a high international reputation.

1986 saw the opening of a visitor centre at Highland Park, and in 2000 it was awarded the accolade of 'Five Star Visitor Attraction' by Visit Scotland, after some £2 million was spent upgrading the centre and areas of the distillery itself. Highland Distilleries was renamed Highland Distillers, and in 1999 it became part of the Edrington Group.

POINTS OF SPECIAL INTEREST

The most northerly distillery in Scotland, Highland Park continues to malt around 20 per cent of its requirements on traditional floor maltings, with the remainder of the malt coming from the mainland.

The distillery's own malt is peated to approximately the same level as that at Bowmore. Peat is cut from Hobbister Hill to fire the distillery kiln, giving the whisky its characteristic heathery, smoky profile.

ISLAND (NORTHERN)

SECTION INDEX ON PAGE 71

VISITOR EXPERIENCE

Highly regarded guided tours of the distillery itself, featuring the rare opportunity to see a working malting floor. Complementary dram and excellent post-tour video, plus shop and cafe.

In 2008 the five-star visitor centre underwent a £250,000 upgrade, and it now offers a bespoke tasting bar and a 'cask education' area.

In addition to the 'standard' distillery tour, a Connoisseurs' Tour is also now on offer, giving a more in-depth experience. This option ends with a vertical tasting of Highland Park expressions in the Tasting Room, which features Orcadian furniture and a fascinating collection of Highland Park bottlings and whisky literature.

Another option for the serious enthusiast is the Magnus Eunson Tour, which embraces older and rarer single malts as part of the nosing and tasting experience.

LOCATION

Holm Road, Kirkwall, Orkney KW15 1SU
The distillery is situated on Holm Road, a mile from the centre of Kirkwall, along the A960, then the A961.

🕐 May - August
  Monday to Saturday 10:00 to 17:00
  Sunday 12:00 to 17:00
🕐 April & September
  Monday to Friday 10:00 to 17:00
🕐 October - March
  Monday to Friday 13:00 to 17:00

Contacts
Tel: 01856 874619
E-mail: distillery@ highlandpark.co.uk

Website
www.highlandpark.co.uk

Admission
£ Standard Tour: £6.00
£ Connoisseurs' Tour: £35.00
£ Magnus Eunson Tour: £75.00

The two more in-depth tours should be booked in advance.

T Set times/Flexible
C Hot and cold drinks
S Whisky and some gift and book items

Personal notes relating to visit:

Whiskies tasted notes/opinions:

Manager/guide signature:

Date visited:

SECTION INDEX ON PAGE 71

147

TALISKER

Meaning of name and pronunciation guide
'Sloping rock'
- TAL-is-ker

Owner
Diageo plc

House style
Full-bodied, with peat smoke, seaweed, spice and pepper.

Principal single malts
Talisker 10 and 18-year-old, Talisker Distiller's Edition and 57° North (bottled at 57% abv).

Principal blends
Johnnie Walker.

Getting technical
Stills: two wash and three spirit

Capacity: 2.7m litres

Malt: peated to 18-22ppm

Casks: ex-Bourbon plus some ex-Sherry

Water: springs on Cnoc nan Speirag

HISTORY

The history of Talisker began in 1830 when brothers Hugh and Kenneth MacAskill leased a site at Carbost in north-west Skye and built a distillery there.

Numerous changes of ownership followed, until in 1894 The Talisker Distillery Co Ltd was founded. Four years later, Talisker merged with Dailuaine-Glenlivet Distillers and Imperial Distillers to create the Dailuaine-Talisker Distilleries Ltd.

In 1916 the company was acquired by a consortium which included John Walker & Sons Ltd, W P Lowrie & Co, and John Dewar & Sons Ltd, ultimately passing into the hands of The Distillers Company Ltd in 1925.

In common with many distilleries, the history of Talisker includes a serious fire. In 1960 a valve on a coal-fired spirit still was left open during distillation. Spirit escaped from the still and caught fire, resulting in serious damage. The entire still house burned to the ground, but was subsequently rebuilt and equipped with new stills that were exact copies of the originals.

In 1988 then owners United Distillers included Talisker in its new Classic Malts selection, and a visitor centre was opened.

POINTS OF SPECIAL INTEREST

Talisker practised tripe distillation, more usually associated with Lowland distilleries, from 1896 until 1928.

At a time when single malt whisky was a rarity, Talisker was already highly regarded, with the novelist Robert Louis Stevenson writing in 1880 "The King o'drinks, as I conceive it, Talisker, Isla or Glenlivet"

ISLAND (WESTERN)

VISITOR EXPERIENCE

The 'Misty Isle' of Skye has been romanticised in story and song, but the scenery really lives up to expectations. Talisker Distillery is magnificently positioned on the shores of Loch Harport and in the shadow of the brooding Cuillin Hills. One cannot help but feel a sense of awe upon arrival.

Once inside, the distillery tour is a pleasure, with friendly, helpful staff and a slightly unusual pre-tour dram of 'the lava of the Cuillins' itself.

In addition to the Classic Tour, there is also the Talisker Tasting Tour option, which includes a more in-depth distillery visit and five-sample tasting session. This tour is run in the afternoon on selected days only.

Written guides are available in Dutch, French, German, Italian, Japanese and Spanish.

LOCATION

Carbost, Isle of Skye IV47 8SR
The distillery is located by the shores of Loch Harport in the remote north-west of the island. It is 24 miles from the village of Broadford, along the A87, then the A863 and B8009. The journey can take up to an hour, and that does not including stopping to enjoy the stunning scenery.

🕐 April – October
Monday to Saturday 9:30 to 17:00
plus Sunday 12:00 to 17:00 (July and August)
🕐 November – March
Monday to Friday 10:00 to 17:00

Contacts
Tel: 01478 614308
Email: talisker.distillery@diageo.com

Website
www.discovering-distilleries.com

Admission
£ Classic Tour: £5.00
£ Talisker Tasting Tour: £15.00 (advance booking required and includes a limited edition nosing and tasting glass)

Both tours include a voucher redeemable on 70cl bottles purchased in the shop.

T Every 15 mins during the summer, set times in the winter
C No
S Whisky and some gift and book items

Personal notes relating to visit:

Whiskies tasted notes/opinions:

Manager/guide signature:

Date visited:

TOBERMORY

Meaning of name and pronunciation guide
'Mary's Well'
- TOBER-mor-ay

Owner
Burn Stewart Distillers
(CL World Brands Ltd)

House style
1) Light to medium-bodied, quite dry, delicate peat smoke, malt, fruit and nuts.
2) Pungent, sweet, tarry, smoky, spicy and medicinal.

Principal single malts
Tobermory 10-year-old, 15-year-old (unpeated).
Ledaig 10-year-old (peated).

Principal blends
Scottish Leader.

Getting technical
Stills: two pairs

Capacity: 1m litres

Malt: both peated (around 35ppm) and unpeated

Casks: ex-Bourbon and ex-Sherry

Water: private lochan in hills a mile from Tobermory

HISTORY

The only licensed distillery on the Hebridean island of Mull, Tobermory is located in the picturesque island capital and is one of Scotland's oldest distilleries, being established by John Sinclair in 1798. It was originally named Ledaig, the Gaelic for 'safe haven.'

To say that Tobermory has a chequered past would be an understatement, as, despite its antiquity, the plant has actually been silent for more than half its total existence.

The first period of closure lasted from 1837 until 1878, and then in 1916 Tobermory was acquired by the Distillers Company Ltd, who ceased distilling in 1930. Subsequently the site served as a canteen for sailors and even as a power station!

Production recommenced in 1972 under Ledaig Distillery Ltd, but that company went bankrupt three years later, precipitating another four years of closure. The Yorkshire-based Kirkleavington Property Company Ltd bought Tobermory in 1979, but they also found it difficult to make the distillery pay, selling off the warehouse building for residential development and closing the plant from 1982 until 1989.

1993 saw the distillery's fortunes start to revive, when Burn Stewart Distillers purchased it for £600,000, plus £200,000 worth of stock. Under the ownership of Burn Stewart Distillers there has been a conscious move to raise the profile and status of Tobermory single malt, and in 2007 a small, on site warehouse was created in a former tun room so that some spirit could be matured on its native island.

POINTS OF SPECIAL INTEREST

In addition to the unpeated Tobermory single malt, the distillery also produces the heavily-peated Ledaig variant (around 35/45ppm). This was first introduced in 1996 and now accounts for some 50 per cent of annual output

ISLAND (WESTERN)

VISITOR EXPERIENCE

Tobermory draws obvious parallels with Oban in terms of being a seaside distillery which enjoys stunning views and is crammed into a tight site in a busy little town and port. It is a charming and pleasant distillery offering relaxed informal tours.

Admission includes a tour of the distillery itself, complementary dram, audio-visual presentation and historic displays. There is a small but well-stocked shop and relaxed members of staff are on hand.

Contacts
Tel: 01688 302647

Website
www.tobermorymalt.com

Admission
£ Standard Tour: £3.50

T Set times
C No
S Whisky and some gift and book items

LOCATION

Tobermory, Isle of Mull, Argyllshire PA75 6NR
The distillery is situated in the heart of Tobermory on the Isle of Mull, to the south side of the bay.

🕐 Easter - October
Monday to Friday 10:00 - 17:00
🕐 October to Easter by appointment.

Personal notes relating to visit:

Whiskies tasted notes/opinions:

Manager/guide signature:

Date visited:

ARDBEG

Meaning of name and pronunciation guide
'Small promontory'
- ard-BEG

Owner
The Glenmorangie Co
(Louis Vuitton Moët
Hennessy)

House style
Full-bodied, peaty,
salty and smoky, with
medicinal notes, fruit,
liquorice and spice.

Principal single malts
Ardbeg 10-year-old,
Blasda, Uigeadail,
Corryvreckan.

Principal blends
Black Bottle.

Getting technical
Stills: one pair

Capacity: 1.1m litres

Malt: peated to 45-
55ppm

Casks: ex-Bourbon plus
some ex-Sherry

Water: Loch Uigeadail
and Airigh Nam Beist

HISTORY

Ardbeg can trace its origins back to 1794, though the present distillery was established in 1815 by John MacDougall. After being in private hands for more than a century and a half, Ardbeg was effectively under the controlled of Hiram Walker & Sons Ltd and the Distillers Company Ltd, with Hiram Walker assuming full control in 1976.

However, the late 1970s and early '80s were hard times for the Scotch whisky industry, and Ardbeg was mothballed from 1982 to 1989, becoming part of Allied Distillers when Hiram Walker was taken over by them in 1987. Despite putting most of its Islay energies into neighbouring Laphroaig, Allied did reopen Ardbeg two years later, making comparatively small quantities of whisky until finally closing the distillery in 1996.

The following year, Ardbeg was acquired by Glenmorangie plc, who spent in excess of £10 million buying and restoring the site. Today, with Islay malts so firmly in the ascendancy, and Ardbeg one of the most iconic of them all, it is difficult to believe that just a few years ago the distillery seemed likely to be lost forever. Ardbeg is the most regularly heavily-peated single malt available, although Bruichladdich has experimented with higher levels in recent years.

POINTS OF SPECIAL INTEREST

Ardbeg devotees may join the Ardbeg Committee, which entitles them to purchase exclusive bottlings and receive regular updates relating to the brand.

ISLAY

VISITOR EXPERIENCE

With a feeling of being situated at the end of the world, Ardbeg exudes an aura of timelessness, so a visit here should not be rushed. Allow time to sit on the rocks, gaze out to sea and contemplate the history of the place.

Ardbeg offers highly-regarded tours of a small, cosy distillery, complete with complementary dram, and the excellent Old Kiln Café. It is so good that even the locals eat there!

LOCATION

Ardbeg, Port Ellen, Islay PA42 7EA
Ardbeg is located on the southern shores of the island of Islay, some four miles east of the ferry terminal at Port Ellen and past its neighbours, Laphroaig and Lagavulin.

🕐 June – August
Monday to Sunday 10:00 to 17:00
🕐 September - May
Monday to Friday 10:00 to 16:00

Contacts
Tel: 01496 302244
E-mail:
website@ardbeg.com

Website
www.ardbeg.com

Admission
£ Standard Tour: £4.00 (redeemable on shop purchases in excess of £20.00)

T Set times
C Light meals
S Whisky and some gift and book items

Personal notes relating to visit:

Whiskies tasted notes/opinions:

Manager/guide signature:

Date visited:

153

BOWMORE

HISTORY

The oldest distillery on Islay, Bowmore was founded in 1779 in the recently-established settlement of Bowmore by farmer and distiller David Simson. He sold the plant in 1837 to Glasgow-based William & James Mutter, previously owners of Jura distillery. Having expanded the distillery it remained in family control until 1892.

Changing ownership several times and having been requisitioned during World war II, the distillery ultimately came into the hands of whisky-brokers Stanley P Morrison Ltd in 1963, and in 1987 the firm, which also operates Auchentoshan and Glengarioch distilleries, changed its trading name to Morrison Bowmore Ltd. Two years later, Japanese distilling giant Suntory acquired a 35 per cent stake in the company, and in 1994 took full control.

POINTS OF SPECIAL INTEREST

Bowmore is one of only a handful of Scottish distilleries which still operates its own floor maltings, with three currently in use. They provide up to 40 per cent of the distillery's malt requirements.

Bowmore is proud of its fine environmental record, and in 1990 a warehouse was donated to the local community for conversion into a swimming pool. It is heated by hot water from the stillroom's condensers

Meaning of name and pronunciation guide
'The big bend/curve'
– bow-MORE

Owner
Morrison Bowmore Distillers Ltd (Suntory Ltd)

House style
Medium-bodied, smoky, slightly medicinal, with a hint of Sherry and chocolate.

Principal single malts
Bowmore Legend, 12-year-old, 15-year-old Darkest, 18 and 25-year-old.

Principal blends
Rob Roy, Black Bottle.

Getting technical
Stills: two pairs

Capacity: 2.2m litres

Malt: peated to 20-25ppm

Casks: ex-Bourbon and ex-Sherry

Water: River Laggan

ISLAY

VISITOR EXPERIENCE

Immaculate and accessible, Bowmore boasts excellent visitor facilities, substantially revamped during 2006. The distillery tour includes an informative and entertaining video presentation, complementary dram, and a rare chance to see working floor maltings, while a specialist 'Craftsman's Tour' is also available. This gives visitors an opportunity to learn from members of staff with hands-on experience of making whisky.

A fascinating exhibition of rare and old Bowmore bottling, which the distillery purchased from a private collector in 2004, are now on display in the visitor centre.

If you just can't bear to leave Bowmore distillery after your visit, there are six fully-renovated cottages, of varying sizes, available to let. All are located within, or beside, the distillery complex.

Contacts
Tel: 01496 810441
E-mail: info@morrison bowmore.co.uk

Website
www.bowmore.com

Admission
£ Standard Tour: £4.00 (includes a voucher redeemable on any 70cl bottle purchased at the shop)
£ Craftsman's Tour: £40.00 (by appointment only)

T Set times
C No
S Whisky and some gift and book items

LOCATION

School Street, Bowmore, Isle of Islay PA43 7JS
The distillery is located in the centre of Bowmore, midway between Port Ellen and Port Askaig.

🕐 Easter – August
Monday to Saturday 9:00 to 17:00
plus Sunday 12:00 to 16:00 (July and August)
🕐 September – Easter
Monday to Friday 9:00 to 17:00
Saturday 9:00-12:00

INSIDE MASHTUN AT BOWMORE

Personal notes relating to visit:

Whiskies tasted notes/opinions:

Manager/guide signature:

Date visited:

SECTION INDEX ON PAGE 71

BRUICHLADDICH

Meaning of name and pronunciation guide
'The shore bank'
- BROOK-laddie

Owner
The Bruichladdich
Distillery Co Ltd

House style
Elegant, floral, lighter-bodied, briny, honey, malt, fruit and spice.

Principal single malts
Bruichladdich Peat, Rocks, Waves, Organic, 12 Year Old, 16 Year Old Bourbon, 18 Year Old, Port Charlotte, Octomore.

Principal blends
N/A

Getting technical
Stills: two pairs

Capacity: 1.5m litres

Malt: 3-5ppm for most distillations, 40ppm for Port Charlotte and 80+ ppm for Octomore

Casks: American and French oak - new and Ex-Bourbon, ex-Sherry and wine

Water: A loch in the hills behind distillery for mashing. A spring on Octomore farm for bottling

HISTORY

Bruichladdich was built in 1881 by the Harvey family of Glasgow, who also owned Dundashill and Yoker distilleries in their home city. It was set up to produce a new type of Islay spirit, one that was pure, elegant and floral. The Harveys remained major shareholders in Bruichladdich until it fell silent in 1929.

Subsequently reopening in 1936, Bruichladdich was acquired the following year by Joseph Hobbs and associates. After a number of further changes in ownership, Bruichladdich was bought by Invergordon Distillers Ltd in 1968, and a second pair of stills was installed seven years later.

Whyte & Mackay Ltd took over Invergordon in 1993 after a bitter battle, and went on to close Bruichladdich. Despite worked briefly for a few months in 1998 it remained silent until December 2000 when it was acquired by a private company, headed by Mark Reynier of independent bottler Murray McDavid. Since then Bruichladdich has thrived, offering non-chill-filtered and colouring-free whisky in an intriguingly wide range of small scale and limited release bottlings. This 'progressive Hebridean distiller' has never been afraid to experiment, producing both triple and quadruple-distilled spirit and using various peating levels. The company also installed the only bottling line on Islay in 2003, giving it the flexibility to bottle a huge range.

POINTS OF SPECIAL INTEREST

Since the Second World War, Bruichladdich has been a minimally-peated Islay malt. Now batches of heavily-peated spirit are also distilled, namely Port Charlotte, peated to 40ppm, and Octomore 'the most heavily peated whisky in the world,' peated to at least 80ppm. Barley is exclusively Scottish grown, and is produced on 23 farms. Almost half is cultivated on Islay and the rest is organically grown on the mainland.

ISLAY

VISITOR EXPERIENCE

Enterprising and innovative, Bruichladdich boasts many firsts and provides a rare chance to see inside a distillery which has changed remarkably little since it opened in the Victorian era. Still "...run by people, not computers," visitors need only look into the enormous open mash tun with its mechanical gearing to see why. It is the only one of its kind on Islay, and just a handful of them are still in use anywhere in Scotland. One wash still is, in part, 130 years old, and a recent addition is 'Ugly Betty,' the only working Lomond spirit still in existence. The distillery tour includes a visit to a traditional dunnage warehouse and Islay's only bottling hall.

A well stocked shop offers a wide range of naturally-bottled whiskies, both from the Murray McDavid range and distillery offerings. These include a rare selection of earlier bottlings and some which are unique to the shop. Visitors may even fill their own 50cl 'valinch' bottle from a specially selected cask, which is then hand-labelled.

If you are unable to visit Bruichladdich in person, it is possible to log on to the distillery website and view all the processes of whisky-making via a series of live webcams.

Contacts
Tel: 01496 850190
E-mail: info@ bruichladdich.com

Website
www.bruichladdich.com

Admission
£ Standard Tour: £5.00 (including a voucher redeemable on 70cl purchases in the shop)

Extended tours and tastings by arrangement.

T Flexible
C No
S Whisky and some gift and book items

Personal notes relating to visit:

LOCATION
Bruichladdich, Isle of Islay Argyll PA49 7UN Overlooking Loch Indaal on its western shoreline, the distillery sits alongside the A847 Bridgend to Portnahaven road in the small Bruichladdich village.

Whiskies tasted notes/opinions:

🕐 Easter - September
Monday to Friday 9:00 to 17:00
Saturday 10:00 to 16:00
🕐 October - Easter
Monday to Friday 9:00 to 17:00
Saturday 10:00 to 14:00

Manager/guide signature:

Date visited:

SECTION INDEX ON PAGE 71

BUNNAHABHAIN

Meaning of name and pronunciation guide
'Mouth of the river'
– BUNNA-hah-ven

Owner
Burn Stewart Distillers
(CL World Brands Ltd)

House style
Quite light-bodied, aromatic, fresh, sweet, fruity and nutty, with a whiff of smoke.

Principal single malts
Bunnahabhain 12, 18 and 25-year-old.

Principal blends
The Famous Grouse, Black Bottle, Cutty Sark.

Getting technical
Stills: two pairs

Capacity: 2.5m litres

Malt: usually peated to 1-2ppm

Casks: ex-Bourbon plus some ex-Sherry

Water: River Margadadale and Loch Staoisha

HISTORY

Bunnahabhain was founded in 1881 by William and James Greenlees and William Robertson. Its spectacular site was chosen for the local availability of pure water and high quality peat, along with its sheltered coastal location which was ideal for communication by sea. Six years after its establishment, Bunnahabhain became part of the newly-formed Highland Distilleries Company Ltd, with whom it remained until 1999, when The Edrington Group took control. Output was doubled in 1963 when a second pair of stills was added.

The distillery suffered periods of silence during the 1930s and the early 1980s, when the level of surplus spirit in what the press dubbed the 'whisky loch' was at its highest. From 1999 to 2001 production was also sporadic. Ultimately, Edrington took the strategic decision to concentrate its marketing efforts on a number of key brands such as The Macallan and Highland Park, and disposed of Glengoyne and Bunnahabhain distilleries, with the latter being acquired by Burn Stewart Distillers plc for £10 million in 2003. Also included in the deal was the Black Bottle blended whisky brand, which has Islay malts at its core.

POINTS OF SPECIAL INTEREST

Although it may not seem obvious at first glance, Bunnahabhain was constructed in the style of a Bordeaux watchtower, or *castel*.

Since 2003 quantities of more heavily peated spirit have been distilled annually at Bunnahabhain, for blending purposes and a single malt bottling of this whisky is due to appear at a future date.

ISLAY

VISITOR EXPERIENCE

Situated in a beautiful and remote setting with stunning views across the Sound of Islay to neighbouring Jura, Bunnahabhain appears somewhat harsh and uncomfortable on its rugged shoreline. However, the vast stills and warm welcome makes the journey worthwhile.

Tours are run by distillery workers, rather than professional guides, which adds to the authenticity of the experience. VIP tours, featuring rare whiskies and cask samples, led by a senior operator or manager, can be arranged by contacting the distillery.

Tea and coffee are complementary, as is the post-tour dram. Essentially, this is a distillery for the enthusiast rather than the casual visitor with little knowledge of whisky. Bunnahabhain has refurbished a number of distillery cottages, which are available to rent. They offer a truly remote getaway for the enjoyment of a warming dram or two.

Contacts
Tel: 01496 840646

Website
www.bunnahabhain.com

Admission
£ Standard Tour: £4.00 (£2.00 refundable on 70cl purchases of Bunnahabhain whisky)
£ VIP Tour: £25.00

T Set times
C No
S Whisky and some gift and book items

LOCATION

Port Askaig, Isle of Islay, Argyll PA46 7RP
The distillery is situated at the end of a four miles-long, unclassified road off the A846, just outside Port Askaig.

🕐 March – October
Monday to Friday 10:00 to 16:00

Other months by appointment only

Personal notes relating to visit:

Whiskies tasted notes/opinions:

Manager/guide signature:

Date visited:

BUNNAHABHAIN DISTILLERY

CAOL ILA

Meaning of name and pronunciation guide
'Sound of Islay'
– cul-EEL-ah

Owner
Diageo plc

House style
Full-bodied, smoky, slightly medicinal, with peat, pepper and tobacco notes.

Principal single malts
Caol Ila 12 and 18-year-old, Cask Strength, Distillers Edition.

Principal blends
Bells, Johnnie Walker, White Horse.

Getting technical
Stills: three pairs

Capacity: 3.6m litres

Malt: peated to 30-35ppm

Casks: ex-Bourbon

Water: Loch nam Ban

HISTORY

Caol Ila was established by distillery magnate Hector Henderson in 1846, and came into the ownership of the Glasgow blending firm of Bulloch Lade & Co in 1863, subsequently being rebuilt in 1879.The new distillery was the first on Islay to be constructed from a revolutionary new substance called concrete!

In 1927 it became part of the ever-expanding Distillers Company Ltd's portfolio of distilleries, and between 1972 and 1974 the entire plant was rebuilt in ultra-modern style at a cost of £1 million, with six large new stills being installed in place of the original pair. The distillery may be stark, but its setting on the shores of the Sound of Islay is exquisite.

Only the warehouse of the 19th century distillery was left intact, though today all the make of Caol Ila is transported by road tanker to the mainland for filling into casks and maturation in the Central Belt. Caol Ila has long enjoyed an excellent reputation as a blending malt, which explains why it operates on a large scale, though its popularity and availability as a single malt has increased in recent years. It is now part of Diageo's extended 'Classic Malts' line up.

POINTS OF SPECIAL INTEREST

Caol Ila is the largest distillery on Islay in terms of output and total capacity.

In addition to the usual style of make, a quantity of unpeated spirit is distilled each year, principally for blending purposes, though a number of eight-year-old bottling of this 'Caol Ila Highland' have been released since 2006.

ISLAY

VISITOR EXPERIENCE

Caol Ila Distillery shares with nearby Bunnahabhain the distinction of enjoying one of the most remote locations of all the Islay distilleries.

The plant is hidden away in a small cove at the foot of a hill, and its sheer modernity comes as a surprise at first glance in this wild and rugged landscape. However, the longer you spend at Caol Ila, the more the buildings seem to complement the countryside, and the warehouse at least is reassuringly traditional!

On offer is a professional distillery tour, shop and visitor centre, plus the finest view - across the Sound of Islay to Jura - from any still house in Scotland.

Premium tours and tastings at £10 per person can be arranged by prior appointment.

LOCATION

Port Askaig, Islay, Argyll PA46 7RL
The distillery is located at the end of a mile-long single track, off the A846 Bowmore to Port Askaig road. Just south-west of Port Askaig, the junction is at the top of the steep hill leading from the ferry port.

🕐 April - November
Monday to Friday 9:15 to 17:00
plus Saturday 13:30 to 16:30 (April - May)
and Saturday 10:00 to 16:30 (June - October)
🕐 December - March
Monday to Friday 13:30 to 16:30

Contacts
Tel: 01496 302760
Email: caolila.distillery
@diageo.com

Website
www.discovering-
distilleries.com

Admission
£ Standard Tour:
£6.00 (includes a complementary Caol Ila whisky glass and free entry to Lagavulin Distillery. It is also part redeemable on 70cl bottles purchased in the shop)

T Set times
C No
S Whisky and some gift and book items

Personal notes relating to visit:

Whiskies tasted notes/opinions:

Manager/guide signature:

Date visited:

CAOL ILA

SECTION INDEX ON PAGE 71

JURA

Meaning of name and pronunciation guide
'Deer island'
– JEW-ra

Owner
Whyte & Mackay Ltd

House style
Medium to light-bodied, quite dry, with pine, hazelnuts, spice and a whisper of peat smoke.

Principal single malts
Isle of Jura 10, 16 and 21-year-old, Superstition. Prophecy.

Principal blends
Whyte & Mackay Special.

Getting technical
Stills: two pairs

Capacity: 2.2m litres

Malt: usually unpeated

Casks: ex-Bourbon plus some Sherry butts for older single malt expressions

Water: Bhaile Mhargaidh Spring

HISTORY

It is sometimes claimed that whisky-making in the area can be traced back to 1502 and the original Jura distillery is thought to have been established in 1810. It was first licensed in 1831 to William Abercrombie. Distilling continued at Craighouse under a number of different licensees until James Ferguson & Co took over in 1876. The operation ceased in 1901, due to a dispute between Ferguson and his landlord, Colin Campbell. Ferguson stripped the distillery of its equipment, and Campbell removed the roofs of the buildings in 1920 to avoid having to pay tax.

Jura appeared to be a lost distillery, until 1960, when Charles Mackinlay & Co set out to restore whisky-making to the island. Recruiting the notable distillery designer William Delmé-Evans for the project, some of the existing buildings were incorporated into the new site. The whisky distilled in the old Jura distillery had been heavily peated, like that of its Islay neighbours, but the 'new' Jura plant was equipped with taller stills and used lightly peated malt to produce spirit closer to the Highland style.

By the time the first spirit flowed in 1963, Mackinlay & Co had become part of Scottish & Newcastle Breweries Ltd, which ran the distillery until its acquisition by Invergordon Distillers Group plc in 1985. In 1993 Invergordon Distillers was taken over by Whyte & Mackay Ltd, which continues to operate the distillery today.

POINTS OF SPECIAL INTEREST

George Orwell wrote his novel *Nineteen Eighty-Four* while living at Barnhill, in the north of Jura, between 1946 and 1948, and a Jura Malt Whisky Writer's Retreat Programme now operates. It has given authors of the calibre of Will Self, Kathleen Jamie, John Burnside and Liz Lochhead the opportunity to spend time living and working on the island.

ISLAY

VISITOR EXPERIENCE

Even compared to other island distilleries, Isle of Jura is remote, but the effort of getting there is well worth it, thanks to stunning scenery and a friendly welcome.

Tours are low key and knowledgeable, with a complementary dram also on offer.

Apartments within the sumptuously refurbished Jura Lodge, formerly the manager's residence, are available to rent.

LOCATION

Craighouse, Ise of Jura PA60 7XT
The distillery is located beside the A846, in the small island 'capital' of Craighouse, eight miles around the south side of the island from the ferry terminal.

🕐 April – September
Monday to Friday 10:00 to 16:00
Saturday 10:00 to 14:00
🕐 October - March
Monday to Friday 11:00 to 14:00

Contacts
Tel: 01496 820385
Email: sue.pettit@
whyteandmackay.com

Website
www.isleofjura.com

Admission
£ Standard Tour:
free

T Set times
C No
S Whisky and some
gift and book items

**Personal notes
relating to visit:**

**Whiskies tasted
notes/opinions:**

**Manager/guide
signature:**

Date visited:

SECTION INDEX ON PAGE 71

KILCHOMAN

Meaning of name and pronunciation guide
'Coman's church'
- kil-HO-man

Owner
Kilchoman Distillery
Co Ltd

House style
Peaty, mildly medicinal, with citrus fruits, toffee and spices.

Principal single malts
Kilchoman Inaugural Release (2009), Autumn 2009 Release.

Principal blends
N/A

Getting technical
Stills: one pair

Capacity: 100,000 litres

Malt: peated to 40-50ppm

Casks: ex-Bourbon and ex-Sherry

Water: Allt Glean Osmail Burn

HISTORY

Kilchoman is the first new distillery to be created on Islay since Malt Mill was built at Lagavulin (see p 166) in 1908. It represents a return to grass roots, farm-based distilling, with barley being grown on land at Rockside Farm, where the distillery is based, and malted at the distillery. Ultimately, a bottling line is also to be installed, fulfilling founder Anthony Wills' ambition of being able to describe his product as 'One hundred per cent Islay from barley to bottle.'

In the 19th century there were as many as 18 farm-based distilleries on Islay, and Kilchoman proudly follows in that tradition. The first casks were filled on 14th December 2005, and the aim is to create a comparatively light, fruity style of spirit, but with high peating levels.

In September 2009 the first release of Kilchoman as legally-defined 'Scotch whisky' (a minimum of three years old) took place.

POINTS OF SPECIAL INTEREST

When it opened, Kilchoman replaced Bruichladdich as the westernmost distillery in Scotland, but that mantle has now been passed to Abhainn Dearg on the island of Lewis.

ISLAY

VISITOR EXPERIENCE

Tours of this small-scale distillery do not take long, but they provide an interesting opportunity to see one of Scotland's newest distillery and on-site maltings, and there is an excellent café and gift shop, which showcases local products. The visitor centre tells the story of farm distilling on Islay, and explores the theory that distilling was actually introduced to Scotland via Islay.

A regular five day, hands on 'Distillery Experience' is also available for serious whisky aficionados who can experience every aspect of making whisky from malting through to bottling.

Printed guides are available in Dutch, French, German, Japanese, Spanish and Swedish.

LOCATION

Rockside Farm, Isle of Islay, PA49 7UT
Eight and a half miles from Bowmore, the distillery is situated off the B8018, and is signposted from the A847 Bridgend to Portnahaven road.

🕐 April – October
Monday to Saturday 10:00 to 17:00
🕐 November - March
Monday to Friday 10:00 to 17:00

Contacts
Tel: 01496 850011
E-mail: info@ kilchomandistillery .com

Website
www.kilchoman distillery.com

Admission
£ Standard Tour: £3.50

T Flexible
C Light meals
S Whisky and some gift and book items

Personal notes relating to visit:

Whiskies tasted notes/opinions:

Manager/guide signature:

Date visited:

SECTION INDEX ON PAGE 71

LAGAVULIN

Meaning of name and pronunciation guide
'The hollow by the mill'
-Laga-VOO-lin

Owner
Diageo plc

House style
Full-bodied and complex, dry, peaty and medicinal, with liquorice and Sherry notes.

Principal single malts
Lagavulin 12-year-old (cask strength), 16-year-old, Lagavulin Distillers Edition.

Principal blends
White Horse.

Getting technical
Stills: two pairs

Capacity: 2.3m litres

Malt: peated to 35-40ppm

Casks: ex-Bourbon plus some ex-Sherry

Water: Solum Lochs

HISTORY

Lagavulin was established in an area of the southern shores of Islay well-known for illicit whisky-making, and was first licensed in 1816 to John Johnston. The following year a distillery by the name of Ardmore was built alongside Lagavulin by Archibald Campbell. However, Johnston took over Ardmore in 1825 and ultimately combined it within the Lagavulin operation.

In 1867 Lagavulin was acquired by James Logan Mackie & Co, with Mackie's nephew, Peter, going on to develop the famous White Horse blended whisky brand, with Lagavulin at its heart.

Peter Mackie died in 1924, the same year in which the company changed its name to White Horse Distillers. Three years later the firm became part of the Distillers Company Ltd.

A 16-year-old expression of Lagavulin was selected as one of the original United Distillers' Classic Malts in 1988 and continues to be the principal bottling from the distillery. Such is its international cache that some 90 per cent of the distillery's output is bottled as single malt.

POINTS OF SPECIAL INTEREST

From 1908 until 1960 a second distillery, known as Malt Mill, operated as part of the Lagavulin complex. It had been created by Peter Mackie in an attempt to replicate the old-style, illicit whiskies of the area, and used peat rather than coal. The Malt Mill stills were incorporated into Lagavulin distillery in 1962.

ISLAY

VISITOR EXPERIENCE

In common with its neighbours, Laphroaig and
Ardbeg, Lagavulin enjoys a stunning location on the
southern shore of Islay, with views across Lagavulin
Bay to the ruins of Dunnyveg Castle, once held by the
chiefs of Clan Donald.

Lagavulin visitor centre is located in the former
Malt Mill maltings, and in characteristic Diageo style it
is well-equipped and appointed, with friendly,
knowledgeable staff.

'The Warehouse Demonstration' provides a greater
insight into Lagavulin distillery and its spirit. It follows
9:30am tours and includes sampling whisky straight
from duty-paid casks in one of the traditional
warehouses. Booking is advisable.

*Tours are available in English and Gaelic and there
are also translation boards in various languages.*

LOCATION

Port Ellen, Isle of Islay, Argyll PA42 7DZ
Situated beside the A846 road, two and a half
miles east of Port Ellen.

🕐 April – June
Monday to Friday 9:00 to 17:00
Saturday 9:00 to 12:30

🕐 July – October
Monday to Saturday 9:00 to 17:00 (staying open until
19:00 on weekdays in July and August)
plus Sunday 12:30 to 16:30 (July - August)

LAGAVULIN

Contacts
Tel: 01496 302749
E-mail: lagavulin.
distillery@diageo.com

Website
www.discovering-
distilleries.com

Admission
£ Standard Tour:
£6.00 (includes a
complementary
Lagavulin whisky
glass and free entry
to Caol Ila Distillery.
It is also part
redeemable on 70cl
bottles purchased
in the shop)

£ Warehouse
Demonstration:
£15.00 (includes
Standard Tour)

T Set times
C Hot and cold drinks
S Whisky and some
gift and book items

**Personal notes
relating to visit:**

**Whiskies tasted
notes/opinions:**

**Manager/guide
signature:**

Date visited:

SECTION INDEX ON PAGE 71

LAPHROAIG

HISTORY

Laphroaig was first licensed in 1815, by brothers Alexander and Donald Johnston, though it is believed that the Johnstons had actually been distilling at Laphroaig for several years prior to this date.

Family control continued until 1954, when the last Johnston family member, Ian Hunter died, having run the operation since 1927. He was succeeded in the role of managing director of D Johnston & Co Ltd by Bessie Williamson, who had previously been his PA.

Seager Evans & Company purchased D Johnston & Co in its entirety through its Long John Distillers Ltd subsidiary in 1972, having already acquired an interest in the firm in 1962.

The brewers Whitbread & Co Ltd then bought Seager Evans in 1975 and in 1989 Allied Distillers Ltd took over Whitbread's spirits' division. When the Allied empire was split up in 2005, Laphroaig, along with Ardmore distillery in Speyside, was purchased by Jim Beam Brands of the USA.

POINTS OF SPECIAL INTEREST

Laphroaig continues to make some 15 per cent of its total malt requirements on site, and is the only distillery to hold a Royal warrant, having been granted one by HRH The Prince of Wales in 1994.

Meaning of name and pronunciation guide
'The beautiful hollow by the broad bay'
- La-FROY-g

Owner
Beam Global UK Ltd

House style
Full-bodied, smoky, salty, earthy and medicinal.

Principal single malts
Laphroaig 10-year-old, Laphroaig 10-year-old cask strength, Laphroaig Quarter Cask, Laphroaig 18-year-old.

Principal blends
Teachers.

Getting technical
Stills: three wash and four spirit

Capacity: 2.85m litres

Malt: peated to 35-40ppm

Casks: ex-Bourbon and ex-Sherry

Water: Kilbride Dam

ISLAY

VISITOR EXPERIENCE

An attractive visitor centre and shop has been created in the bottom floor of a former maltings and tours of the distillery are conducted by very knowledgeable staff. Highlights include the floor maltings and idiosyncratic still house.

Additionally, a Standard Tutored Tasting is available on weekdays, by prior arrangement. It comprises a tasting of four drams across the core range, and lasts for some around 45 minutes. There is also a Premium Tutored Tasting, which offers four older and rarer Laphroaigs. This, too, must be pre-booked.

Real aficionados can join the Source, Peat, Malt Experience, which is a bespoke tour that takes enthusiasts beyond the distillery. It starts with a short walk to the water source, where there is an opportunity to sample a 10-year-old Laphroaig cut, the way it should be, with water directly from the distillery source. This is followed by a drive to the peat banks where, with a wee dram of Cask Strength, visitors can try out their peat-cutting skills. Back at the distillery, the experience is rounded off by turning the malt on the traditional malting floors, accompanied by a dram of Quarter Cask. This tour lasts around two hours and is available only during certain months. It accommodates up to six people at a time and should be booked in advance.

The Friends of Laphroaig organisation exists to keep aficionados in touch with the distillery and its whiskies, and now boasts more than 400,000 members.

LOCATION

Port Ellen, Isle of Islay PA42 7DU
Situated off the A846 road, one and a half miles east of Port Ellen

🕐 All year except Christmas and New Year
Monday to Friday 9:30 to 17:30
plus Saturday and Sunday 10:00 to 16:00
(March to December)

Reduced opening times between Christmas and New Year

Contacts
Tel: 01496 302418
E-mail: visitor.centre@laphroaig.com

Website
www.laphroaig.com

Admission
£ Standard Tour: £3.00 (redeemable on 70cl bottles purchased in the shop)
£ Standard Tutored Tasting: £10.00
£ Premium Tutored Tasting: £25.00
£ Source, Peat, Malt Experience: £20.00

The three more in-depth tours should be booked in advance.

T Set times
C No
S Whisky and some gift and book items

Personal notes relating to visit:

Whiskies tasted notes/opinions:

Manager/guide signature:

Date visited:

SECTION INDEX ON PAGE 71

SPRINGBANK

HISTORY

Springbank was the 14th distillery to be established in the old 'whisky capital' of Campbeltown, with the first spirit flowing in 1828. It was founded by the Reid family, whose in-laws, the Mitchells, purchased the distillery from them during a period of financial difficulty in 1837. It has remained in the Mitchell family to the present day, and is the oldest family-owned distillery in Scotland. Since 2004, J&A Mitchell & Co Ltd has also owned and operated the nearby Glengyle distillery.

Springbank fell victim to the depression of the inter-war years, which decimated Campbeltown's distilling industry. Closing in 1926, it reopened seven years later, unlike most of its rivals. The distillery was also silent from 1979 until 1987, when limited production resumed, followed two years later by a full distilling programme.

Despite the overall optimism of the Scotch whisky industry at the time, Springbank again closed temporarily in 2008 in order to allow stocks to fall into line with future sales projections, with limited production taking place during 2009 and 2010.

POINTS OF SPECIAL INTEREST

One of the last family-owned distilleries in Scotland, Springbank is superbly idiosyncratic, continuing to malt its own barley on traditional malting floors and to bottle on site. Three distinct types of spirit are produced, namely Springbank (distilled two and a half times), Longrow (heavily-peated and distilled twice) and Hazelburn (unpeated and triple-distilled). The wash still is unique in being heated both by internal steam coils and direct-fired by oil.

Meaning of name and pronunciation guide
'The bank of the spring'
- spring-BANK

Owner
J&A Mitchell & Co Ltd

House style
Medium-bodied, oily, with toffee, spice, coconut and some peat smoke.

Principal single malts
Springbank CV, 10, 15 and 18-year-old, 12-year-old cask strength. Longrow CV, 10 and 14-year-old. Hazelburn 8 and 12-year-old.

Principal blends
Campbeltown Loch.

Getting technical
Stills: one wash and two 'low wines'

Capacity: 750,000 litres

Malt: 'in-house' peating level varies from 12-55ppm. Unpeated for Hazelburn

Casks: ex-Bourbon and ex-Sherry

Water: Crosshills Loch

CAMPBELTOWN

VISITOR EXPERIENCE

Springbank is one of the 'must-see' distilleries in Scotland, as it is truly unique in so many ways, with most of the processes taking place in one room. This distillery really gives an impression of a bygone age.

Tours are friendly and informal, and admission includes a complementary dram in the Whisky Shop, a retail area which offers not only whiskies distilled at Springbank, but also other malts produced by independent bottler William Cadenhead, which has been owned by J&A Mitchell & Co Ltd since 1969.

The Tour and Tasting includes sampling of four whiskies, while the Silver Tour includes six samples. The Gold Tour offers the additional experience of visiting Glengyle, the company's sister distillery in Campbeltown.

LOCATION

Well Close, Campbeltown, Argyllshire PA28 6ET
The distillery is situated just off the A83 as it approaches the centre of Campbeltown, 130 miles south-west of Glasgow. Tucked away behind the shops and housing that line the west side of the street.

🕐 All year except Christmas and New Year
Monday to Friday 9:00 to 5:00
plus summer weekends by appointment only

For tickets and reservations contact
Cadenhead's Whisky Shop on Bolgam Street
Tel: 01586 551710
E-mail: tours@jandamitchell.com

Contacts
Tel: 01586 552085
E-mail: info@spring
bankwhisky.com

Website
www.springbank
distillers.com

Admission
£ Standard Tour:
£5.00
£ Tour and Tasting:
£10.00
£ Silver Tour:
£15.00
£ Gold Tour:
£20.00

The three more
in-depth tours should
be booked in advance.

T Set times
C No
S Whisky only

**Personal notes
relating to visit:**

**Whiskies tasted
notes/opinions:**

**Manager/guide
signature:**

Date visited:

SECTION INDEX ON PAGE 71

DISTILLERIES NOT USUALLY OPEN TO THE PUBLIC

Approximately 50 per cent of the distilleries in Scotland have visitor facilities, which is quite a remarkable percentage and should fulfil most visitors demand to 'bag' distilleries. The remaining operational malt whisky distilleries are listed in this section, though the majority do not cater for visitors. Some, however, do open for special occasions, such as during whisky festivals, while others may be able to accommodate members of the public if they have staff available and an advance request is made.

We have endeavoured to show how likely it is that you will be able to visit distilleries in this section, but the decision will be based on the circumstances at the time of your planned trip. It should always be born in mind that these are operational plants and distilling is the primary objective.

Travelling around Scotland, you will undoubtedly come across some of these distilleries, either by a roadside, in a hidden valley, or away in the distant hills. If you are in Speyside, you are likely to find several distilleries within a mile of each other, and sometimes even more than one on the same site.

SYMBOLS
T Timing of distillery tours, whether set or flexible
C Catering options for visitors
S Shopping facilities, indicating whether whisky is sold and scale of the shop

---

GLEN SCOTIA DISTILLERY

SECTION INDEX

LISTED ALPHABETICALLY WITHIN WHISKY REGIONS

Each page in this section is colour coded in the top corner to reflect the whisky region. See the map on the inside front and back covers for the distillery location.

ABBREVIATIONS

PRINCIPAL SINGLE MALT The primary expressions of malt whisky widely available.

PRINCIPAL BLENDS The main blends to which the distilleries whisky is used in.

STILLS The number of stills with which a distillery is equipped. However, this is not necessarily an indication of volume output, as still sizes vary considerably.

CAPACITY The output of each distillery is given in thousands or millions (m) of litres per annum.

MALT Indicates the level of peat influence in the malting process.

CASK Most Scotch whisky is matured in American Oak casks which formerly held Bourbon whiskey, produced in the USA . European Oak casks which previously contained Sherry are used to a lesser degree due to their comparatively high cost.

AILSA BAY

Meaning of name and pronunciation guide
Ailsa Craig is a rocky islet off the Ayrshire coast, in the Firth of Clyde. 'Island of seafowl' or 'island of elf victory' - AYLSA - bay

Owner
William Grant & Sons Ltd

House style
Estery sweetness and fruitiness, with some complexity. Similar to Balvenie.

Principal single malts
N/A

Principal blends
N/A

Getting technical
Stills: eight pairs

Capacity: 5m litres

Malt: mostly unpeated

Casks: ex-Bourbon

Water: Penwapple Reservoir

Visiting
No visitor tour/facilities

Contacts
Tel: 01465 713091

Date visited:

HISTORY

Ailsa Bay malt distillery was created within the existing Girvan grain distilling, blending and maturation complex of William Grant & Sons Ltd during 2007.

The Girvan operation itself was established in 1963/64, and between 1966 and 1975 a small, pot still facility made malt whisky under the Ladyburn name.

Ailsa Bay was developed within an existing structure that had previously housed a plant making glucose syrup for the confectionery industry until 2003.

The stills were modelled on those at William Grant's Balvenie distillery on Speyside, with similar pot size, shape and lyne arm angles, while the spirit 'cut points' are also modelled on those in place at Balvenie.

According to William Grant's CEO Roland van Bommel, Ailsa Bay was created to produce "...a high quality single malt for blending".

Although the vast majority of the spirit distilled at Ailsa Bay is peated to less than 2ppm, some two per cent of the distillery's annual output comprises lightly peated (5-8ppm) and heavily peated (+15ppm) spirit.

POINTS OF SPECIAL INTEREST

Ailsa Bay was developed in a total of just nine months, the same time it took to build the original Girvan grain distillery. The first spirit flowed from the Ailsa Bay stills on 24th September 2007. One distinctive feature of the distillery is its unique, octagonal spirit safe.

LOCATION

Grangestone Ind Estate, Girvan, Ayrshire KA26 9PT
Situated 23 miles south of Ayr, off the A77 then B741, on the outskirts of Girvan.

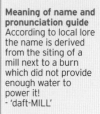

DAFTMILL

HISTORY

The Cuthbert family have farmed and quarried on a substantial scale near the historic Fife town of Cupar for generations. In 2003 they decided to convert an unused mill and adjacent farm buildings into a 'boutique' distillery. Brothers Ian and Francis Cuthbert run the distillery, which fills an average of one cask per day when the plant is working.

The stills were commissioned from leading coppersmiths Forsyth's of Rothes, on Speyside, but all other equipment and specialist skills were sourced as close to home as possible. Barley grown on the Cuthbert's own land is used for distillation, with the first spirit flowing from the Daftmill stills on 16 December 2005. 14,000 litres were distilled during the initial year of production, and the first single malt is not expected to be bottled before 2015.

POINTS OF SPECIAL INTEREST

Daftmill became the first new Lowland distillery to be created since William Grant's Girvan grain plant opened in 1963. With Daftmill in operation, the sorely depleted ranks of working Lowland malt whisky distilleries rose from three (Auchentoshan, Bladnoch and Glenkinchie) to four, and subsequently Ailsa Bay came on stream within the Girvan complex during 2007.

LOCATION

By Cupar, Fife KY15 5RF
Some four miles west of Cupar, the distillery is located at the end of a farm road, off the A91 Stirling to St Andrews road, just west of its junction with the A92.

Meaning of name and pronunciation guide
According to local lore the name is derived from the siting of a mill next to a burn which did not provide enough water to power it!
- 'daft-MILL'

Owner
The Cuthbert family

www.daftmill.com

House style
The new spirit is biscuity, slightly smoky, with a malty nose and floral, fruity characteristics.

Principal single malts
N/A

Principal blends
N/A

Getting technical
Stills: one pair

Capacity: 90,000 litres

Malt: unpeated

Casks: ex-Bourbon plus some ex-Sherry

Water: an artesian well

Visiting
May be possible by prior arrangement

Contacts
Tel: 01337 830303
E-mail:
info@daftmill.com

Date visited:

SECTION INDEX ON PAGE 173

DEANSTON

Meaning of name and pronunciation guide
'The hill (fort) or Dean's Farm'
- DEANS-ton

Owner
Burn Stewart Distillers (CL World Brands Ltd)

House style
Fragrant, medium bodied, malty, honeyed and nutty.

Principal single malts
Deanston 12-year-old.

Principal blends
Scottish Leader, Black Bottle.

Getting technical
Stills: two pairs

Capacity: 3m litres

Malt: unpeated

Casks: ex-Bourbon and ex-Sherry

Water: The River Teith

Visiting
Ideally by prior arrangement.

Contacts
Tel: 01786 841422
E-mail:
ann.shackell@burn-stewartdistillers.com

Date visited:

HISTORY

Deanston was established in 1965/66 by Brodie Hepburn Ltd, owners of Tullibardine distillery, and James Finlay & Co, and traded as Deanston Distillery Co Ltd. Uniquely, the distillery was created in the former Adelphi cotton mill, a listed complex, in part dating back to 1785 and designed by Richard Arkwright, creator of the world's first steam-driven spinning frame. When conversion to a distillery took place, four internal floors were removed to make way for the stills and other distilling plant.

In 1972 Invergordon Distillers acquired Deanston, and two years later the distillery name appeared on a single malt bottling for the first time. The distillery fell silent in 1982, when Scotch whisky stocks were very high and many distillers cut back on production, but in 1990 Burn Stewart Distillers purchased Deanston and production resumed the following year.

Deanston is a very traditional plant, with not a computer in sight, boasting one of the last open-topped mashtuns in the Scotch whisky industry.

POINTS OF SPECIAL INTEREST

One of the warehouses at Deanston is the magnificent, vaulted former weaving shed, constructed in 1836. The distillery is self sufficient in hydro-electric power, with water fed to two turbines, installed during the 1940s. Creating more than four times its own energy requirements, the excess is sold back to the National Grid.

LOCATION

Deanston, by Doune, Perthshire FK16 6AG
Situated on the banks of the River Teith and an unclassified road, just off the B8032 and A84, one mile south-west of Doune.

Small group tours only. £5.00 per person.

PHOTOGRAPH ON PAGE 9

LOCH LOMOND

HISTORY

Loch Lomond distillery was founded in 1965 by the Littlemill Distillery Company Ltd. In 1971 Barton Distilling (Scotland) Ltd was formed, with the US distiller Barton Brands having previously been part-owner of the company. Loch Lomond operated under its auspices until closure in 1984.

The following year the independent blender and bottler Glen Catrine Bonded Warehouse Ltd, headed by Sandy Bulloch, took over the distillery, with production resuming in 1987. In 1993 a Coffey still was installed to produce grain spirit.

Loch Lomond distillery is one of the most complete and versatile distilling operations in Scotland. The permutations of distilling plant enable a variety of spirit styles to be produced, from the unpeated Glen Douglas single malt to a heavily peated (40ppm) expression called Croftengea.

POINTS OF SPECIAL INTEREST

Loch Lomond is the only distillery in Scotland to make both grain and malt whisky.

LOCATION

Lomond Industrial Estate, Alexandria, Dunbartonshire G83 OTL
18 miles north-west of Glasgow, the distillery is situated in Alexandria, next to the Antartex Village. From the B857 North Main St and Luss Road, take Heather Ave, then Bowie Rd.

Meaning of name and pronunciation guide
'Loch beacon'
- loch LOW-mond

Owner
Loch Lomond
Distillery Co Ltd

www.lochlomonddistillery.com

House style
Light-bodied, floral, sweet, malty and fruity.

Principal single malts
Inchmurrin 4-year-old and 12-year-old, Loch Lomond (no age statement), Old Rhosdhu 5-year-old.

Principal blends
Loch Lomond (single blend), Scots Earl.

Getting technical
Stills: 2 conventional pot stills, 4 adjustable rectifying columns and a Coffey still

Capacity: malt spirit 2.5m litres, grain spirit 10m litres

Malt: peating levels vary

Casks: ex-Bourbon

Water: Loch Lomond and on-site boreholes

Visiting
No visitor
tour/facilities

Contacts
Tel: 01389 752781
E-mail: mail@lochlomonddistillery.com

Date visited:

ARDMORE

Meaning of name and pronunciation guide
'Big height'
– ard-MORE

Owner
Beam Global UK Ltd

House style
Medium-bodied and medium-sweet, slightly smoky, with a buttery, malty character, plus nuts, honey and spice.

Principal single malts
Ardmore Traditional Cask, Ardmore 12-year-old (Gordon & MacPhail).

Principal blends
Teacher's.

Getting technical
Stills: four pairs

Capacity: 5.1m litres

Malt: peated 10-15ppm

Casks: ex-Bourbon

Water: Springs on Knockandy Hill

Visiting
May be possible by prior arrangement

Contacts
Tel: 01464 831213

Date visited:

HISTORY

Ardmore distillery was built by Adam Teacher, son of William, in 1897/98, close to the main Inverness-Aberdeen railway line. It was intended to provide a significant amount of the malt requirements of the increasingly popular Teacher Highland Cream blend, launched in 1884, in much the same way as Aberfeldy served Dewar's White Label.

Ardmore remained with the Teachers until the firm's acquisition by Allied Breweries in 1976, by which time capacity had been increased from two to four stills (1955) and from four to eight stills (1974).

Along with Laphroaig, Ardmore was acquired in 2005 by the US-based Jim Beam Brands as part of the break up of Allied Domecq plc; successor company to Allied Breweries. Production was subsequently increased by 25 per cent to around the four million litres per annum mark, largely in order to service the requirements of the Teacher's blend. A further increase in capacity has since taken place.

POINTS OF SPECIAL INTEREST

Ardmore was one of the last distilleries to change over from direct-fired coal stills, which it did in 2001, when a switch was made to steam heating. Enthusiasts wait to see whether the further change has noticeably altered the character of the whisky.

LOCATION

Kennethmont, Huntly, Aberdeenshire AB54 4NH
Situated alongside the B9002, just east of the small village of Kennethmont, 8 miles south of Huntly.

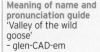

GLENCADAM

HISTORY

Glencadam was established by George Cooper in 1825, in the wake of the revolutionary Excise Act of 1823. After several changes of ownership, Glencadam was purchased by Gilmour Thomson & Co Ltd in 1891, with the Glasgow blending company owning it until 1954. In that year the distillery was acquired by Hiram Walker (Scotland) Ltd, who undertook a major reconstruction programme five years later.

Through a series of takeovers, Glencadam came into the possession of Allied Lyons in 1987, and in 2000, the company, by now Allied Domecq, closed the Brechin distillery as surplus to requirements.

However, in 2003 Glencadam was bought by London-based Angus Dundee plc, who also own Tomintoul distillery, and who specialise in producing own label malt and blended whiskies for sale abroad. Production recommenced that same year, and a 'house' bottling of 15-year-old Glencadam was released in 2005.

POINTS OF SPECIAL INTEREST

During the early 20th century, Glencadam was one of the component malts in Gilmour Thomson's Royal Blend, one of King Edward VII's favourite drams. The historic town of Brechin formerly boasted two distilleries, but North Port closed in 1983, and was subsequently demolished.

LOCATION

Park Road, Brechin, Angus DD9 7PA
Situated to the north-east of the centre of Brechin, off Park Road and the crossroads with the A935.

Meaning of name and pronunciation guide
'Valley of the wild goose'
– glen-CAD-em

Owner
Angus Dundee plc

www.angusdundee.co.uk

House style
Medium-bodied, comparatively sweet and nutty, creamy, with summer fruits on the palate.

Principal single malts
Glencadam 10, 15 and 30-year-old.

Principal blends
Dundee, Parker's.

Getting technical
Stills: one pair

Capacity: 1.5m litres

Malt: unpeated

Cask: ex-Bourbon

Water: springs in the Unthank Hills

Visiting
By prior arrangement

Contacts
Tel: 01356 622217

Date visited:

KNOCKDHU

Meaning of name and pronunciation guide
'Black hill'
- knock-DOO

Owner
Inver House Distillers
Ltd (Thai Beverage
plc)

www.ancnoc.com

House style
Sweet and fruity, with
nuts, light malt and a
hint of smoke.

Principal single malts
anCnoc 12-year-old
and 16-year-old.

Principal blends
Haig, Hankey
Bannister, Pinwhinnie.

Getting technical
Stills: one pair

Capacity: 900,000
litres

Malt: lightly peated

Casks: ex-Bourbon

Water: lochs on
Knock Hill

Visiting
May be possible by
prior arrangement

Contacts
Tel: 01466 771223
E-mail:enquiries@inve-
rhouse.com

Date visited:

HISTORY

Knockdhu was constructed in 1893/94 by the Distillers Company Ltd (DCL), and has the distinction of being the only distillery built by the organisation itself, rather than acquired from existing operators.

DCL had a contract to supply malt whisky for the increasingly popular Haig blend, and required additional distilling capacity, hence the establishment of Knockdhu. The location was chosen partly due to locally available supplies of barley and peat, but also because the new owner of Knock estate, John Morrison, found several high quality springs on Knock Hill, and DCL got to hear about the discovery.

After operating for almost 90 years, Knockdhu was one of the casualties of DCL's drastic round of distillery closures in 1983, but five years later the plant was acquired by Inver House Distillers Ltd. They recommenced whisky-making in February 1989, and in 1993 began to market its single malt under the An Cnoc label, thus avoiding confusion with fellow Speysider Knockando.

POINTS OF SPECIAL INTEREST

Knockdhu was used to billet troops during the Second World War and from 1940 until 1945 it played host to a unit of the Indian Army, which even developed a halal slaughterhouse for the preparation of food.

LOCATION

Knock, by Huntly, Aberdeenshire AB54 7LJ
Some 9 miles from Huntly, the distillery is located off the B9022 mid way to Portsoy. Keith is 9 miles via the A95.

HIGHLAND (EASTERN)

MACDUFF

HISTORY

Sometimes known as Glen Deveron distillery, because of its location beside the River Deveron, Macduff dates from 1962. It was constructed by Macduff Distillers Ltd in order to provide malt spirit to satisfy the growing demand for blended Scotch whisky.

Production started in 1963, and the original pair of stills was increased to four during the next few years, with ownership passing to William Lawson Distillers Ltd in 1972.

In 1980 Lawson's was purchased by Martini Rossi, and the tun room and stillhouse at Macduff were rebuilt in 1990, when a fifth still was added. Only Macduff and Talisker operate with a pair of wash stills and three spirit stills.

1992 saw Martini Rossi taken over by the Bacardi Corporation, who transferred Macduff to its John Dewar & Sons Ltd Scotch whisky subsidiary.

POINTS OF SPECIAL INTEREST

Macduff is notable for pioneering a number of innovations in the Scotch whisky industry.

It was the first distillery to install a steel mash tun, the first to use steam coils to heat the stills, and the first to fit 'shell and tube' condensers instead of the customary worm tubs.

LOCATION

Banff, Banffshire AB45 3JT
23 miles from Keith and Huntly, the distillery is situated beside the A947 and off the A98 on the eastern side of the estuary that separates the towns of Banff and Macduff.

Meaning of name and pronunciation guide
'Son of Duff'

Owner
John Dewar & Sons Ltd (Bacardi Limited)

House style
Sweet, medium-bodied, a little Sherry and smoke, plus vanilla and spice.

Principal single malts
Glen Deveron 10-year-old.

Principal blends
William Lawson's.

Getting technical
Stills: two wash and three spirit

Capacity: 3.2m litres

Malt: unpeated

Casks: ex-bourbon and ex-Sherry

Water: The Gelly Burn

Visiting
May be possible by prior arrangement

Contacts
Tel: 01261 812612

Date visited:

SECTION INDEX ON PAGE 173

181

ALLT-À-BHAINNE

Meaning of name and pronunciation guide
'Burn of milk'
– alta-VAN-ya,'
although the owners
opt for 'alta-vain'

Owner
Chivas Bros Ltd
(Pernod Ricard)

House style
Light-bodied, sweet,
floral, and slightly
spicy. An aperitif
whisky.

Principal single malts
Not bottled by the
owners. Independent
bottlings occasionally
appear.

Principal blends
Chivas Regal, 100
Pipers, Passport.

Getting technical
Stills: two pairs

Capacity: 4.5m litres

Malt: unpeated

Casks: ex-Bourbon

Water: Rowantree and
Scurran Burns

Visiting
No visitor
tour/facilities

Contacts
Tel: 01542 783200

Date visited:

HISTORY

Allt-à-Bhainne was constructed in distinctively modern style during 1975 by Chivas Brothers, then a subsidiary of Seagram. The distillery was built, along with nearby Braeval, to provide malt whisky for Chivas' blends at a time when the Scotch whisky industry was enjoying a period of growth. In 1989 capacity at the distillery was doubled.

The distillery was designed to require minimal levels of staffing, and one man per shift is able to control all the processes of whisky making with the aid of a computer. Once produced, the spirit is tankered away to Chivas' vast bonding facility at Keith.

In 2002 Allt-à-Bhainne was one of four Speyside distilleries to be mothballed by Chivas Bros, in the wake of the acquisition of many Seagram assets by parent company Pernod Ricard.

However, Pernod subsequently made a strategic decision to try to take the world's number one deluxe Scotch whisky spot from Johnnie Walker Black Label with its Chivas Regal brand, and Allt-à-Bhainne was reopened in May 2005 to supply malt for the blend.

POINTS OF SPECIAL INTEREST

Although Allt-à-Bhainne was built several years after most distilleries stopped operating floor maltings, the architect incorporated four decorative 'pagodas' into his design to offer a touch of tradition.

LOCATION

Glenrinnes, Dufftown, Banffshire AB55 4DB
Five miles south-west of Dufftown, situated alongside the B9009 Dufftown to Glenlivet road.

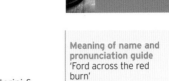

AUCHROISK

HISTORY

Constructed between 1972 and 1974 by Justerini & Brooks Ltd (part of International Distillers & Vintners) in order to supply malt whisky for the company's best-selling flagship J&B blend. However, after maturing for a number of years, the resultant spirit was found to be of a very high quality, and quantities were subsequently released as single malt as well as finding their way into the blending vats. Although singularly modern, Auchroisk was designed to fit well into the landscape. The white-harled buildings include such nice touches as circular towers in the Scottish vernacular style, although they serve no practical purpose.

Through a series of mergers and takeovers, Auchroisk became part of the newly-formed Diageo's portfolio of distilleries in 1997. The site comprises not only Auchroisk distillery but also a very large range of bonded warehouses, capable of accommodating 265,000 casks. Here spirit from a number of other Diageo distilleries on Speyside is stored as well as the Auchroisk make. Some malts are also vatted together on site before being tankered away for blending.

POINTS OF SPECIAL INTEREST

When the distillery's single malt first came on the market, it was branded as 'the Singleton' as it was felt that the distillery name would be too difficult to pronounce. This name was dropped in 2001.

LOCATION

Mulben, Banffshire AB55 6XS
Situated alongside the B9103, west of Mulben and the A95, midway between Rothes and Keith.

Meaning of name and pronunciation guide
'Ford across the red burn'
- Oth-RUSK

Owner
Diageo plc

House style
Medium-bodied, sweet, honeyed and fragrant, with slightly smoky and nutty notes.

Principal single malts
Auchroisk 10-year-old (Flora & Fauna Series).

Principal blends
J&B.

Getting technical
Stills: four pairs

Capacity: 3.8m litres

Malt: unpeated

Casks: ex-Bourbon, while spirit destined to be bottled as single malt is 'finished' in ex-Sherry

Water: Dorie's Well

Visiting
No visitor tour/facilities

Contacts
Tel: 01466 795650

Date visited:

AULTMORE

Meaning of name and pronunciation guide
'The big burn'
– olt-MORE

Owner
John Dewar & Sons
Ltd (Bacardi Limited)

House style
Medium-bodied,
comparatively sweet,
malty, fruity and floral.

Principal single malts
Aultmore 12-year-old.

Principal blends
Dewar's White Label.

Getting technical
Stills: two pairs

Capacity: 2.9m litres

Malt: unpeated

Casks: ex-Bourbon and
ex-Sherry

Water: Auchinderran
Burn

HISTORY

Aultmore was constructed in an area noted for illicit distilling by Speyside distillery entrepreneur Alexander Edward, coming on stream in 1897. The following year production was doubled, but the distillery was hit by the general slump that affected the Scotch whisky industry around the turn of the century, with over-production being a serious problem.

In 1923 Alexander Edward's Oban & Aultmore Glenlivet Distilleries Ltd was sold to John Dewar & Sons Ltd, being absorbed into the Distillers Company Ltd two years later.

The distillery was totally rebuilt in 1971, when capacity was doubled, and virtually all of the original Victorian structure has now disappeared.

In 1998 Aultmore returned to the ownership of John Dewar, when it was one of four distilleries sold to Dewar's parent company, Bacardi Limited, by Diageo.

POINTS OF SPECIAL INTEREST

Much of the pioneering work in creating high-protein animal feed from pot ale was carried out at Aultmore in the early 1950s. A plant was subsequently developed there in the mid-1960s to process pot ale and draff into 'dark grains'.

> ### LOCATION
> Keith, Banffshire AB55 6QY
> Standing close to the B9016 Keith to Buckie road,
> off the main A95, just west of Keith.

Visiting
May be possible by
prior arrangement

Contacts
Tel: 01542 881800

Date visited:

BALMENACH

HISTORY

Balmenach was one of the first distilleries to be granted a licence in the wake of the influential 1823 Excise Act, though distilling had been taking place at this remote location not far from the River Spey for some years previously. The distillery was in the hands of the founding McGregor family until the 1920s, when difficult economic conditions forced its sale. Both Whisky Galore author Sir Compton Mackenzie and diplomat and writer Sir Robert Bruce-Lockhart were members of the McGregor family.

Acquired by the Distillers Company Ltd (DCL) in 1925, Balmenach's make contributed to the Johnnie Walker and Crabbie's blends. Consequently, the capacity of the plant was increased in 1962 by the introduction of a third pair of stills, while its mash house was reconstructed six years later.

Balmenach was mothballed in June 1993, but Inver House Ltd purchased it from DCL in 1997, with distilling recommencing the following year. Inver House invested a considerable amount of money in restoring Balmenach to good working order, but the distillery remains very traditional in working practices.

It is one of just 14 working Scottish distilleries still using 'worm tubs' to condense its spirit, rather than more modern 'shell and tube' condensers.

POINTS OF SPECIAL INTEREST

Balmenach single malt enjoyed strong sales in the British colonies during the Victorian era, and it is recorded that in 1878 Queen Victoria herself drank Balmenach while staying at the Gairloch Hotel in the West Highlands.

LOCATION

Cromdale, Grantown-on-Spey, Morayshire PH26 3PF
Nestled away, one mile along an unclassified road, just south of the village of Cromdale, which is four miles north-east of Grantown-on-Spey and some 21 miles south-west of Aberlour, on the A95.

Meaning of name and pronunciation guide
'Middle farm'
– bal-MEN-ach

Owner
Inver House Distillers Ltd (Thai Beverage plc)

House style
Full-bodied, quite sweet, slightly peaty and herbal, aromatic, spicy and nutty.

Principal single malts
Balmenach 12-year-old ('Flora & Fauna' series).

Principal blends
Hankey Bannister, Inver House.

Getting technical
Stills: three pairs

Capacity: 2.7m litres

Malt: unpeated

Casks: ex-Bourbon

Water: Rasmudin Burn

Visiting
By prior arrangement

Contacts
Tel: 01479 872569
E-mail: enquiries@inver-house.com

Date visited:

SECTION INDEX ON PAGE 173

BENRIACH

HISTORY

BenRiach was established in 1898 by John Duff & Co, owners of the neighbouring, and much higher profile, Longmorn distillery. However, recession soon hit the Scotch whisky industry, which had expanded dramatically during the 1890s, and Benriach closed in 1900.

It remained silent until the next whisky boom of the 1960s, being substantially rebuilt before re-opening in 1965 in the new hands of The Glenlivet Distillers Ltd. Glenlivet Distillers later became part of the Seagram Company Ltd subsidiary Chivas Brothers, and capacity was doubled with the installation of a second pair of stills in 1985.

Benriach was one of the Chivas' assets acquired by Pernod Ricard in 2001, and the distillery was shut down the following October. However, in 2004 The BenRiach Distillery Company Ltd was formed by a consortium of businessmen, led by whisky industry veteran Billy Walker, and production recommenced later that year. The new regime has been responsible for a vigorous and varied programme of releases.

POINTS OF SPECIAL INTEREST

Despite the distillery being closed in 1900, its floor maltings continued to operate, helping to serve the needs of its larger neighbour, Lomgmorn. Chivas habitually made batches of heavily-peated whisky in Benriach from 1983. Some of this has now been marketed as Curiositas (10-year-old) and Authenticus (21-year-old). The maltings ceased to be used in 1999.

LOCATION

Longmorn, Elgin, Morayshire IV30 8SJ
Some three miles south of Elgin, located alongside the A941, Elgin to Craigellachie road.

Meaning of name and pronunciation guide
'Hill of the red deer' or 'Speckled mountain' – ben-REE-ach

Owner
The BenRiach - GlenDronach Distilleries Company Ltd

www.benriachdistillery.co.uk

House style
Light to medium-bodied, sweet, spicy and fruity, with cereal.

Principal single malts
Benriach 12, 16 and 20-year-olds, Curiositas, Authenticus and Heart of Speyside.

Principal blends
Chivas Regal, Queen Anne, 100 Pipers.

Getting technical
Stills: two pairs

Capacity: 2.8m litres

Malt: mostly unpeated

Casks: ex-Bourbon and ex-Sherry

Water: Burnside Spring

Visiting
May be possible by prior arrangement

Contacts
Tel: 01343 862888
E-mail: info@benriachdistillery.co.uk

Date visited:

PHOTOGRAPH ON PAGE 13

BENRINNES

HISTORY

The original Benrinnes distillery was established by Peter Mckenzie in 1826, being known as Lyne of Ruthrie. However, it was destroyed by a flood just three years later. In 1834 a replacement was established close by, and it was fire rather than flood that decimated this one, necessitating a major reconstruction programme in 1896. By this time the distillery was in the hands of the whisky entrepreneur Alexander Edward (see Aultmore, Dallas Dhu, Craigellachie and Oban), whose father had purchased it in 1864.

In 1922 Benrinnes was acquired by John Dewar & Sons Ltd, becoming part of Distillers Company Ltd when Dewar's was absorbed three years later. The present distillery dates from 1955/56 when the plant was totally rebuilt, with capacity being doubled from three to six stills in 1966. Until that time, it had worked as a combined farm and distillery.

Benrinnes is one of a comparatively small number of Scottish distilleries which continues to use worm tubs to condense the spirit. This tends to give a heavier and more 'meaty' character.

POINTS OF SPECIAL INTEREST

Since the distillery was rebuilt in the 1950s, Benrinnes has operated an unusual form of partial distillation, with the stills grouped into threes, rather than pairs. Usually, triple distillation gives a comparatively light spirit, but the use of small low wines/intermediate stills coupled with the effect of worm tubs means that Benrinnes is a much 'bigger' whisky than might be expected.

The distillery is 700 feet above sea level, on the edge of Ben Rinnes.

LOCATION

Aberlour, Banffshire AB38 9NN
Three miles south of Aberlour, along an unclassified road leading of the A95.

Meaning of name and pronunciation guide
'Promontory hill'
– ben RIN-is

Owner
Diageo plc

House style
Full-bodied, smoky yet also sweet, with malt and cereal notes.

Principal single malts
Benrinnes 15-year-old (Flora & Fauna Series).

Principal blends
Johnnie Walker, J&B.

Getting technical
Stills: two sets of three stills

Capacity: 2.5m litres

Malt: unpeated

Casks: ex-Bourbon and ex-Sherry

Water: Scurran and Rowantree Burns

Visiting
No visitor tour/facilities

Contacts
Tel: 01340 871215

Date visited:

SECTION INDEX ON PAGE 173

PHOTOGRAPH ON PAGE 70

(ROYAL) BRACKLA

HISTORY

Founded in 1812 by Captain William Fraser, Brackla distillery was situated in an area notorious for the production and consumption of illicit whisky. Fraser complained that although everyone in the area drank whisky, he could not sell so much as 100 gallons a year!

Brackla ended up in the ownership of DCL in 1943, and in 1970 production was doubled with the installation of a second pair of stills. However, production ceased in 1985, only to resume six years later.

In 1997 DCL's successor company United Distillers & Vintners invested £2 million in upgrading Brackla, but the following year it was one of four distilleries sold to John Dewar & Sons, who currently operate it.

POINTS OF SPECIAL INTEREST

Brackla is one of only three distilleries to have been allowed to use the 'royal' prefix or suffix, the others being Glenury and Lochnagar. Brackla was the first to be granted a Royal Warrant, with King William IV bestowing the honour in 1834 for the brand named 'The King's Own Whisky.'

Brackla also has the distinction of being one of the malts chosen by Andrew Usher for his pioneering work in creating blended whiskies during the 1860s.

> **LOCATION**
> Cawdor, Nairn, Inverness-shire IV12 5QY
> Situated off the B9090, four miles south of Nairn.

Meaning of name and pronunciation guide
'Speckled hillslope' or 'badgers' sett'
– BRACK-la

Owner
John Dewar & Sons Ltd (Bacardi Ltd)

House style
Medium-bodied, sweet, floral and fruity, with a hint of smoke.

Principal single malts
Royal Brackla 10-year-old.

Principal blends
Dewar's White Label.

Getting technical
Stills: two pairs

Capacity 3.7m litres

Malt: unpeated

Cask: ex-Bourbon plus some ex-Sherry casks

Water: Cursack Springs

Visiting
May be possible by prior arrangement

Contacts
Tel: 01667 402002

Date visited:

BRAEVAL

HISTORY

Braeval was constructed in 1972/73 by the Canadian distilling giant Seagram's Chivas Brothers Ltd subsidiary to supply bulk malt for the Chivas Regal brand. Its style is uncompromisingly modern, yet not unattractive, rather like its 'sister' distillery of Allt-à-Bhainne, which was built two years later.

Until 1994 the distillery was known as Braes of Glenlivet, but in that year the name was changed to Braeval, so as not to dilute the exclusivity and cache of the Glenlivet name.

In 1975 a further pair of stills was added to the original three, and in 1978 another individual still was installed, taking the total to six.

Braeval was mothballed in October 2002 by new owners Pernod Ricard, who had acquired it as part of Chivas Brothers' assets the previous year. However, increasing global demand for Chivas Regal saw Braeval come back on stream in July 2008.

POINTS OF SPECIAL INTEREST

Braeval is one of just three distilleries within the actual glen of the River Livet (along with The Glenlivet and Tamanvulin). Despite this, no fewer than 36 distilleries in total have at one time or another added the 'Glenlivet' suffix to their own names.

Braeval is the highest working distillery in Scotland.

LOCATION

Chapeltown, Ballindalloch, Banffshire AB37 9JS
Seven miles north-east of Tomintoul or 17 miles south of Dufftown, the distillery is located in the hamlet of Chapeltown, three miles from the B9008.

Meaning of name and pronunciation guide
'Mountain slope'
- bray-VARL

Owner
Chivas Bros Ltd
(Pernod Ricard)

House style
Quite sweet, grassy and fruity, with spice and a hint of smoke.

Principal single malts
Deerstalker 10 and 15-year-old (independent bottlings).

Principal blends
Chivas Regal.

Getting technical
Stills: two pairs

Capacity: 4m litres

Malt: unpeated

Casks: ex-Bourbon

Water: Preenie Well

Visiting
No visitor tour/facilities

Contacts
Tel: 01542 783042

Date visited:

SECTION INDEX ON PAGE 173

CRAIGELLACHIE

HISTORY

Constructed in 1891, Craigellachie was designed by Charles Doig and was part-owned by Peter Mackie - of White Horse fame - and Speyside distillery entrepreneur Alexander Edward. Production did not commence until 1898.

In 1916, Mackie & Co (Distillers) Ltd took complete control of Craigellachie, and the firm - now renamed White Horse Distillers Ltd - was acquired by the Distillers Company Ltd in 1927.

Much of the original distillery was demolished in 1964/65, when the present buildings were created and the number of stills was doubled to four, however the distinctive pagoda-head of the maltings survives.

In 1998 Craigellachie was one of four distilleries sold to Dewar's parent company, Bacardi Limited, by Diageo, and the prominent White Horse logo which had adorned the distillery for many years was finally removed.

POINTS OF SPECIAL INTEREST

The distillery is located close to the Craigellachie Hotel, renowned for its Quaich Bar, which boasts a range of more than 600 whiskies.

LOCATION

Hill St, Craigellachie, Banffshire AB38 9ST
The distillery stands beside the A941
Craigellachie to Dufftown road, in Craigellachie village.

Meaning of name and pronunciation guide
'Rock of the stony place'
- Craig-ELL-ach-ee

Owner
John Dewar & Sons Ltd (Bacardi Ltd)

House style
Medium-bodied, floral, sweet and slightly smoky, with nuts and spice.

Principal single malts
Craigellachie 14-year-old.

Principal blends
Dewar's White Label and Special Reserve.

Getting technical
Stills: two pairs

Capacity: 3.5m litres

Malt: lightly peated

Casks: ex-Bourbon plus some ex-Sherry

Water: springs on Little Conval

Visiting
May be possible by prior arrangement

Contacts
Tel: 01340 872971

Date visited:

DAILUAINE

HISTORY

Dailuaine was established by William Mackenzie in 1852, and in 1884 the distillery was rebuilt and substantially enlarged, making it one of the largest in the north of Scotland. Five years later the Dailuaine maltings were fitted with the first Doig Ventilator - better known as the 'pagoda' roof - by Elgin architect Charles Doig.

In 1898 Dailuaine-Talisker Distilleries Ltd was formed, bringing together not only Dailuaine and the famous Isle of Skye distillery, but also the North of Scotland distillery in Aberdeen. By 1916 the company was acquired by James Buchanan & Co, John Dewar & Sons and John Walker & Sons, but the following year a major fire seriously damaged the distillery, destroying Doig's original pagoda.

Dailuaine did not reopen until 1920, and five years later it became part of the Distillers Company Ltd. In 1959/60 the number of stills was increased from four to six, Saladin maltings were installed, and a dark grains plant was constructed. Today Dailuaine's effluent plant treats waste from a total of eight distilleries in the area.

POINTS OF SPECIAL INTEREST

For many years, Dailuaine was one of a large number of distilleries that used the railway for much of its transport requirements. The small, 'puggie' engine which moved wagons between the main Strathspey Railway line and the distillery until 1967 is now on display at Aberfeldy distillery.

LOCATION

Carron, Aberlour, Banffshire AB38 7RE
Situated quarter of a mile along an unclassified road off the A95, three miles south-west of Aberlour.

Meaning of name and pronunciation guide
'The green valley'
– dall-YEW-in

Owner
Diageo plc

House style
Full bodied, aromatic, with Sherry, malt, fruits and spice.

Principal single malts
Dailuaine 16-year-old (Flora & Fauna series).

Principal blends
Johnnie Walker.

Getting technical
Stills: three pairs

Capacity: 2.9m litres

Malt: unpeated

Casks: ex-Bourbon, while spirit destined to be bottled as single malt is 'finished' in ex-Sherry

Water: Bailliemullich Burn

Visiting
No visitor tour/facilities

Contacts
Tel: 01340 810361

Date visited:

DUFFTOWN

HISTORY

'Rome was built on seven hills, Dufftown was built on seven stills,' according to the old rhyme. Dufftown distillery was the sixth of them, and the fourth to become operational during the great whisky boom of the 1890s.

It was converted from a meal mill in 1895/96 by an enterprising group of businessmen, including the mill owner, John Symon. However, within a year they had sold the fledgling distillery to P Mackenzie & Co, already owners of Blair Athol distillery in Pitlochry.

In 1933 the Perth blending firm of Arthur Bell & Sons acquired Mackenzie & Co for £56,000, and ran Dufftown until the company was taken over by Guinness in 1985, ultimately becoming part of Diageo in 1997. The distillery has been enlarged on several occasions, with the number of stills rising from its original pair to a total of six.

POINTS OF SPECIAL INTEREST

Until the construction of Roseisle distillery in 2009, Dufftown had the greatest capacity of any malt whisky distillery in Diageo's portfolio.

> ### LOCATION
>
> Dufftown, Keith, Banffshire AB55 4BR
> The distillery is to be found on Church Street, off Fife Street, close to the centre of Dufftown. Eighteen miles south of Elgin.

Meaning of name and pronunciation guide
Named after James Duff, 4th Earl of Fife, who built the town from 1817 onwards - 'DUFF-ton'

Owner
Diageo plc

House style
Aromatic, quite light, sweet, malty and floral.

Principal single malts
Dufftown 15-year-old (Flora & Fauna series), Singleton of Dufftown.

Principal blends
Bell's.

Getting technical
Stills: three pairs

Capacity: 5.6m litres

Malt: unpeated

Casks: ex-Bourbon and ex-Sherry

Water: Jock's Well

Visiting
No visitor tour/facilities

Contacts
Tel: 01340 822960

Date visited:

GLENALLACHIE

HISTORY

Glenallachie was established in 1967/68 by the Scottish & Newcastle Breweries subsidiary Mackinlay-McPherson Ltd, and was constructed principally to supply malt whisky for the popular Mackinlay blend.

In 1985, Glenallachie and Jura distilleries were sold to Invergordon Distillers Group, and Glenallachie fell silent two years later. In 1989 Pernod Ricard acquired Glenallachie through its Campbell Distillers Ltd subsidiary and capacity was doubled with the introduction of a second pair of stills. Campbell Distillers already owned nearby Aberlour distillery.

Glenallachie tends to be underrated as a single malt, and has not been regularly bottled by its proprietors for some years.

POINTS OF SPECIAL INTEREST

Glenallachie was the final distillery to be fully designed by William Delmé-Evans, sometimes described as a latter day Charles Doig, due to his contribution to the post-Second World War Scotch whisky industry boom.

LOCATION

Near Aberlour, Banffshire AB38 9LR
Along an unclassified road off the A95. The distillery is in the hamlet of Glenallachie, just over a mile south-west of Aberlour.

Meaning of name and pronunciation guide
'Glen of the rocky place'
– glen-ALLACH-ee

Owner
Chivas Bros Ltd
(Pernod Ricard)

House style
Light bodied, sweet and floral, with fresh fruits and a sweet, honeyed finish.

Principal single malts
Glenallachie 16-year-old Cask Strength Edition (matured in first fill Oloroso Sherry casks).

Principal blends
Clan Campbell.

Getting technical
Stills: two pairs

Capacity: 3m litres

Malt: unpeated

Casks: ex-Bourbon

Water: springs on Ben Rinnes

Visiting
No visitor tour/facilities

Contacts
Tel: 01340 810361

Date visited:

GLENBURGIE

Meaning of name and pronunciation guide
'Glen of the fort'
– glen-BURGY

Owner
Chivas Bros Ltd
(Pernod Ricard)

House style
Sweet, fragrant,
medium-bodied, with
toffee and a final note
of liquorice.

Principal single malts
Glenburgie 15-year-
old.

Principal blends
Ballantine's.

Getting technical
Stills: three pairs

Capacity: 4.2m litres

Malt: unpeated

Casks: ex-Bourbon

Water: springs on
Burgie Hill

Visiting
No visitor
tour/facilities

Contacts
Tel: 01343 554120

Date visited:

HISTORY

Glenburgie was probably established in 1810 by William
Paul as Kilnflat distillery, although official records of
whisky production do not appear until 1829. The
distillery was silent between 1870 and 1878, reopening
under the name Glenburgie-Glenlivet.

The Canadian distilling company Hiram Walker & Sons
(Scotland) Ltd acquired 60 per cent of Glenburgie's
owners James & George Stodart Ltd in 1930, but the
distillery was not active between 1927 and 1935. The
following year Hiram Walker gained control of the rest of
Stodart Ltd and production at Glenburgie recommenced.

Hiram Walker's main Scottish blend was Ballantine's,
and Glenburgie has been a principal constituent of that
blend right up to the present day. In 1958 two Lomond
stills were installed at Glenburgie, turning out a second
single malt named Glencraig which was principally used
for blending purposes. The Lomond stills were removed
in 1981.

1987 saw Hiram Walker purchased by Allied Lyons
plc, and in 2004 Allied Domecq, as the company had
become, demolished the existing distillery and spent
£4.3 million creating a new, state-of-the-art plant on the
site. Remarkably, just five months of production were
lost during the reconstruction programme.

In 2005 Chivas Bros took control of Glenburgie and
the Ballantine's brand as part of its acquisition of a large
part of Allied's assets. Another pair of stills was installed
in May 2006 to further boost capacity.

POINTS OF SPECIAL INTEREST

Since its reconstruction and subsequent expansion,
Glenburgie is now the third largest distillery in Chivas'
portfolio, with only The Glenlivet and Miltonduff having
greater capacity.

LOCATION

Forres, Morayshire IV36 2QY
Situated off the A96 Inverness to Aberdeen road,
five miles east of Forres or some eight miles west
of Elgin.

GLENDULLAN

HISTORY

The seventh distillery to be built in Dufftown, Glendullan came on stream in 1897, and was owned by the Aberdeen-based whisky blenders William Williams & Sons. It managed to survive the dramatic recession that hit the whisky industry almost as soon as the plant was in operation, but like so many other distilleries during the difficult inter-year wars, it was purchased in 1926 by the Distillers Company Ltd.

In 1962 major reconstruction work was undertaken on Glendullan, and a decade later a completely new distillery was built alongside the old one. Both ran simultaneously until 'Old' Glendullan was closed in 1985. Part of the silent distillery is now used by Diageo as its Glendullan Engineering Centre.

Despite having quite different stills, the two Glendullans produced surprisingly similar style of spirit when running in tandem. Today, Glendullan is one of Diageo's principal blending malts, and was a key component of the short-lived Cardhu Pure Malt venture (see Cardhu).

POINTS OF SPECIAL INTEREST

After Roseisle, Auchroisk and nearby Dufftown, Glendullan is the fourth largest of Diageo's operating malt whisky distilleries. The malt was one of King Edward VII's favourite whiskies.

LOCATION

Dufftown, Keith, Banffshire AB55 4DJ
Situated alongside Low Road and the B9014 on the eastern side of Dufftown.

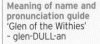

Meaning of name and pronunciation guide
'Glen of the Withies'
– glen-DULL-an

Owner
Diageo plc

House style
Medium-bodied, fruity, malty, quite dry.

Principal single malts
Glendullan 12-year-old, (Flora & Fauna Series), Singleton of Glendullan.

Principal blends
Bell's, Dewar's, Johnnie Walker, Old Parr.

Getting technical
Stills: three pairs

Capacity: 3.4m litres

Malt: unpeated

Casks: ex-Bourbon and ex-Sherry

Water: Goatswell Spring

Visiting
No visitor tour/facilities

Contacts
Tel: 01340 822303

Date visited:

SECTION INDEX ON PAGE 173

GLEN ELGIN

HISTORY

Construction of Glen Elgin began in 1898 for the banker James Carle and former Glenfarclas manager William Simpson, who invested £13,000 in the project. Unfortunately, their timing could hardly have been worse, since the distillery began production in May 1900, just as the whisky industry collapsed into recession. Glen Elgin operated for a mere five months before closing.

It was subsequently sold at auction to the Glen Elgin-Glenlivet Distillery Co Ltd but remained silent until 1904, only then to operate for a very short period. In 1907 it was acquired by the Glasgow blender JJ Blanche & Co but was ultimately purchased in 1930 by the Distillers Company Ltd.

In 1964, still capacity was increased from two to six, and the mash house, tun room and still house were all rebuilt. Glen Elgin is one a small number of Scottish distilleries which continues to operate with worm tubs rather than modern condensers, giving rise to the whisky's characteristic floral note.

Glen Elgin became one of Diageo's expanded range of Classic Malts in 2005, having previously featured in the company's Flora & Fauna and Hidden Malts series.

POINTS OF SPECIAL INTEREST

At the time of Glen Elgin's construction, architect Charles Doig predicted that no new distillery would be built on Speyside for half a century, and his words were to be remarkably prophetic, as the next to be created was Glen Keith in 1957/58.

LOCATION

Longmorn, Elgin, Morayshire IV30 8SL
Four miles south of Elgin or 11 miles north of Aberlour, the distillery stands off the A941, in the village of Fogwatt.

Meaning of name and pronunciation guide
'Glen of little Ireland'
– glen-ELG-in

Owner
Diageo plc

House style
Medium bodied, sweet, malty and notably floral, with fruit and spice notes.

Principal single malts
Glen Elgin 12-year-old.

Principal blends
Bell's, White Horse.

Getting technical
Stills: three pairs

Capacity: 1.7m litres

Malt: unpeated

Casks: ex-Bourbon and ex-Sherry

Water: springs below Millbuies Loch

Visiting
May be possible by prior arrangement

Contacts
Tel: 01343 860212

Date visited:

GLENLOSSIE

HISTORY

Glenlossie was founded in 1876 by local innkeeper and former GlenDronach distillery manager John Duff and two partners. The new plant was built on a slope in order to harness gravity for a number of production processes, and a waterwheel at the distillery dam meant that Glenlossie did not have to rely on steam power in order to operate.

The distillery was largely rebuilt in 1896, and being located close to the railway line from Perth to Elgin, a dedicated siding was created. In 1919 the Distillers Company Ltd took over Glenlossie, and a decade later a serious fire caused considerable damage. One of the fire engines used to fight the blaze, dating back to the 1860s, is on display at the distillery.

As demand for Scotch whisky grew in the decades following the Second World War, the number of stills at Glenlossie was increased from four to six in 1962, and in 1971 a new distillery, called Mannochmore, was constructed beside Glenlossie, largely to provide malt for DCL's Haig blends. Although elusive as a single malt, Glenlossie has long been prized by blenders as one of the top dozen blending whiskies.

POINTS OF SPECIAL INTEREST

Between 1968 and 1971 a 'dark grains' plant was installed to process the by-products of distillation into cattle feed. It is now able to process 2.6 million tonnes of draff and 8 million litres of pot ale per week, serving around a dozen local distilleries.

LOCATION

Glenlossie Rd, Thornshill, Elgin, Morayshire
IV30 8SS
Located in Thornshill along minor unclassified roads, west of the A941, some three miles south of Elgin or 12 miles north of Aberlour.

Meaning of name and pronunciation guide
'Glen of the Lossie'
– glen-LOSSY

Owner
Diageo plc

House style
Medium-bodied, elegant, floral, sweet, malty, spicy and nutty.

Principal single malts
Glenlossie 10-year-old (Flora & Fauna bottling).

Principal blends
Haig, Haig Dimple.

Getting technical
Stills: three pairs

Capacity: 1.8m litres

Malt: unpeated

Casks: ex-Bourbon

Water: Bardon Burn

Visiting
May be possible by prior arrangement

Contacts
Tel: 01343 862000

Date visited:

SECTION INDEX ON PAGE 173

PHOTOGRAPH ON PAGE 206

GLENROTHES

Meaning of name and pronunciation guide
'The glen of the ring-fort'
– glen-ROTH-is

Owner
The Edrington Group

www.glenrotheswhisky.com

House style
Medium-bodied, fragrant, sweet, spicy, fruity. A dram which comes in many guises thanks to a vigorous 'vintage release' programme.

Principal single malts
Glenrothes Select Reserve plus various vintages.

Principal blends
Cutty Sark, The Famous Grouse.

Getting technical
Stills: five pairs

Capacity: 5.6m litres

Malt: lightly peated

Casks: ex-Bourbon and ex-Sherry

Water: Ardcanny Spring

Visiting
May be possible by prior arrangement

Contacts
Tel: 01340 872300

Date visited:

HISTORY

In 1878 Macallan distillery leaseholder James Stuart began to plan a new distillery in Rothes, in company with local bankers Robert Dick and William Grant, plus Elgin solicitor John Cruikshank. However, due to financial problems encountered by Stuart, the three other partners formed William Grant & Co, leaving Stuart to concentrate on Macallan.

The first spirit flowed from the Glenrothes stills in December 1879, but the early years of its operation were precarious, and economic stability only arrived in 1887, when William Grant & Co amalgamated with the Islay Distillery Company. The new concern was called Highland Distilleries, which today, as Highland Distillers, is part of the Edrington Group.

Glenrothes suffered a serious fire in December 1897, but capacity was doubled during reconstruction. In 1963 an additional pair of stills was installed, giving a total of six, and a further two pairs were added in 1980, when a major programme of modernisation was undertaken.

Glenrothes is one of only three Speyside malts to be credited by blenders as 'Top Class,' and it has only become widely available as a single malt during the past decade. In 2010, ownership of the Glenrothes brand, though not the actual distillery, passed to Berry Bros & Rudd.

POINTS OF SPECIAL INTEREST

After a new stillhouse was constructed in 1980 the apparition of Biawa Makalanga (see Glen Grant) began to appear to distillery workers. However, the ghost of Biawa was never seen again after a visit from the celebrated psychic investigator Professor Cedric Wilson to his grave in the neighbouring cemetery.

LOCATION

Burnside Street, Rothes, Morayshire AB38 7AA
Five miles north of Aberlour, located off the A941 in Rothes, just over a small bridge and beside the town cemetery.

PHOTOGRAPH ON PAGE 15

GLEN SPEY

HISTORY

Glen Spey was the second distillery (after Glen Grant) to be established in Rothes, and it was developed by James Stuart & Co in 1878 alongside Stuart's oatmeal mill, originally trading as Mill of Rothes. Stuart was a corn merchant and licensee of Macallan from 1868, as well as taking an interest in the planning of Glenrothes distillery.

When the London firm of W & A Gilbey Ltd acquired Glen Spey from Stuart for £11,000 in 1887, they became the first English company to purchase a Scotch whisky distillery. In 1962, Gilbey combined with United Wine Traders (owners of the J&B blended whisky brand) to form International Distillers & Vintners (IDV), and eight years later production capacity at Glen Spey was doubled by the installation of a second pair of stills.

In 1972, IDV was acquired by the brewers Watney Mann, who were themselves taken over by Grand Metropolitan Hotels the same year. In 1997 'Grand Met' and Guinness merged to form Diageo, the present owners of Glen Spey.

POINTS OF SPECIAL INTEREST

In common with its near neighbour of Glenrothes, Glen Spey also has a resident ghost. In this case the distillery is said to be haunted by a former soldier, who was electrocuted while billeted there during the Second World War.

LOCATION

Rothes, Aberlour, Banffshire AB38 7AY
The distillery stands back from the main street, the A941, in the centre of Rothes, five miles north of Aberlour.

Meaning of name and pronunciation guide
'The glen of the hawthorn'
– glen-SPEY

Owner
Diageo plc

House style
Light-bodied, floral, sweet and malty, with a hint of spice.

Principal single malts
Glen spey 12-year-old (Flora & Fauna series).

Principal blends
J&B, Spey Royal.

Getting technical
Stills: two pairs

Capacity: 1.5m litres

Malt: unpeated

Casks: ex-Bourbon

Water: Doonie Burn

Visiting
No visitor tour/facilities

Contacts
Tel: 01340 832000

Date visited:

SECTION INDEX ON PAGE 173

GLENTAUCHERS

HISTORY

In 1897 James Buchanan and Co Ltd and the Glasgow whisky merchants WP Lowrie & Co Ltd formed Glentauchers Distillery Co to build Glentauchers, which came on stream in June the following year. The site was chosen partly for the excellent water supply, but also because of its proximity to the nearby railway line. In 1906 Buchanan took total control of Glentauchers and also acquired 80% of WP Lowrie, which had been experiencing financial difficulties for several years.

Between 1923 and 1925 a new spirit store was built to the design of Charles Doig, supervisor of the original construction project, when alterations to the maltings and mash house were also undertaken. James Buchanan & Co Ltd became part of the Distillers Company Ltd in 1925, operating under the auspices of DCL's Scottish Malt Distillers subsidiary from 1930.

The number of stills was increased from two to six during 1965/66, when the still house, mash house and tun room were reconstructed in their present form. Glentauchers was silent from 1985 to 1989, when it was purchased by Allied Distillers, and production recommenced three years later. The distillery became part of Chivas Brothers following that company's acquisition of Allied Domecq assets in 2005.

Glentauchers remains largely non-automated, and is therefore used to train Chivas' staff in the hands-on practicalities of distilling before they are assigned to sites which boast greater degrees of automation.

POINTS OF SPECIAL INTEREST

James Buchanan, co-founder of Glentauchers, was one of the pioneers of blended Scotch whisky from the 1880s, marketing his 'Buchanan Blend' – formulated by WP Lowrie - in an eye-catching black bottle with a white label. He later registered it as the Black & White brand and it remains a popular seller for Diageo in a number of key export markets.

Meaning of name and pronunciation guide
Derivation unclear, but 'tocher' is Gaelic for dowry or treasure chest – glen-TOCK-ers

Owner
Chivas Bros Ltd
(Pernod Ricard)

House style
Light-bodied, fragrant, floral and fruity, with malt and nuts.

Principal single malts
Glentauchers 15-year-old.

Principal blends
Ballantines.

Getting technical
Stills: three pairs

Capacity: 3.5m litres

Malt: unpeated

Casks: ex-Bourbon

Water: The Rosarie Burn

Visiting
May be possible by prior arrangement

Contacts
Tel: 01542 860272

Date visited:

LOCATION

Mulben, Keith, Banffshire AB55 6YL
Four miles west of Keith, the distillery is situated by the A95, Keith to Aberlour road.

INCHGOWER

HISTORY

Inchgower distillery was founded in 1871 by Alexander Wilson & Co, in a location close to the fishing port of Buckie and once renowned for illicit distilling. When fitting out Inchgower, Wilson used equipment from Tochineal distillery, which the firm had also operated and which was located near Cullen, some eight miles east of Buckie.

Inchgower remained in the hands of Wilson & Co until the company went bankrupt in 1936, when the site was purchased by Buckie Town Council for £1,000. Not only did the council safeguard jobs at Inchgower, but it also profited greatly by its investment, selling the distillery on to Arthur Bell & Sons Ltd for a reputed £4,000 just two years later.

At the height of the mid-20th century Scotch whisky boom, Inchgower's capacity was doubled by the installation of a second pair of stills, though structurally the distillery remains largely original.

When Guinness acquired Arthur Bell & Sons in 1985, Inchgower was one of three malt distilleries (along with Blair Athol and Dufftown) included in the deal. Today it operates as part of the Diageo empire.

POINTS OF SPECIAL INTEREST

The only Scottish distillery ever to be owned by a town council!

LOCATION

Buckie, Banffshire AB56 5AB
Some 11 miles north of Keith, the distillery stands beside the A98 Fochabers to Fraserburgh road, half a mile south of Buckie.

Meaning of name and pronunciation guide
'Goat's meadow'
- inch-GOW-er

Owner
Diageo plc

House style
Comparatively sweet, with spice, malt and oak notes, drying in a salty finish.

Principal single malts
Inchgower 14-year-old (Flora & Fauna series).

Principal blends
Bell's.

Getting technical
Stills: two pairs

Capacity: 2.8m litres

Malt: unpeated

Casks: ex-Bourbon

Water: springs in the Menduff Hills

Visiting
No visitor tour/facilities

Contacts
Tel: 01542 836700

Date visited:

SECTION INDEX ON PAGE 173

INCHGOWER DISTILLERY

KININVIE

Meaning of name and pronunciation guide
'The end of the fair plain'
- kin-IN-vie

Owner
William Grant & Sons Ltd

House style
Floral. Sweeter, fruitier and heavier in body than Balvenie.

Principal single malts
Limited edition bottling in 2006 as 'Hazelwood 105,' and 500 bottles issued in 2008 to celebrate the opening of Heathrow's Terminal 5.

Principal blends
William Grant's Family Reserve.

Getting technical
Stills: three wash & six spirit

Capacity: 4.4m litres

Malt: unpeated

Casks: ex-Bourbon and ex-Sherry

Water: Robbie Dhu Spring

Visiting
No visitor tour/facilities

Contacts
Tel: 01340 820373
E-mail: info@wgrant.com

Date visited:

HISTORY

Officially opened on 18th July 1990 by Mrs Janet Roberts, the grand-daughter of William Grant, Kininvie was designed principally to produce malt whisky for use in Grant's range of blends and for reciprocal trading within the Scotch whisky industry. Kininvie is also one of the key components of William Grant's blended malt Monkey Shoulder. The distillery takes its name from the Kininvie Estate which borders the Balvenie grounds.

Essentially, Kininvie is just a stillhouse, with its nine Oregon pine washbacks being located in a purpose-built extension to Balvenie. Initially, there were two wash and four spirit stills, but in 1992 one new wash and two new spirit stills were added. The spirit stills with their bulbous 'waists' are not dissimilar to the originals purchased by William Grant from Cardow (Cardhu) and installed at Glenfiddich back in 1886/87.

POINTS OF SPECIAL INTEREST

Kininvie was the ninth distillery to be established in Dufftown, and is one of six currently in production.

When sold for blending purposes outwith the company, Kininvie is vatted with one per cent Balvenie and called 'Aldunie' to prevent independent bottlers from releasing it as Kininvie single malt.

> ### LOCATION
>
> Dufftown, Banffshire AB55 4BB
> On the northern outskirts of Dufftown, located behind Balvenie Distillery, just off the A941 to Craigellachie.

KNOCKANDO

HISTORY

Knockando was established in 1898/99 on a wooded bank of the River Spey for Elgin spirits broker John Thompson to the design of Elgin architect Charles Doig. It operated initially as the Knockando-Glenlivet Distillery Company. Knockando began to produce spirit in May 1899, just before the end of the great Victorian whisky 'boom,' which spawned so many new distilleries, especially on Speyside.

Knockando was only active for some 10 months before being forced to close, and in 1904 it was purchased by London-based gin specialist W&A Gilbey Ltd for just £3,500.

Distilling re-commenced in October 1904, and Gilbey continued to operate the distillery until 1962, when the company merged with United Wine Traders to form International Distillers & Vintners (IDV). In 1969 the distillery's capacity was doubled by the installation of a second pair of stills, and three years later IDV was acquired by the brewer Watney Mann, which in turn became part of Grand Metropolitan Ltd. 1997 saw 'Grand Met' merge with Guinness to form Diageo, and Knockando remains in the Diageo portfolio today.

POINTS OF SPECIAL INTEREST

From the 1970s onwards, Knockando has been bottled for most markets according to vintage, rather than carrying a specific age statement, though a 12-year-old expression is also now widely available.
The distillery's former railway station has been redeveloped and is now used by Diageo as a trade centre.

LOCATION

Knockando, Morayshire AB38 7RT
9 miles from Aberlour, the distillery is situated at the end of a steep unclassified road off the B9102 Grantown-on-Spey to Craigellachie road.

Meaning of name and pronunciation guide
'Small black hill'
– knock-AN-do

Owner
Diageo plc

House style
Medium-bodied, sweet, floral, spicy and nutty, with berries and a hint of smoke.

Principal single malts
Knockando 12-year-old.

Principal blends
J&B Rare.

Getting technical
Stills: two pairs

Capacity: 1.3m litres

Malt: lightly peated

Casks: ex-Bourbon, while some spirit destined as single malt is matured in ex-Sherry

Water: Cardnach Spring

Visiting
No visitor tour/facilities

Contacts
Tel: 01479 874660

Date visited:

SECTION INDEX ON PAGE 173

LINKWOOD

Meaning of name and pronunciation guide
Named after Linkwood House, on the estate where the distillery was built
- LINK-wood

Owner
Diageo plc

House style
Sweet, fragrant, fruity and floral, with gentle malt and spice.

Principal single malts
Linkwood 12-year-old (Flora & Fauna series).

Principal blends
Bell's, Haig, White Horse.

Getting technical
Stills: three pairs

Capacity: 3.5m litres

Malt: unpeated

Casks: ex-Bourbon

Water: springs near Millbuies Loch

Visiting
May be possible by prior arrangement

Contacts
Tel: 01343 547004

Date visited:

HISTORY

Linkwood was established in 1821 by Peter Brown, factor for the Seafield Estates, with the first spirit flowing four years later. After Brown's death in 1868, his son, William, inherited the distillery, proceeding to rebuilt it in 1872/74.

1933 saw Linkwood join so many other once-independent distilleries in the Scottish Malt Distillers' fold, a subsidiary of the Distillers Company Ltd, and forerunner of current owner Diageo plc.

During the whisky 'boom' of the 1960s and '70s Linkwood was significantly expanded, with major refurbishment taking place in 1962. This was followed nine years later by a rebuilding programme that created a new stillhouse, kitted out with four stills.

This was known as 'Linkwood B' while the old, two-still unit was 'Linkwood A,' and the former closed in 1985, subsequently being used on occasions to produce experimental batches of spirit and to augment overall output.

POINTS OF SPECIAL INTEREST

Distillery manager Roderick Mackenzie (1946-63) was a firm believer in what would now be called 'micro-climate,' and refused to allow even a spider's web to be removed from his distillery in case it somehow altered the character of the spirit.

> ### LOCATION
>
> Linkwood Road, Elgin, Morayshire IV30 8RD
> On the south-eastern edge of Elgin, the distillery is best accessed via the A941, Reiket Lane, then Linkwood Road.

LONGMORN

HISTORY

Longmorn dates from the 1890s 'whisky boom,' when so many of the Speyside distilleries that we see today were constructed.

It was developed by John Duff, who had built Glenlossie distillery, in association with George Thomson and Charles Shirres, and initially traded as the Longmorn-Glenlivet Distillery Company. The first spirit flowed in December 1894, and four years later, the neighbouring distillery of Benriach was also constructed by Duff, who was now the sole owner.

When 'boom' turned to 'bust' Duff was forced to sell his shares in the distillery to James Grant. Private ownership of Longmorn continued until 1970, when The Glenlivet Distillers Ltd was formed.

In 1978 Seagram of Canada acquired The Glenlivet Distillers Ltd, and in 2001 Longmorn was one of the former Seagram assets purchased by Pernod Ricard subsidiary Chivas Bros.

During the 1970s, the number of stills was progressively increased to eight in order to cope with high demand for its whisky for blending purposes.

POINTS OF SPECIAL INTEREST

Until the comparatively late date of 1994, the distillery's wash stills continued to be direct-fired, using coal, while the spirit stills, located in a separate still house, were heated by steam.

LOCATION

Lithe Lochan, Elgin, Morayshire IV30 8SJ
Some three miles south of Elgin or 11 miles north of Aberlour, the distillery is situated along a single track road, off the A941, just north of Fogwatt village.

Meaning of name and pronunciation guide
'Place of the Holy Man'
- long-MORN

Owner
Chivas Bros Ltd
(Pernod Ricard)

House style
Floral, fruity, quite full-bodied and complex, with malt and nuts.

Principal single malts
Longmorn 16-year-old.

Principal blends
Chivas Regal, Queen Anne, Something Special.

Getting technical
Stills: four pairs

Capacity: 3.5m litres

Malt: unpeated

Casks: ex-Bourbon and ex-Sherry

Water: local springs

Visiting
No regular visitor tour/facilities, but sometimes open to the public for short, seasonal, periods

Contacts
Tel: 01343 554120

Date visited:

SECTION INDEX ON PAGE 173

MANNOCHMORE

Meaning of name and pronunciation guide
'Big Mannoch (hill)'
- man-och-MORE

Owner
Diageo plc

House style
Quite light-bodied, floral and fruity, with malt and nutty notes, plus a hint of mint.

Principal single malts
Mannochmore 12-year-old (Flora & Fauna series).

Principal blends
Haig.

Getting technical
Stills: three pairs

Capacity: 2.4m litres

Malt: lightly peated

Casks: ex-Bourbon

Water: Loch Dhu

Visiting
No visitor tour/facilitiest

Contacts
Tel: 01343 862000

Date visited:

HISTORY

Mannochmore was established in 1971 by the Distillers Company Ltd to help satisfy the growing international thirst for blended Scotch whisky.

Built alongside the firm's Glenlossie distillery which was almost a century older, it was licensed to John Haig & Co Ltd. Much of the spirit produced was destined for the Haig blend.

Mannochmore shares warehousing with Glenlossie, and both utilise the vast on-site dark grains plant. The distillery was mothballed between 1985 and 1989, when the Scotch whisky industry was endeavouring to reduce stock surpluses created by the over-optimistic production levels perpetuated during the 1970s.

POINTS OF SPECIAL INTEREST

The now infamous, but highly collectable, black-coloured Loch Dhu 10-year-old single malt whisky was distilled at Mannochmore. It was launched in 1996, at a time when United Distillers & Vintners was experimenting by pushing the boundaries of what was perceived as 'conventional' Scotch whisky, but it was only marketed for a short period, hence its rarity value.

LOCATION

Glenlossie Rd, Thornshill, Elgin, Morayshire IV30 8SS
Located in Thornshill along minor, unclassified roads, west of the A941, some three miles south of Elgin or 12 miles north of Aberlour.

GLENLOSSIE DISTILLERY WHICH SITS NEXT TO MANNOCHMORE

MILTONDUFF

HISTORY

Robert Bain and Andrew Peary licensed Miltonduff in 1824, with the distillery having previously operated illicitly, in common with many stills in the area.

It was subsequently run by William Stuart, co-owner of Highland Park and later also by Thomas Yool & Co. It was extended during the 1890s whisky boom, then, in 1935, it was acquired by the largest distilling company in Canada, Hiram Walker, who went on to run it under their George Ballantine & Son subsidiary.

Miltonduff was largely rebuilt during 1974/75 and in 1986/87 Allied Lyons plc took over Hiram Walker's distilling interests. In 2005 Miltonduff was one of the distilleries to come into the possession of Chivas Brothers Ltd as a result of their purchase of what had by that time become the Allied Domecq Group.

Today, Miltonduff is home to Chivas' 'Northern Division' administrative function, previously located at Strathisla in Keith, along with its engineering department and a dark grains plant.

POINTS OF SPECIAL INTEREST

A pair of Lomond stills was installed at Miltonduff in 1964 to produce a heavier, oilier spirit, intended to give the company's blenders greater variety. The whisky produced was known as Mosstowie. The Lomond stills were removed in 1981.

LOCATION

Miltonduff, Elgin, Morayshire IV30 8TQ
Alongside an unclassified road in the Muir of Miltonduff, off the B9010, some three miles south-west of Elgin.

Meaning of name and pronunciation guide
'Mill town owned by the Duff family'
- mill-ton-DUFF

Owner
Chivas Bros Ltd
(Pernod Ricard)

House style
Floral, elegant, sweet, malty and quite light-bodied. Aperitif.

Principal single malts
Miltonduff 10-year-old
(Gordon & MacPhail).

Principal blends
Ballantine's.

Getting technical
Stills: three pairs

Capacity: 5.5m litres

Malt: unpeated

Casks: ex-Bourbon

Water: The Black Burn

Visiting
No visitor
tour/facilities

Contacts
Tel: 01343 554120

Date visited:

SECTION INDEX ON PAGE 173

MORTLACH

Meaning of name and pronunciation guide
'Bowl-shaped valley'
- MORT-lack

Owner
Diageo plc

House style
Full-bodied and complex, with Sherry, spices, nuts and a whiff of smoke.

Principal single malts
Mortlach 16-year-old (Flora & Fauna series).

Principal blends
Johnnie Walker.

Getting technical
Stills: three wash & three spirit

Capacity: 3.6m litres

Malt: unpeated

Casks: ex-Sherry

Water: springs in the Conval Hills

Visiting
No visitor tour/facilities

Contacts
Tel: 01340 822100

Date visited:

HISTORY

The first distillery to be established in what was to become the great Speyside distilling centre of Dufftown, Mortlach was licensed in the immediate aftermath of the 1823 Excise Act by James Findlater.

Subsequent owners came and went, with the distillery enduring periods of silence, being used as both a church and a brewery during the 1840s! Then, in 1853, George Cowie became part-owner of the distillery, with the Cowie family retaining possession of Mortlach until selling it to John Walker & Sons in 1923. The distillery became part of the Distillers Company Ltd two years later, when Walker's was absorbed into the distilling giant's empire.

The number of stills had been increased from three to six in 1897, during a period of expansion and upgrading, and in 1963/64 a major rebuilding programme was undertaken. Further upgrading took place in 1996.

POINTS OF SPECIAL INTEREST

Mortlach operates what is possibly the most complicated distilling regime in Scotland, with six stills working individually rather than in pairs. A form of partial triple distillation is practiced.

William Grant worked as distillery manager at Mortlach for some 20 years before leaving to build his own Glenfiddich distillery in 1886.

> **LOCATION**
>
> Dufftown, Banffshire AB55 4AQ
> Located just off the A941, Fife Street, east of the centre of Dufftown.

ROSEISLE

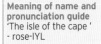

HISTORY

Roseisle distillery was constructed between 2007 and 2009 on a site adjacent to Diageo's Roseisle Maltings, close to the Moray Firth coast. The first production run took place in January 2009. Roseisle Maltings date from 1979/80, and the original plans included the provision of a neighbouring single malt distillery, but the problems of over-production which beset the Scotch whisky industry during the 1980s meant that it was almost three decades before this distillery was finally added.

Roseisle operates on a vast scale, and is extremely flexible in terms of the spirit character it can produce. Designed to embrace the latest environmentally-friendly technology, the plant is as carbon-neutral and water-neutral as possible.

It is intended to supplement the output of Diageo's existing 27 malt distilleries as demand for the company's key blended whiskies, such as Johnnie Walker, has risen significantly in recent years

POINTS OF SPECIAL INTEREST

Roseisle is the largest of Scotland's malt whisky distilleries in terms of potential output.

LOCATION

Roseisle, Elgin, Morayshire IV30 5YP
Seven miles north-west of Elgin, Roseisle is situated alongside the B9089 road, off the A96 and B9013.

Meaning of name and pronunciation guide
'The isle of the cape '
- rose-IYL

Owner
Diageo plc

House style
Roseisle makes two styles of malt whisky, namely a lighter, perfumed, grassy, fruity Speyside type, similar to Glenlossie and Cardhu and a heavier, more complex type in the mould of Cragganmore, Mortlach and Benrinnes.

Principal single malts
N/A

Principal blends
N/A

Getting technical
Stills: seven pairs

Capacity: 10.2m litres

Malt: unpeated

Casks: ex-Bourbon

Water: springs on site

Visiting
No visitor tour/facilities

Contacts
Tel: 01343 832106

Date visited:

SPEYBURN

HISTORY

Speyburn was a relative latecomer to the 'whisky boom' scene, being constructed in 1897/98 to the design of the great distillery architect Charles Doig..

It's founder was John Hopkin & Co, already owner of Tobermory distillery on the Isle of Mull. The new distillery operated under the auspices of the Speyburn-Glenlivet Distillery Co Ltd.

In 1916 ownership passed to the Distillers Company Ltd, and with the exception of a period of silence from 1930 to 1934 and again during the Second World War, Speyburn turned out malt for blending purposes for DCL until 1991. In that year, Inver House Distillers Ltd acquired Speyburn, and proceeded to make it available as a 10-year-old single malt, most notably in the USA, where it enjoys strong sales.

POINTS OF SPECIAL INTEREST

The founders of Speyburn were anxious to distil some spirit during Queen Victoria's Diamond Jubilee year (1897) for a special commemorative release. This was only achieved by distilling during a snowstorm toward the end of December, before the doors or windows had been fitted to the newly-constructed stillhouse!

In 1900 Speyburn became the first distillery in Scotland to install drum maltings in place of floor maltings, although they remain unused since 1968.

> ### LOCATION
>
> Rothes, Aberlour, Morayshire AB38 7AG
> Situated off the B9015 Rothes to Garmouth road as it leave the A941 through Rothes.

Meaning of name and pronunciation guide
'Spey' may be derived from the Gaelic for 'thorn' or 'hawthorn' -SPEY-burn

Owner
Inver House Distillers Ltd (Thai Beverage plc)

House style
Sweet, medium-bodied, with fudge and malt notes, plus a gentle tang of smoke.

Principal single malts
Speyburn 10 and 25-year-old.

Principal blends
Inver House.

Getting technical
Stills: one pair

Capacity: 2m litres

Malt: unpeated

Casks: ex-Bourbon

Water: The Granty Burn

Visiting
May be possible by prior arrangement

Contacts
Tel: 01340 831213
E-mail: enquiries@inverhouse.com

Date visited:

SPEYSIDE

HISTORY

The origins of the present Speyside distillery go back to 1956, when whisky broker George Christie and his Speyside Distillery & Bonding Co purchased a plot of land on which a barley mill had previously operated at Drumguish, close to the River Spey. Six years later Christie commissioned local drystone waller Alex Fairlie to build a distillery for him on the site, though in the meantime he had established the North of Scotland grain distillery at Alloa in Clackmannanshire.

It took no less than 34 years from Christie buying the land to the first spirit flowing from the new Speyside distillery in December 1990, and a decade later Speyside Distillers Co Ltd was established by a group of private investors, although the actual distillery remained in the hands of members of the Christie family.

The group that set up Speyside Distillers Co Ltd included the founder's son, Ricky Christie, and Sir James Ackroyd, and has its headquarters in Glasgow, where blending bottling and bonding operations for a variety of brands are carried out.

2001 saw the release of a 10-year-old bottling of Speyside single malt, though younger whisky had previously been marketed under the Drumguish label, which carried no age statement.

POINTS OF SPECIAL INTEREST

The present Speyside distillery is actually the second to bear the name, with the original being established in nearby Kingussie in 1895. It was only productive for a decade before falling silent and eventually being demolished.

LOCATION

Tromie Mills, Glentromie, Kingussie, Inverness-shire PH21 1NS
15 miles south-west of Aviemore and three miles from Kingussie, the distillery is situated at the end of a private track, off the B970 Kingussie road.

Meaning of name and pronunciation guide
'Spey' may be derived from the Gaelic for 'thorn' or 'hawthorn' - SPEY-side

Owner
Speyside Distillery Co Ltd

www.speysidedistillery.co.uk

House style
Medium-bodied and medium-sweet, floral, with malt, fruit and nuts.

Principal single malts
Speyside 10 and 12-year-old, Drumguish.

Principal blends
Speyside.

Getting technical
Stills: one pair

Capacity: 600,000 litres

Malt: unpeated

Casks: ex-Bourbon and ex-Sherry

Water: The River Tromie

Visiting
No visitor tour/facilities

Contacts
Tel: 01540 661060
E-mail: info@speyside-distillery.co.uk

Date visited:

PHOTOGRAPH ON PAGE 14

STRATHMILL

Meaning of name and pronunciation guide
'The mill in the valley' - strath-MILL

Owner
Diageo plc

House style
Fragrant and fruity, medium-bodied, sweet, fruity and spicy.

Principal single malts
Strathmill 12-year-old (Flora & Fauna series).

Principal blends
J&B, Spey Royal.

Getting technical
Stills: two pairs

Capacity: 1.7m litres

Malt: unpeated

Casks: ex-Bourbon

Water: on-site spring

Visiting
No visitor tour/facilities

Contacts
Tel: 01542 882295

Date visited:

HISTORY

One of the lowest-profile of all Diageo's distilleries, Strathmill is tucked away in a small glen by the River Isla, across town from Keith's much better known distillery of Strathisla.

Strathmill was established during 1891/92 as Glenisla-Glenlivet in a former flour and corn mill, and was bought by London-based gin distillers WA Gilbey in 1895 for £9,500. Gilbey's subsequently changed the name to Strathmill.

In 1962, Gilbey combined with United Wine Traders (owners of the J&B blended whisky brand) to form International Distillers & Vintners (IDV), and six years later production capacity at Glen Spey was doubled by the installation of a second pair of stills. Purifiers were also fitted to the stills in order to produce a lighter style of spirit.

IDV was acquired by the brewers Watney Mann in 1972, who were themselves taken over by Grand Metropolitan Hotels the same year. In 1997 'Grand Met' and Guinness merged to form Diageo.

POINTS OF SPECIAL INTEREST

Strathmill has always been elusive as a single malt, but in 1993 it became available for the time since 1909 when Oddbins bottled a 1980 expression.

LOCATION

Keith, Banffshire AB55 5DQ
Located off the A96 Aberdeen to Inverness road, the distillery is situated at the end of Union Street in the centre of Keith.

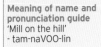

TAMNAVULIN

HISTORY

Tamnavulin was a product of the 1960s Scotch whisky boom, being established in 1966 by the Tamnavulin-Glenlivet Distillery Company, which was a subsidiary of Invergordon Distillers Ltd.

In 1993 Whyte & Mackay Ltd acquired Invergordon, principally for its eponymous grain distillery on the Cromarty Firth in the eastern Highlands, so May 1995 saw Tamnavulin mothballed.

The distillery was not to fully reopen for 12 years, finally making spirit again in the summer of 2007, though in 2000 some 400,000 litres of spirit was distilled during a six week period by employees of nearby Tomintoul distillery in order to maintain stock levels of the malt.

POINTS OF SPECIAL INTEREST

Although located in a stunning area of Speyside, not far from Glenlivet distillery, Tamanvulin can best be described as 'functional' in appearance. However, a nearby traditional mill building, complete with waterwheel, served as a notably attractive visitor centre until the late 1990s.

LOCATION

Tomnavoulin, Banffshire AB37 9JA
Some 12 miles south-west of Dufftown or six miles north-east of Tomintoul, the distillery is located just off the B9008 in the village of Tomnavoulin.

Meaning of name and pronunciation guide
'Mill on the hill'
- tam-naVOO-lin

Owner
Whyte & Mackay Ltd

House style
Medium-bodied, sweet, fruity and floral, with nuts and gentle smoke.

Principal single malts
Tamnavulin 12-year-old.

Principal blends
Whye & Mackay, Mackinlays.

Getting technical
Stills: three pairs

Capacity: 4m litres

Malt: unpeated

Casks: ex-Bourbon

Water: underground springs at Easterton

Visiting
No visitor tour/facilities

Contacts
Tel: 01479 818031

Date visited:

SECTION INDEX ON PAGE 173

TOMINTOUL

HISTORY

Constructed during 1964/65, Tomintoul was only the third new Scottish distillery to be built in the 20th century. It was commissioned by two Glasgow whisky broking and blending companies, namely Hay & Macleod & Co Ltd and W&S Strong & Co Ltd.

In 1973 Scottish & Universal Investment Trust acquired both Tomintoul Distillery Ltd and also the Glasgow-based distillers and blenders Whyte & Mackay Distillers Ltd, with Whyte & Mackay taking control of the Tomintoul operation. The following year a second pair of stills was added and a12-year-old single malt was launched.

London-based blenders and bottlers Angus Dundee plc acquired Tomintoul in 2000, going on to purchase Glencadam three years later.

In addition to its distilling capacity, the Tomintoul site also serves as a 'blend centre,' where Angus Dundee mixes a range of grain and malt whiskies, ready for bottling or bulk export, notably to various European markets.

POINTS OF SPECIAL INTEREST

Such are the extremes of winter weather in this area that during construction of Tomintoul distillery, the building contractors always ensured they had at least two weeks' worth of materials on site in case they became cut off from the outside world!

In addition to its 'regular' range, Tomintoul has also enjoyed success courtesy of heavily-peated spirit, marketed as Old Ballantruan and Peaty Tang.

Meaning of name and pronunciation guide
'Small hill of the barn' - Tom-in-TOWEL

Owner
Angus Dundee Distillers plc

www.tomintouldistillery.co.uk

House style
Sweet, easy-drinking, with vanilla, spice, floral and fruit notes.

Principal single malts
Tomintoul 10, 14, 16 and 33-year-old, 12-year-old Oloroso, Old Ballantruan, Peaty Tang.

Principal blends
Dundee and Parker's.

Getting technical
Stills: two pairs

Capacity: 3.3m litres

Malt: usually unpeated

Casks: ex-Bourbon and ex-Sherry

Water: The Ballantruan Spring

Visiting
May be possible by prior arrangement

Contacts
Tel: 01907 590274

Date visited:

LOCATION

Ballindalloch, Banffshire AB37 9AQ
17 miles south-west of Dufftown, the distillery sits alongside the B9136 between Tomintoul and Ballindalloch.

TORMORE

HISTORY

Designed to be an eye-catching, showpiece distillery, Tormore was built on virgin land (rather than a conversion of former buildings) between 1958 and 1960. It was built to a design by former Royal Academy president Sir Albert Richardson for US distillers Schenley International, owners of the Long John blended whisky brand.

By contrast with some of the less than aesthetically pleasing distilleries that followed in its wake, Tormore's architecture was worthy of its splendid surroundings, and the structures are now 'B' listed.

In 1975 Schenley sold its Scotch whisky assets, including Tormore, to the brewing giant Whitbread & Co Ltd, and from there it passed into the hands of Allied Lyons plc in 1989. Allied Lyons ultimately became the Allied Domecq Group, and in 2005 Pernod Ricard took control of Allied's Scotch whisky distilleries and brands, placing them under its Chivas Brothers Ltd subsidiary.

POINTS OF SPECIAL INTEREST

The architect included a unique clock, which plays a different traditional Scottish tune each 15 minutes. Had it not been for technical difficulties, Richardson's distillery chimney would have resembled a giant whisky bottle!

LOCATION

Advie, Grantown on Spey, Morayshire PH26 3LR
Some ten miles south-west of Aberlour or twelve miles from Grantown on Spey, the distillery sits beside the A96, midway between the two towns.

Meaning of name and pronunciation guide
'The big hill'
- Tor-MORE

Owner
Chivas Bros Ltd
(Pernod Ricard)

House style
Sweet, medium-bodied, with malt, honey, spice and sherry notes.

Principal single malts
Tormore 12-year-old.

Principal blends
Ballantine's, Long John, Cream of the Barley.

Getting technical
Stills: four pairs

Capacity: 3.7m litres

Malt: unpeated

Casks: ex-Bourbon

Water: Achvochkie Burn

Visiting
No visitor tour/facilities

Contacts
Tel: 01807 510244

Date visited:

BALBLAIR

HISTORY

Distilling is said to have been practised at Balblair as long ago as 1749, but its formal history begins in 1790, when John Ross established a distillery at Balblair Farm, about half a mile from the current site. The distillery was rebuilt in 1872, but the present structure dates from 1894/95, and was the work of Alexander Cowan, who chose a location beside the Inverness to Wick railway line to facilitate deliveries to and from the plant.

The distillery was silent from 1915 until 1947, when Keith solicitor Robert 'Bertie' Cumming purchased it for £48,000, recommencing distilling the following year. In 1970 Cumming sold Balblair to the Canadian distilling giant Hiram Walker & Sons Ltd, who already owned five Scottish distilleries.

Hiram Walker merged with Allied Vintners to become Allied Distillers in 1988, and Allied sold Balblair to Inver House in 1996, having considered closing it down.

Balblair is a very attractive, traditional distillery in external appearance, and is one of oldest operating in Scotland. Only Bowmore, Glenturret and Strathisla claim greater antiquity.

POINTS OF SPECIAL INTEREST

The air around Edderton is considered to be the purest in all of Scotland, and is said to contribute to the whisky's smooth yet invigorating character, presumably due to its influence during maturation.

> ### LOCATION
>
> Edderton, Tain, Ross-shire IV19 1LB
> Situated half a mile beyond the village of Edderton, which is just off the A836 and A9, some five miles from Tain and the Glenmorangie Distillery.

Meaning of name and pronunciation guide
'The farm on the moor'
– bal-BLAIR

Owner
Inver House Distillers Ltd (Thai Beverage plc)

House style
Medium-bodied, fruity and nutty, with gentle smoke and spice.

Principal single malts
Balblair offers a range of 'vintage' bottling, currently from 1975, 1989 and 1997.

Principal blends
Inver House, Hankey Bannister, Pinwinnie Royal.

Getting technical
Stills: one pair

Capacity: 1.75m litres

Malt: unpeated

Casks: plus some ex-Sherry

Water: Allt Dearg Burn

Visiting
By prior arrangement

Contacts
Tel: 01862 821273
E-mail: enquiries@ inverhouse.com

Date visited:

PHOTOGRAPH ON PAGE 8

TEANINICH

HISTORY

One of Scotland's older distilleries, Teaninich dates back to 1817, when it was established at Alness by local landowner Captain Hugh Munro, partly in an attempt to thwart the activities of prolific local illicit distillers.

The distillery passed through a number of hands, and was modernised and extended in 1899, before being sold to the Distillers Company Ltd in 1933.

The 1960s and '70s were heady years for Scotch whisky, with two additional stills being installed at Teaninich in 1962. Eight years later an entirely new production unit, known as the 'A Side' and equipped with six stills, was added to the site. This gave the distillery an impressive annual capacity of six million litres

However, when the problem of over-production reached a critical point in the 1980s, both the old 'B Side' and then the newer 'A Side' were closed down.

The latter reopened in 1991, but the 'B Side' was demolished in 1999, leaving a series of modern structures in what had by that time become an industrial estate. In 2008, a new pair of stainless steel washbacks was installed to allow seven days a week working practices and thereby increase output at Teaninich once more.

POINTS OF SPECIAL INTEREST

Teaninich is the only distillery in Scotland to use a mash filter (more common in the brewing industry) instead of a mash tun, which reduces the mashing time and offers greater processing efficiency.

LOCATION

Riverside Drive, Alness, Ross-shire IV17 0XB
21 miles north of Inverness, Teaninich is located on an industrial estate on the southern outskirts of Alness. The best access from the A9 is via the second exit to the town, then right along River Drive.

Meaning of name and pronunciation guide
'The house on the moor'
- TEA-an-in-ich

Owner
Diageo plc

House style
Medium-bodied, slightly oily, quite sweet, with citrus fruits, spice and a hint of smoke.

Principal single malts
Teaninich 10-year-old (Flora & Fauna series).

Principal blends
Johnnie Walker.

Getting technical
Stills: three pairs

Capacity: 4m litres

Malt: unpeated

Casks: ex-Bourbon

Water: Dairywell Spring

Visiting
No visitor tour/facilitiest

Contacts
Tel: 01349 885001

Date visited:

ABHAINN DEARG

Meaning of name and pronunciation guide
The Red River
- A-veen ja-RIGG

Owner
Mark Tayburn

www.abhainndearg.co.uk

House style
The new make spirit is sweet, smooth and cerealy. It begins to take on spicy, Bourbon characteristics, plus peach and apricot notes, after a short time in the cask.

Principal single malts
A small release of three-year-old spirit will take place in 2011, followed by five and seven-year-olds.

Principal blends
N/A

Getting technical
Stills: one pair

Capacity: 25,000 litres

Malt: lightly peated

Casks: first fill ex-Bourbon

Water: Abhainn Dearg

Visiting
May be possible by prior arrangement

Contacts
Tel: 01851 672429

Date visited:

HISTORY

Scotland's westernmost distillery was created on the site of a former salmon hatchery close to the Atlantic coast of the Isle of Lewis and opened in September 2008. It is owned and run by Stornoway businessman Mark Tayburn, who learnt the finer points of whisky-making at the Bruichladdich Academy on Islay.

He was inspired to develop a distillery on his native island in order to continue its long history of both legal and illicit distilling. A licensed distillery operated in Stornoway from 1829/30 until 1840, and a number of unlicensed stills were working until comparatively recently. Indeed, the idiosyncratic 'cylinder' still design at Abhainn Dearg is based on a 'scaled up' version of a local, illicit still.

In addition to the 'bespoke' pair of stills in general operation, Mark Tayburn was granted permission to make whisky using a genuine, 27 gallon illicit still, left at the distillery entrance by an anonymous donor. He also plans to increase production significantly in future, and in 2010 released bottles of 'New Spirit' on to the market.

POINTS OF SPECIAL INTEREST

Abhainn Dearg is the only licensed distillery in the Outer Hebrides, and Mark Tayburn plans to install a small malting unit, experimenting with locally-grown barley, along with a hydro-electric plant to provide greener and cheaper fuel. For every cask filled, an oak sapling is planted at nearby Loch Scaslavat.

A three-day 'Whisky Experience' package is now available at Abhainn Dearg, which gives participants a hands-on taste of whisky-making. At the end of their time at the distillery they can take home a bottle of 'Spirit of Lewis' or purchase a 30-litre cask.

LOCATION

Carnish, Isle of Lewis HS2 9EX
30 miles west of Stornoway, situated close to the hamlet of Carnish, along an unclassified road beyond the B8011 from Garrynahine.

SCAPA

HISTORY

Scapa enjoys an altogether lower profile than its Orcadian neighbour Highland Park, having been used almost exclusively to provide spirit for blending purposes throughout most of its history.

The distillery was founded in 1885 by the Glasgow firm of Macfarlane and Townsend, and after several changes of ownership it closed in 1934 when the Scapa Distillery Company Ltd went into voluntary liquidation. Production resumed two years later under Bloch Brothers Ltd, owners of Glen Scotia in Campbeltown, followed in 1954 with Hiram Walker & Sons (Scotland) Ltd taking control. The distillery was subsequently rebuilt in 1959 and further modernised in 1978.

Hiram Walker merged with Allied Vintners to become Allied Distillers in 1988, and in 1994 Scapa was mothballed. Three years later a programme of sporadic production was instigated, utilising staff from Highland Park.

Then, in 2004, some £2 million was spent restoring Scapa to its former glory, and the following year the upgraded and revitalised distillery passed into the hands of Chivas Bros Ltd, who launched a 14-year-old 'house' bottling in 2006. This was superseded by a 16-year-old in 2009.

POINTS OF SPECIAL INTEREST

In common with several other Hiram Walker plants, a 'Lomond' still was installed at Scapa in 1959 in order to give the company a different style of spirit for blending purposes. Suitably modified for standard distillation, this wash still continues in use today, and is one of only two remaining operational examples of its type.

LOCATION

St Ola, Kirkwall, Orkney KW15 1SE
Two miles south-west from the centre of Kirkwall, Scapa is situated off the A964, Old Scapa Road.

Meaning of name and pronunciation guide
From the Old Norse scalp, meaning boat - SCAPP-ah

Owner
Chivas Bros Ltd (Pernod Ricard)

www.scapamalt.com

House style
Floral, grassy, medium-dry, honey, nuts and vanilla.

Principal single malts
Scapa 16-year-old.

Principal blends
Ballantine's.

Getting technical
Stills: one pair

Capacity: 1m litres

Malt: unpeated

Casks: ex-Bourbon

Water: The Lingro Burn

Visiting
May be possible by prior arrangement

Contacts
Tel: 01856 875430
Email: info@scapamalt.com

Date visited:

GLENGYLE

Meaning of name and pronunciation guide
'Glen of the stranger'
– glen-GYLE

Owner
Mitchell's Glengyle Ltd

www.kilkerran.com

House style
Malty and spicy, slightly oily, with cereal, peach and pineapple notes (based on 4-year-old sample).

Principal single malts
Kilkerran 4-year-old, (available from a solera cask of 2004 spirit at The Tasting Room, Springbank distillery, 2008/09.

Principal blends
Mitchell's.

Getting technical
Stills: one pair

Capacity: 750,000 litres

Malt: lightly peated

Casks: ex-Bourbon

Water: Crosshills Loch

Visiting
By appointment

Contacts
Tel: 01586 551710
E-mail:
info@kilkerran.com

Date visited:

HISTORY

The original Glengyle distillery was established in 1872/73 by William Mitchell, previously co-owner of Springbank with his brother, John. The recessionary years following the First World War were severe for the entire Scottish distilling industry, but Campbeltown suffered particularly badly, and Glengyle closed in 1925.

The distillery buildings were subsequently used for several years by Campbeltown Miniature Rifle Club, before the Bloch brothers, who owned Glen Scotia distillery, acquired the site in 1941, intending to recommence distilling. The Second World War prevented that from happening and in 1951 Campbell Henderson applied for planning permission to restore and reopen Glengyle as a distillery, but those plans also came to nothing.

Then, in 2000, Springbank supremo Hedley Wright, a descendant of the Mitchell family who had originally built Glengyle, formed Mitchell's Glengyle Ltd to purchase the distillery site and restore it to its former glory. New equipment was commissioned, though the two stills had formerly been part of Ben Wyvis malt distillery, located within the Invergordon grain distilling complex.

Production began at Glengyle in March 2004, making it the first new distillery of the millennium and the first in Campbeltown for 125 years. The single malt produced there is bottled as Kilkerran, rather than Glengyle, as the name Glengyle is already registered for a blended malt.

POINTS OF SPECIAL INTEREST

In 1994 the Scotch Whisky Association (SWA) dropped the historic Campbeltown classification of whiskies, but with five single malts (Springbank, Hazelburn, Longrow, Glengyle and Glen Scotia) now being produced in the former whisky capital of Scotland, the SWA has reinstated Campbeltown to its rightful place as a distinctive whisky-making region.

LOCATION

Glengyle St, Campbeltown, Argyll PA28 6EX
In the centre of Campbeltown, just off Longrow road and the A83 as it enters the town.

GLEN SCOTIA

HISTORY

The Campbeltown distillery of Glen Scotia was established in 1832, when around a dozen distilleries were already working in the town. It was founded by the Galbraith family, who owned the distillery until 1895, after which it changed hands on several occasions before falling silent in 1928. This was a time when the Scotch whisky industry in general, and the Campbeltown region in particular, was suffering badly from economic recession. No fewer than 20 distilleries in Campbeltown closed between 1921 and 1934. Only Springbank and Glen Scotia were to reopen.

Distilling at Glen Scotia recommenced in 1933, in the ownership of the Bloch brothers, who sold the distillery to Hiram Walker (Scotland) Ltd in 1954, along with Scapa on Orkney. However, the following year, Hiram Walker sold Glen Scotia on to A Gillies & Co, and the Glasgow blending company became part of Amalgamated Distillers Products (ADP) in 1970. Between 1979 and 1982 more than £1 million was spent refurbishing Glen Scotia, but the distillery closed two years later.

Production began again in 1989 under ADP's new owners Gibson International, but a further change of ownership saw the distillery mothballed once more by Glen Catrine Bonded Warehouse Ltd (also operators of Loch Lomond Distillery) in 1994. Distilling recommenced in May 1999, and has continued – with modest volumes being produced - to the present time.

POINTS OF SPECIAL INTEREST

The distillery is said to be haunted by the ghost of Duncan MacCallum, owner of Glen Scotia from 1924 to 1928. The story goes that MacCallum was defrauded of the enormous sum of £40,000 by a group of confidence tricksters. What is known for certain is that MacCallum drowned himself in Crosshill Loch, aged 83, in 1930.

LOCATION

2 High Street, Campbeltown, Argyll PA28 6DS
Situated on the B842, High Street in the centre of Campbeltown.

Meaning of name and pronunciation guide
'Glen of the Scots'
 – glen-SCO-sha

Owner
Loch Lomond
Distillery Co Ltd

www.lochlomonddis-tillery.com

House style
Medium-bodied, briny, spirity, nutty, with notes of light smoke.

Principal single malts
Glen Scotia 12 and 17-year-old.

Principal blends
Black Prince, Royal Escort.

Getting technical
Stills: one pair

Capacity: 750,000 litres

Malt: usually unpeated

Casks: ex-Bourbon

Water: Crosshill Loch

Visiting
May be possible by prior arrangement

Contacts
Tel: 01586 552288
E-mail: mail@lochlomonddistillery.com

Date visited:

SECTION INDEX ON PAGE 173

PHOTOGRAPH ON PAGE 172

CLOSED DISTILLERIES

Like all commercial enterprises, whisky production is susceptible to the vagaries of international economics and the health, or otherwise, of individual national economies. One of the difficulties faced by the Scotch whisky industry is that is has to predict likely sales levels well in advance of consumption, due to the time lapse while maturation takes place. It will be three years at the very least before spirit distilled today can be bottled as whisky. Historically, the industry has expanded and contracted with severe cutbacks in production. The most notable occasions were following the end of the Victorian 'boom' era in the early years of the 20th century, during times of world war, the economic depression of the inter-war years, and over-production during the 1970s and early 1980s.

Sometimes distilleries have worked at less than full capacity, sometimes they have been 'silent' for several months at a time while remaining on a 'care and maintenance' basis, and sometimes they have closed down for years, only to reopen during periods of industry expansion. Many of the distilleries featured in this book have endured lengthy spells of inactivity, and several have been brought back from the dead, as it were, having apparently ceased whisky-making forever.

Others, however, have not been so fortunate, and have fallen silent never to distil again. Many of these distilleries have been demolished to make way for new developments, with the Inverness duo of Glen Alyn and Glen Mhor, for example, disappearing beneath a retail park, while the site of Glenury Royal in the east coast port of Stonehaven, is occupied by an estate of houses; tenanted principally by commuters who work in nearby Aberdeen.

But some dormant distilleries have survived against the odds, either being retained in case one day their spirit is required again or because they have been granted a new lease of life, with a different function. When selecting the distilleries to be profiled in this section it was decided that there should be something to make the trip worthwhile – something more than just one crumbling still house wall or an extant warehouse.

Before exploring the individual distilleries presented here it is worth considering why these particular distilleries were chosen for redundancy while others survived and thrived. One crucial factor was the value of the land. A town centre site is usually worth more than a remote, rural one for commercial or even residential development. If two distilleries with similar profiles were being considered for closure, one rural and one urban, the odds would be stacked against the distillery in an urban location.

Other factors taken into account when closure was under discussion were the amount of modernisation and/or expansion that had been carried out at the distillery, the scope for further expansion, and even the availability of additional water supplies as part of any future expansion programme. It was also often the case that a distillery which produced a whisky with some reputation would be spared, while one that produced a more obscure malt, perhaps relatively easy to replace with a substitute in blends, would be sacrificed.

The distilleries profiled here are to be found the length and breadth of Scotland, and while a closed distillery is a sad distillery, all are worth a visit to help gain an insight into the overall heritage of the Scotch whisky industry.

SECTION INDEX

LISTED ALPHABETICALLY WITHIN WHISKY REGIONS

Each page in this section is colour coded in the top corner to reflect the whisky region. See the map on the inside front and back covers for the distillery location.

> SYMBOLS
> **T** Timing of distillery tours, whether set or flexible
> **C** Catering options for visitors
> **S** Shopping facilities, indicating whether whisky is sold and scale of the shop

ROSEBANK

Meaning of name and pronunciation guide
'Bank of roses'
- ROSE-bank

Owner
Last operated by
Distillers Co Ltd

House style
Floral, sweet, and grassy, quite light-bodied, with spices and malt.

Principal single malts
Rosebank 12-year-old (Flora & Fauna series), Rosebank 1991 (Gordon & MacPhail Connoisseurs' Choice range) and other independent bottlings.

HISTORY

Rosebank distillery is located beside the Forth-Clyde Canal at Camelon, on the outskirts of the industrial town of Falkirk, midway between Edinburgh and Glasgow. Its origins are confused, with claims being made for an establishment date of 1798. What is known for certain is that James Rankine constructed a distillery on the present site in 1840, based on the maltings of the Camelon distillery, which operated principally on the opposite bank of the Forth-Clyde Canal.

Rankine expanded the distillery in 1845, going on to purchase Camelon distillery in 1861. Three years later his son rebuilt Rosebank, subsequently demolishing most of Camelon and keeping only the maltings, which he connected with Rosebank by way of a swing bridge across the canal.

In 1914, Rosebank, along with the fellow Lowland distilleries of Clydesdale, Glenkinchie, Grange and St Magdalene, merged to form Scottish Malt Distillers (SMD), which became part of The Distillers Company Ltd (DCL) five years later. When DCL was taken over by Guinness plc in 1986, Rosebank was absorbed into United Distillers (UD).

Prior to the formation of United Distillers, Rosebank had survived DCL's drastic closure programme of 1983 and '85, but ultimately it was doomed, being one of four UD distilleries mothballed in mid-1993.

In May 2002 Rosebank was purchased by British Waterways, which subsequently sold off some of the property for conversion into a series of canal-side apartments, while other buildings have been transformed into offices and a pub/restaurant.

POINTS OF SPECIAL INTEREST

Rosebank was equipped with three stills and, like Auchentoshan (see p 72), practiced triple distillation in classic Lowland style.

LOCATION

Camelon Road, Falkirk, Stirlingshire FK1 5BX
Located one mile west of Falkirk centre on the A803 (Camelon Road) at the junction with the A9 and B816.

Personal notes relating to visit:

Date visited:

ST MAGDALENE

HISTORY

St Magdalene was located in the historic West Lothian royal burgh of Linlithgow, birthplace of Mary Queen of Scots and some 20 miles west of Edinburgh.

The site for the distillery had formerly been a leper colony under the auspices of the Knights Templar of St John of Torphichen during the 12th century. The land was later occupied by a convent.

St Magdalene was first licensed in 1797, occupying land beside the Union Canal, which provided ready access for raw materials and the transportation of casks filled with spirit. The distillery also boasted its own railway sidings.

Neighbouring Bonnytoun distillery pre-dated St Magdalene by two years, and in 1800 Bonnytoun's owner, Adam Dawson, purchased St Magdalene from its founder Sebastian Henderson, creating something of a 'super distillery,' embracing both the Bonnytoun and St Magdalene operations. The Dawson family operated the distillery until 1912, when A&J Dawson Ltd went into liquidation, resulting in the Distillers Company Ltd (DCL) acquiring it the same year.

In 1915, St Magdalene became one of the five founding distilleries of the DCL subsidiary Scottish Malt Distillers (SMD), along with Glenkinchie (see p 76), Clydesdale (in Wishaw, Lanarkshire), Grange (in Burntisland, Fife), and Rosebank. However, St Magdalene found itself surplus to requirements during DCL's rationalisation programme, and closed in 1983.

POINTS OF SPECIAL INTEREST

A significant part of St Magdalene found a new lease of life as apartments with the malt kiln pagodas still standing prominently as a reminder that Linlithgow was once home to no fewer than five distilleries.

LOCATION

Edinburgh Road, Linlithgow, West Lothian EH49 6AQ
19 miles north-west of Edinburgh via the M9, the distillery is located half a mile east of Linlithgow centre, along the A803 and B9080. Edinburgh Road (B9080) is just east of the train station.

Meaning of name and pronunciation guide
Built on the site of the convent of St Magdalene's Cross
- Saint MAG-de-len

Owner
Last operated by Distillers Co Ltd

House style
Perfumed and grassy, some fruit, medium-bodied, quite dry.

Principal single malts
Linlithgow 1973 (Diageo Special Releases, 2004), St Magdalene 1975 (Gordon & MacPhail Rare Old range) and other independent bottlings.

Personal notes relating to visit:

Date visited:

SECTION INDEX ON PAGE 223

PHOTOGRAPH ON PAGE 238

CAPERDONICH

Meaning of name and pronunciation guide
'Secret well'
- Capper-DOH-nich

Owner
Chivas Brothers Ltd
(Pernod Ricard)

House style
Light-bodied,
relatively sweet, with
vanilla, tropical fruits
and spice.

Principal single malts
Caperdonich 16-year-
old Cask Strength
Edition.

HISTORY

Caperdonich was established in 1897 at the height of the Victorian Scotch whisky boom by J&G Grant of nearby Glen Grant distillery (see p 114). It was intended to supplement the output of its sibling and was originally named 'Glen Grant No. 2 Distillery.' When 'boom' turned to 'bust,' the plant was closed in 1902.

After more than six decades of silence, the distillery was resurrected under the Caperdonich name in 1965, being substantially rebuilt and mechanised. It operated under the auspices of The Glenlivet & Glen Grant Distilleries Ltd.

In 1967, a second pair of stills was added at Caperdonich, with almost the entire output of the distillery going into the Chivas Regal, Queen Anne, Passport and Something Special blends.

A decade later, Caperdonich became part of the Canadian Seagram empire, and in 2001 found itself in the ownership of Pernod Ricard. A year later, the distillery was mothballed, along with the Allt a Bhainne and Braeval plants.

Although they have both subsequently re-opened, the future looks bleaker for Caperdonich. Most of the equipment remains in place, however, with the exception of the still condensers.

POINTS OF SPECIAL INTEREST

Caperdonich was originally connected to Glen Grant by what was known locally as 'the whisky pipe,' which carried new make spirit across the main road for filling into casks.

Personal notes relating to visit:

Date visited:

LOCATION

Station St, Rothes, Morayshire AB38 7BN
Located opposite Glen Grant Distillery and to the east of New Street (A941), in the heart of Rothes village.

COLEBURN

Meaning of name and pronunciation guide
'Charcoal Burn'
- COLE-burn

Owner
Private. Last operated by the Distillers Co Ltd

House style
Quite dry, lightly fruity, with resin, ginger and spice.

Principal single malts
Coleburn 1981
(Gordon & MacPhail Connoisseurs' Choice range).

HISTORY

Coleburn was born out of the late 19th century whisky 'boom,' being established in 1897/99 to the design of the prolific Elgin 'distillery' architect Charles Doig.

The distillery was commissioned by Dundee whisky blender John Robertson & Son Ltd, who operated it until May 1913, when it fell silent. Production resumed four years later, by which time Coleburn had been sold to the Clynelish Distillery Company Ltd, a partnership comprising the Distillers Company Ltd (DCL), John Walker & Sons, and John Risk.

The distillery came into the full ownership of DCL in 1925, and operated under its Scottish Malt Distillers subsidiary from 1930. Licensed to J&G Stewart Ltd, its make was a significant component of their Usher's Green Stripe Blend.

However, when DCL sought to rationalise its distilling empire during the 1980s, Coleburn was one of those sites chosen for closure, and the last spirit from its pair of stills flowed in March 1985.

POINTS OF SPECIAL INTEREST

Coleburn remains externally relatively intact and the current owners purchased the site in 2004, intending to develop it into a travel lodge and restaurant, with shops and an entertainment centre. However, their plans were turned down by Moray Council in 2008 and the distillery's future remains uncertain.

LOCATION

Longmorn, by Elgin, Morayshire IV30 8SN
Located just off the A941, 5 miles south of Elgin, 2 miles south of Fogwatt, or 10 miles north of Aberlour.

Personal notes relating to visit:

Date visited:

CONVALMORE

Meaning of name and pronunciation guide
'Big Conval hill'
- Conval-MOR

Owner
William Grant & Sons Ltd

House style
Substantial and quite sweet, with malt, fruits and nutty spice.

Principal single malts
Convalmore 1977 (Diageo Special Releases 2005), Convalmore 1984 (Gordon & MacPhail Connoisseur's Choice range).

HISTORY

Convalmore was the fourth distillery to be built in Dufftown, with the Convalmore-Glenlivet Distillery Co Ltd being established in 1893 by the Glasgow blending firm of Peter Dawson Ltd. Distilling began in February the following year.

However, the dramatic downturn that struck the Scotch whisky industry around the turn of the century, due to vast over-production, brought about the demise of the company, and in 1904 the distillery and its stock were bought by WP Lowrie & Co Ltd for £6,000.

Two years later, Lowrie was purchased by James Buchanan & Co Ltd, and in 1925 Convalmore was one of several distilleries acquired from Buchanan's by the Distillers Company Ltd. It operated under DCL's Scottish Malt Distillers subsidiary from 1930, and the number of stills was subsequently increased from two to four during 1964/65.

Convalmore fell victim to the next bout of serious over-production in the Scotch whisky industry, which forced its closure in 1985. Sitting adjacent to Balvenie (see p 102) it was purchased by William Grant & Sons Ltd in 1990 in order to utilise its extensive warehousing capacity. Today, the distillery appears externally quite intact, but is really little more than an empty shell.

POINTS OF SPECIAL INTEREST

In 1909, the distillery was fitted with a continuous still, in addition to its pair of pot stills. While the still boasted a remarkable capacity of 2,273 litres per hour, the results were disappointing, with decidedly variable spirit quality. The continuous still was removed in 1916.

Personal notes relating to visit:

Date visited:

LOCATION

Dufftown, Morayshire AB55 4BB
Located beside the A941 road, one mile north of Dufftown and a short distance north of Glenfiddich.

PHOTOGRAPH ON PAGE 239

DALLAS DHU

HISTORY

Dallas Dhu was designed by that doyen of 'whisky architects' Charles Doig, being constructed during 1898/99. Production commenced in April 1899, and the following year the distillery was sold by its founder, Alexander Edward, to the Glasgow blending firm of Wright & Greig Ltd, principally to provide supplies of malt whisky for their Roderick Dhu blend.

After a brief period in the hands of JP O'Brien & Co Ltd, Dallas Dhu was acquired by Benmore Distilleries Ltd in 1921. Eight years later that company was purchased by the Distillers Company Ltd (DCL).

The following year Dallas Dhu was transferred to DCL's Scottish Malt Distillers (SMD) subsidiary, but it was silent from 1930 to 1936, and three years later a fire necessitated reconstruction of the stillhouse, with its single pair of stills. This was re-commissioned just in time for the distillery to be closed down due to the outbreak of the Second World War, after which production did not recommence until 1947.

The 1960s and '70s saw some upgrading work carried out at Dallas Dhu, but expansion was not possible due to the limited water supply provided by the Altyre Burn. Unsurprisingly, when the time came in the early 1980s for DCL to address the issue of excess whisky stocks by closing plants, Dallas Dhu was on the company's' hit list,' and the last cask was filled on 16th March 1983.

POINTS OF SPECIAL INTEREST

Dallas Dhu is Scotland's only dedicated 'distillery museum,' being acquired by Historic Scotland in 1988. It allows visitors the opportunity to experience a largely unaltered Victorian Scotch whisky distillery.

> ### LOCATION
> Dallas Dhu, nr Forres, Morayshire IV36 2RR
> Located off Manachie Road, off the A940, just south-east of Forres. 14 miles west of Elgin.

Open daily April to October, and Saturday to Wednesday from November to March.

PHOTOGRAPH ON PAGE 238

Meaning of name and pronunciation guide
'Black Water Valley - Dallas-DHU

Owner
Managed by Historic Scotland

House style
Quite full-bodied, with fruit, honey, milk chocolate and gentle spice.

Principal single malts
Dallas Dhu 23 and 24-year-old single cask bottlings, exclusive from Historic Scotland.

Contacts
Tel: 01309 676548

Website
www.historic-scotland.gov.uk

Admission
Tour - £5.20 (includes complementary dram)

T - Flexible
C - N/A
S - Sell whisky and some gift/book items

Personal notes relating to visit:

Date visited:

SECTION INDEX ON PAGE 223

GLEN KEITH

Meaning of name and pronunciation guide
'Glen wood'
- Glen KEITH

Owner
Chivas Bros Ltd
(Pernod Ricard)

House style
Medium-sweet, with spicy fruit, cedar and almonds.

Principal single malts
Glen Keith 10-year-old (last 'house' bottling), Glen Keith 1993 (Gordon & MacPhail Connoisseurs' Choice range).

HISTORY

Along with Tullibardine (see p 88) and Tormore distilleries, Glen Keith was one of the first wave of new, post-war distilleries to be established in Scotland, and the first to be built on Speyside in the 20th century.

It was constructed during 1957/58 on the site of a former corn mill, which occupied the opposite bank of the River Isla to Strathisla Distillery (see p 122). Its owner was the Canadian distiller Seagram Ltd, which already owned Strathisla, and operated the newcomer through its Chivas Brothers subsidiary.

The distillery was deemed surplus to Seagram's requirements in 1999, at which time it boasted an annual capacity of some four million litres. The plant subsequently fell silent, and remains mothballed to this day, although it is structurally intact and distilling equipment remains in place.

Since its closure, Glen Keith has become home to the Chivas Technical Centre, and has been used as a 'test-bed' for trial ingredients and processes.

POINTS OF SPECIAL INTEREST

One of very few distilleries in the Highlands to practice triple distillation, Glen Keith was converted to double distillation in 1970, when the number of stills was increased from three to five. A sixth still was added in 1983. Glen Keith is also notable as the first Scottish distillery to use gas to fire its stills, and an early example of distilling computerisation came in 1980, when a micro-processor was installed in the distillery to automate many of the production practices.

Personal notes relating to visit:

Date visited:

LOCATION

Station Road, Keith, Morayshire AB55 5BU
Located on Station Road, north of the A96, in the centre of Keith. 17 miles south-east of Elgin.

IMPERIAL

HISTORY

Imperial distillery was constructed during 1897/98, just as the great Victorian whisky boom was coming to an end. Unusually, it was built not from stone but from Aberdeen red brick on an iron framework.

It was created to serve as a 'second distillery' to nearby Dailuaine, and was also owned by Thomas Mackenzie's Dailuaine-Talisker Distilleries Ltd, but after operating for just one season it fell silent, remaining closed until 1919.

Imperial closed again six years later, by which time ownership of Dailuaine-Talisker Distilleries Ltd had passed to the Distillers Company Ltd (DCL). 30 years later, distilling restarted in 1955 followed a major rebuilding programme and the development of processes to convert waste products such as draff and pot ale into high-protein cattle feed.

The number of stills was subsequently doubled from two to four in 1964/65 but Imperial ceased production once again in 1985, and four years later was sold to Allied Distillers Ltd. Distilling recommenced in 1991, but seven years later the site entered it present silent period having been sold off in 2005 to Chivas Bros Ltd.

Although most of the plant remains intact, the future of Imperial distillery is uncertain, and there have been proposals to redevelop the site.

POINTS OF SPECIAL INTEREST

The size of the four stills (some of the largest on Speyside) meant that it was not possible to make modest amounts of spirit, leaving the distillery at a disadvantage in terms of flexibility.

> ### LOCATION
> Carron, Aberlour, Morayshire AB38 7QP
> Located four miles south-west of Aberlour, via the A95, then after two miles along an unclassified road to Carron.

Meaning of name and pronunciation guide
Named during Queen Victoria's Diamond Jubilee year (1897)
- im-PERIAL

Owner
Chivas Bros Ltd
(Pernod Ricard)

House style
Full-bodied, medium-sweet, with light smoke and spice.

Principal single malts
Imperial 1991
(Gordon & MacPhail Connoisseurs' Choice range) and other independent bottlings.

Personal notes relating to visit:

Date visited:

PHOTOGRAPH ON PAGE 239

SECTION INDEX ON PAGE 223

PARKMORE

HISTORY

Externally, Parkmore is a very well preserved example of a late Victorian distillery, but it is really little more than a shell, not having produced whisky for some 80 years.

Parkmore was the fifth distillery to be built in Dufftown, being founded by the Parkmore Distillery Company in 1894. Six years later, with the Scotch whisky industry in a somewhat parlous state, it was sold to the Dundee-based distiller and well-known blender James Watson & Co Ltd. In Watson's ownership the distillery subsequently operated under the auspices of the Parkmore-Glenlivet Distilling Co.

In 1923, Watson's was acquired by John Dewar & Sons Ltd, and passed with other Dewar's assets into the hands of the Distillers Company Ltd two years later. The firm's Scottish Malt Distillers subsidiary took over Parkmore in 1930, and closed it the following year, though the malting operated for many years afterwards. Problems with the quality of its water supply are often cited as one of the reasons for Parkmore's demise.

Rumours have circulated in recent years about a possible distilling revival on the site, but at the present time they are no more than rumours.

POINTS OF SPECIAL INTEREST

Although stripped of distilling equipment, Parkmore has remained structurally intact, largely due to its role as an engineering base and cask storage site for the Distillers Company Ltd for many years. Since 1988 it has functioned as a warehousing complex in the ownership of what is now The Edrington Group.

Meaning of name and pronunciation guide
'The big park'
- PARK-mor

Owner
The Edrington Group

House style
N/A

Principal single malts
N/A

Personal notes relating to visit:

Date visited:

LOCATION

Low Road, Dufftown, Keith, Banffshire AB55 4DL
Located beside the B9041 Dufftown to Keith road, a mile north-east of the centre of Dufftown.

PHOTOGRAPH ON PAGE 238

TAMDHU

HISTORY

Tamdhu was established at the height of the late 19th century expansionist movement in the Scotch whisky industry, being constructed during 1896/97 for a consortium of whisky blenders, operating under the name of the Tamdhu Distillery Company. The distillery cost £19,200 to build, and was designed by Charles Doig, the Elgin architect responsible for so much of Speyside's distilling landscape.

Production began in July 1987, and the following year the Highland Distilleries Company acquired Tamdhu, having been heavily involved in the consortium behind its creation. The distillery was subsequently silent between 1911 and 1913, and again for two decades from 1928 until 1948.

The 1970s saw renewed expansion in Scottish distilling, and Tamdhu's single pair of stills was increased to two pairs in 1972 and from four to six three years later. Ultimately boasting a theoretical capacity of four million litres per annum, Tamdhu was a substantial distillery, being acquired in 1999 by The Edrington Group, in association with William Grant & Sons Ltd.

Tamdhu single malt is a significant component of blends like Cutty Sark, Famous Grouse and J&B, but in the spring of 2010, the distillery was put on a 'care and maintenance' basis, being surplus to Edrington's operational requirements.

POINTS OF SPECIAL INTEREST

Tamdhu was the last distillery in Scotland still using Saladin 'box' maltings, installed in 1950. These comprise long, concrete troughs, with perforated floors through which air circulates, while the barley in the troughs is turned on a regular basis by computer-controlled, mechanic turners.

LOCATION

Knockando, Morayshire AB38 7RP
9 miles from Aberlour, the distillery is situated at the end of a steep, unclassified road off the B9102 Grantown-on-Spey to Craigellachie road.

Meaning of name and pronunciation guide
'Black hill'
- tam-DOO

Owner
The Edrington Group

House style
Light-bodied, malty and sweet. Easy drinking.

Principal single malts
Tamdhu (No age statement).

Personal notes relating to visit:

Date visited:

SECTION INDEX ON PAGE 223

BRORA

Meaning of name and pronunciation guide
'The Bridges' River'
- Bror-Ah

Owner
Diageo plc

House style
Big-bodied, earthy and coastal, with fruit and smoke.

Principal single malts
Brora 30-year-old (Diageo Special Releases), Brora 1982 (Gordon & MacPhail Connoisseurs' Choice range).

HISTORY

Brora distillery, stands on the outskirts of the east Sutherlandshire port and holiday resort of Brora, some 50 miles north-east of Inverness.

It was founded – as Clynelish distillery - in 1819 by the Marquis of Stafford, later the 1st Duke of Sutherland, principally to provide an outlet for barley grown by the estate's tenants. Not only was there a plentiful supply of barley to make malt, but there was also an abundance of peat in the area, and even a modest local coal seam, which had been operating from the 16th century.

Ownership of the distillery passed through several hands before John Walker & Sons Ltd bought into the Clynelish Distillery Co Ltd in 1916. Walker's became part of the Distillers Company Ltd (DCL) in 1925, and within five years DCL owned the entire share capital of Clynelish, subsequently moving the distillery into the care of its Scottish Malt Distillers (SMD) subsidiary. However, the distillery was silent for most of the economically troubled 1930s, only resuming production on the eve of the Second World War.

The post-war 'whisky boom' saw an entirely new distillery built alongside the original, and the Clynelish name was transferred to that (see p 126). The original distillery was re-christened Brora, and operated until 1983, when it fell victim to the DCL's swingeing round of distillery closures. The old, stone-built distillery is externally intact, and its two stills remain in situ. A number of its warehouses are still used for the maturation of spirit.

POINTS OF SPECIAL INTEREST

During the early 1970s, DCL was concerned about a potential shortage of Islay-style malts for blending, so Brora was tasked to produce spirit that could replicate the role of Islays in the company's blends.

Heavy peating at the distillery dates principally from the period 1969 to 1973, though later peated batches were also occasionally produced.

Personal notes relating to visit:

Date visited:

LOCATION

Brora, Sutherland KW9 6LR
Situated off the A9, just over a mile north of Brora and 60 miles north of Inverness.

GLENLOCHY

HISTORY

The Glenlochy-Fort William Distillery Co Ltd was formed in 1897, and was headed by David McAndie of Nairn's Glen Cawdor distillery. Production commenced in April 1901, but scenting a quick profit, McAndie sold his share in the distillery within a year of it opening, netting a fourfold return on his initial investment.

Glenlochy fell silent from 1917 until 1924, when it was revived by a consortium of English brewers, who had purchased the distillery from its liquidators in 1920. The new owners proved no more successful than their predecessors, and just two years later Glenlochy fell silent again.

The distillery was sold for a bargain basement price in 1934 and passed on via a third party in 1937 to Train & McIntyre Ltd, a company owned by National Distillers of America Inc and the colourful Scots-born, Canadian entrepreneur Joseph Hobbs. Under their control Glenlochy fared much better, operating from 1938 until 1953, when ownership was transferred to the Distillers Company Ltd's (DCL) Scottish Malt Distillers Ltd.

When the time came for DCL to wield its axe during the early 1980s, Glenlochy was a logical contender for closure, being comparatively un-modernised and equipped with just one pair of stills. The distillery shut down in 1983.

POINTS OF SPECIAL INTEREST

Although some of the site was cleared after distilling ceased, a number of buildings survive, including the 'listed' kiln and malt barn, with the latter having been developed into affordable accommodation units.

LOCATION

North Road, Fort William, Inverness-shire PH33 6LR
Located just off the A82, on the north-eastern outskirts of Fort William.

Meaning of name and pronunciation guide
'Glen of the dark goddess '
- Glen-LOCHIE

Owner
Last operated by Distillers Co Ltd

House style
Medium-bodied, with vanilla, coconut, malt, ripe fruits and hints of peat.

Principal single malts
Glenlochy 1968 (Gordon & MacPhail Rare Old range) and other independent bottlings.

Personal notes relating to visit:

Date visited:

SECTION INDEX ON PAGE 223

PHOTOGRAPH ON PAGE 239

MILLBURN

Meaning of name and pronunciation guide
'The stream of the mill'
- MILL-burn

Owner
Last operated by Distillers Co Ltd

House style
Medium-bodied, rounded, with delicate peat, fresh fruit and nuts.

Principal single malts
Millburn 1972 and 1978 (Gordon & MacPhail).

HISTORY

Millburn was the oldest of the trio of Inverness distilleries. It was established in 1805 by a Mr Welsh under the name Inverness Distillery. It subsequently passed through several sets of hands before being acquired in 1853 by David Rose, an Inverness corn merchant who used the distillery as a mill. However, in 1876 the plant was rebuilt and began to make whisky again two years later, being taken over by Rose's son, George, in 1881. By that time the distillery had secured a sufficiently high reputation to win a lucrative contract to supply whisky to the British military garrison on Cyprus.

In 1892 Andrew Haig & Co purchased the plant, going on to rename it Millburn in 1904. Booth's Distillery Ltd, best known for their London gin, bought Millburn from Haig in 1921, but the following year, the distillery suffered a serious fire.

Despite the severity of the fire, Millburn was rebuilt within a year, and continued to trade through some lean times before becoming part of the Distillers Company Ltd in 1937, operating within the DCL subsidiary Scottish Malt Distillers Ltd until 1985.

POINTS OF SPECIAL INTEREST

Much of the distillery structure remains intact today, having opened as a Beefeater Steakhouse in 1989.

It currently operates as the Auld Distillery Slice restaurant and bar and is owned by Premier Travel Inn.

LOCATION

7 Millburn Road, Inverness IV2 3QX
Located on the B865, off the A9, one and a half miles east of the city centre.

Personal notes relating to visit:

Date visited:

PORT ELLEN

HISTORY

Port Ellen distillery was one of many distilleries that sprang up in the wake of the liberating Excise Act, being established two years later in 1825. Port Ellen was built by Alexander Kerr Mackay, who became bankrupt soon after the distillery opened. It was subsequently operated with little more financial success by various members of the Mackay family, before the youthful John Ramsay from Clackmannanshire was appointed to take control. Ramsay was subsequently granted the distillery lease in 1836, and went on to build up a considerable property holding on Islay. Port Ellen remained in the Ramsay family until 1920, when it was acquired by the blending companies of James Buchanan & Co Ltd and John Dewar & Sons Ltd, passing to the mighty Distillers Company Ltd (DCL) when Buchanan and Dewar merged with it in 1925. In 1930 the distillery closed, having been transferred to the DCL subsidiary Scottish Malt Distillers.

The distillery was granted a second lease of life in 1967, when, after 37 years of inactivity, Port Ellen underwent an 18 months-long, £400,000 rebuilding programme, during which the distillery changed quite dramatically, both internally and externally.

Six years later, the village of Port Ellen was transformed by the construction of a vast new maltings plant beside the distillery, capable of producing 400 tonnes of malted barley per week. Sadly, it was only a decade later that Port Ellen distillery fell silent once again, with the last spirit flowing in May 1983. Most of the 1960s distillery has now been demolished, and what remains are the two original pagodas, maltings, a range of original warehouses and some other structures that have been converted into business units.

POINTS OF SPECIAL INTEREST

Septimus Fox tested and refined his newly-invented 'spirit safe' at Port Ellen during the early 1820s, and the distillery was the first in Scotland to export malt whisky directly to North America.

LOCATION
Port Ellen, Isle of Islay PA42 7AH
Located on the northern outskirts of Port Ellen, just off the A846 to Bowmore.

Meaning of name and pronunciation guide
Named after the wife of 19th century Islay landowner Walter Frederick Campbell
- Port ELL-en

Owner
Diageo plc

House style
Oily, medicinal, with smoke, brine and pepper.

Principal single malts
Port Ellen 30-year-old (Diageo Special Releases 2009), Port Ellen 1982 (Gordon & MacPhail Connoisseurs' Choice range) and other independent bottlings.

Personal notes relating to visit:

Date visited:

ST MAGDALENE DISTILLERY

DALLAS DHU DISTILLERY

PARKMORE DISTILLERY

GLENLOCHY DISTILLERY

IMPERIAL DISTILLERY

CONVALMORE DISTILLERY

INDEX

INDEX OF DISTILLERIES